Under One Tent
Circus, Judaism, and Bible

Ora Horn Prouser
Michael Kasper
Ayal Prouser

Ben Yehuda Press
Teaneck, New Jersey

UNDER ONE TENT ©2023 the authors. All rights reserved. No part of this book may be used or reproduced in any manner whatsoever without written permission except in the case of brief quotations embodied in critical articles and reviews.

Published by Ben Yehuda Press
122 Ayers Court #1B
Teaneck, NJ 07666
http://www.BenYehudaPress.com

To subscribe to our monthly book club and support independent Jewish publishing, visit https://www.patreon.com/BenYehudaPress

Ben Yehuda Press books may be purchased at a discount by synagogues, book clubs, and other institutions buying in bulk.

For information, please email markets@BenYehudaPress.com

Cover art: Azoulay, Guillaume, Le Grand Cirque, 1988, Serigraph on paper. Photo courtesy of Guillaume Azoulay.

The list of photo permissions on page 299 constitutes as extension of this copyright page.

ISBN13 978-1-953829-45-0

23 24 25 / 10 9 8 7 6 5 4 3 2 1 20230308

This book is dedicated with profound love and deep gratitude to my parents, Bill and Dena Horn, my husband, Joe, and my children, Shira, Avi, Eitan, and Ayal. Each of you has played an important role in making me who I am today.
—Ora

This book is lovingly dedicated to my wife, Sylvia, who has supported my work at every turn. And to my three daughters, Lisa, Anika, and Hannah, who have filled my life with all sorts of goodness.
—Michael

This book is dedicated with a full heart and endless gratitude to my parents and grandparents, whose constant support, in all facets of my life, leads me on my journey.
—Ayal

Contents

Acknowledgements	vii
Introduction Michael Kasper, Ayal Prouser, and Ora Horn Prouser	xi
Extracts from the Autobiography of an Ambivalent Ashtangi: The Ambivalent Ashtangi/Camilla Damkjær	1
Circus, *Tzedek*, and *Tikkun Olam* Jessica Hentoff	19
Juggling Across the Ancient World Thom Wall	33
Circus Jews Under National Socialism Stav Meishar	61
Circus.Freiheit.Fleischschaltung. Roxana Küwen	81
Jewish Circus History Ayal Prouser, Ora Horn Prouser, and Michael Kasper	87
An Embodied Epistemology Lori Wynters	103
Early Childhood Hebrew Learning Incorporating Total Physical Response Shirah Rubin	119
An Invitation to Dance Toward our Spiritual Identity Daniella Pressner	137
Dance as a Way of Knowing: Studying Jewish Texts Through Dance Ofra Arieli Backenroth	161
Motor Skills, Creativity, and Cognition in Learning Physics Concepts Roni Zohar, Esther Bagno, Bat-Sheva Eylon, and Dor Abrahamson	183
On Movement and Learning Roni Zohar	205

Bringing Physics to the Circus   219
    Alexander Volfson and Yuval Ben-Abu

Movement is in the Jewish DNA   243
    Michael Kasper, Ayal Prouser, Ora Horn Prouser

Hafokh Bah, For Everything is In It   261
    Ayal Prouser, Michael Kasper, Ora Horn Prouser

Conclusion   289
    Ora Horn Prouser, Michael Kasper, Ayal Prouser

Glossary of Circus Terms   293

About the Authors   295

Acknowledgements

The process of writing and editing is exciting and enriching, but also arduous. The many chapters in this volume are the result of years of thinking, research, and care on the part of many individuals. Thank you to all the contributors to this book for your devotion to your work, and the creative and enlightening research shared in this volume. We are so appreciative for your willingness to keep answering our questions and to rush when we were under deadlines.

Thank you to Larry Yudelson and the staff at Ben Yehuda Press, including our editors Laura Logan and Kira Schwartz, for your painstaking and careful attention to our manuscript. Larry expressed interest in the topic from day one and was a wonderful partner throughout the project.

Sacred Arts began at the Academy for Jewish Religion and continues to grow and thrive there. We are grateful to our colleagues and students who didn't flinch when we first suggested studying Talmud through circus and dance ten years ago! Since that time, our students and colleagues have been true sources of inspiration and collaboration as we continued to develop this work.

Thank you also to our own teachers who, over the years, have opened our eyes to new ideas, supported our learning and development, and who always helped us see the value of creative thinking. We know that we stand on their shoulders in all our work (this is, after all, a circus book!).

While this project took longer than expected, a beautiful byproduct was the time working together. Each one of us came to this idea with excitement and passion; the opportunity to learn together, push each other, and celebrate successes has been a joy and a blessing.

Of course, none of this would have been possible without the support of our spouses, partners, family, and friends. You listened to our concerns, helped us find the perfect word, gave advice, helped with design, and caringly expressed interest. It was a labor of love supported by love.

See you down the road...

Le Cheval de Cirque, 1964. Marc Chagall.
Gouache and brush and India ink on paper.
Image © Artists Rights Society (ARS), New York / ADAGP, Paris.

Introduction

Michael Kasper, Ayal Prouser, and Ora Horn Prouser

Sacred Arts is the Academy for Jewish Religion's name for an entire range of arts-based curricula designed to teach sacred literature in new and exciting ways. It has led to a library of stories about the processes and experiences of the various cohorts who have engaged in this learning. Here are two vignettes which will help introduce the reader to all that will follow.

At a Jewish education conference, we happened to have a number of parent-child pairings in the group. We were studying the Garden of Eden story (Genesis 3). One of the groups created a pyramid in which a child was leaning on a parent, and then, as part of the plan, the parent needed to step away to move to a different part of the pyramid. This was meant to be representative of God's role in the story, first being leaned upon, and then moving into a different position in relationship to the humans. In our structure, the child was really only leaning on the parent in theory; there was no significant weight on the parent, and yet, when discussing it later, the parent had a difficult time changing positions. She felt uncomfortable moving out of the position of being leaned upon, even though she knew her child would not fall. She sympathized with God's potential "parental" anxiety in the Divine relationship with Adam and Eve as they emotionally age through the chapters. Given that there was such a presence of parent-child pairs in the group, this led to a powerful conversation about the roles of parents and children, how to let go, when to let go, etc. We also discussed deeply the relationship of God and the first humans, using parent-child imagery. That is a standard reading of the narrative, yet it was one that we had not shared in that group. We came to it purely through embodying the text, not through teaching. It was a very powerful moment for all attending.

With a gathering of professionals, we decided to examine Genesis 3 through movement. Honing in on the character of Eve, we wanted to research what she might have felt when, in conversation with the snake, she was pushed to eat the forbidden fruit. The dancers/participants were told to step into a position that challenged their balance. They were to repeat the same movement until it became a "step," something they could repeat at will. Moving on, we asked them to make up two or three additional off-balance poses that would resolve in the same way… by coming to an easy and balanced upright position. Stringing the three steps together, they each had a unique phrase of movement. The only instructions given were that no one could step into the middle of the space, though they were encouraged to get as close as they could without encroaching on it. That area was to be the Tree of Life and it was forbidden to all. We repeated the process of making up the movements two separate times. After the first, we stopped to talk about what the experience felt like. Most everyone experienced the emotional weight of staying away from the tree even when their off-balance recovery led them in its direction. The second go-round, however, elicited a different feeling state. Uniformly, each participant felt themselves drawn closer and closer to the tree, as if it was teasing or daring them to come closer. The temptation to be pulled into something forbidden was a very powerful feeling for everyone. With that in mind, we went back to discussing the story.

Sacred Arts
These two words have been at the center of the Academy for Jewish Religion's (AJR's) groundbreaking exploration into modern ways of teaching and learning ancient texts. This volume, almost three years in the making, sheds light on two of the Academy's teaching tools: movement (dance) and circus arts, the latter being the primary focus of these papers. Equally importantly, the collection of scholarship we have curated, edited, and present here represents not only our particular approach, but much more. Reading through each chapter will reap rewards that begin with The Academy for Jewish Religion's particular emphasis but move into related fields, all having to do with the idea that embodied learning is finding expression in early childhood education, primary school classrooms, Jewish day schools, university physics curricula, street theater, social circus, philosophical explorations, and more.

Embodied learning is the central idea of this book. It is the belief and knowledge that our bodies are capable of making sense of all manner of information, and that relying only on the power of the brain to process information effectively reduces our ability to understand the world by an incalculable factor. How much more could we all learn, process, metabolize, and express if we understood the intelligence inherent in our physical beings and the intellectual power our bodies could generate? Circus and dance are the two movement disciplines this volume wants to explore. Circus and dance become not simply art forms to be learned; they are the methodologies and contexts we have explored in our search for embodied ways of learning biblical texts.

We recognize that there are a variety of ways in which the arts can be used in studying sacred text. When we employ dance or circus arts, we are not desiring to make new art; we are not expecting the choreography to represent the story in any way. Rather, we think of them as art forms that help us explore the text in front of us. They are not media that express new ideas on their own, but rather creative and explorative technologies that are active research methodologies in their own right. Ultimately, we take our research data and use it to clarify some piece of meaning held closely within the words of a text.

Others might use the text as a jumping-off place to create a work of art that captures and expresses something about it in a new and beautiful way. Clearly, these two ways are meant to shine light on differing end goals. Our approach at the Academy sees dance and circus as methods of study, while others might see them solely as methods of artistic expression. There is a place for both approaches. The world needs art, and it needs refined and resonant research techniques. It is our hope that this book opens a window that opens a door that opens a world.

The time feels particularly right for this collection. Our colleague and friend, Dr. Job Jindo, has made the point repeatedly that we are living in the golden age of *parashat hashavua*. His point is that we are living in a time when people are searching for opportunities to study. The Bible has been the focus of much of this hunger, and classes, programs, and workshops focusing on biblical study have proliferated. It thus feels even more fitting that we continue to find and refine new and exciting methodologies of approaching the biblical text.

At the same time, the field of Circus Studies is in its early stages, just finding and establishing its rightful place in the academic world. The methodologies being developed through this new field have been instrumental in our Sacred Arts work.

The Role of Sacred Arts at AJR

In order to understand how we all came to this work, and why it's so important to us, we think it would be helpful to understand something about the role of Sacred Arts at the Academy for Jewish Religion, where we have all worked. AJR has two communal programs each year that are required of all matriculated students. In our Fall Retreat, we spend three-and-a-half days together studying, praying, and building community. For many years, we had been including some sort of art session at Retreat, whether it was singing, movement, paper midrash, etc. Our students loved the art sessions, and they were always both meaningful and fun. We even had whole retreats revolving around a single biblical text, bringing in a variety of artists to address that text in one way or another.

At a certain point, we decided that it was time to take the next step, on a few levels. First, we decided to do an arts retreat revolving around a text from the Talmud rather than from the Bible. Additionally, we began to further define and clarify our unique approach, setting out to use the arts to process text rather than to use the text as a jumping off point to create art. Significantly, we were not focusing on the quality of the art we were creating, sometimes not even creating an end product. The importance of the art was in its value to us as a tool to process the texts. We decided to push this theory further by making the object of our study not a gem of a story from the Talmud, but rather a section of

Talmud that was a typical argument about Jewish law. The question became how we could use the arts to help discern the structure of the Talmudic argument.

One of the first ideas we had was to use circus pyramids to process the structure of the Talmudic argument. We realized that we could embody the structure of the *sugya,* a section of the Talmud focusing on a specific issue. For example, one statement could be built upon the statement that came before it. Alternatively, a statement could be turning the previous statement on its head (figuratively, and now, literally). Two statements could be connected as parallel statements that perhaps just barely touch each other, etc. When we brought the students into this, the results were just astounding. There were groups that built up multilayer structures to represent the argument. Others did not want to have anyone get off the ground, so they created a structure that had everyone in one way or another sitting on the ground or with their feet on the ground. There were some who did not feel able to participate physically, and they decided to draw a picture of what their structure would look like. At that point we realized we were the first (or only) group to have studied Talmud through circus arts!

We considered this a real experiment, and the results were amazing. The students made clear that the process of thinking about how to embody the text, and then actually embodying the text, led them to understand the *sugya* more quickly and more fully than they ever had before. We had similar results in the same retreat using dance. We were thrilled and decided this meant we needed to continue this exploration into Sacred Arts, using the arts to process the texts. We continued our work, engaging in a variety of art forms including visual arts, writing, storytelling, music, and more.

Who We Are

Michael Kasper's Personal Statement
I grew up surrounded by music. A portable speaker, tethered to the family phonograph, followed my mother, my father, and me into every room of our house. Wherever we were, there was music. My first instrument was the trumpet, and I was a serious player. Other instruments came later, and music was my path until I found modern dance as a physical education requirement in college. Moving to New York City, I had an enviable career in the dance world until I retired to study social work and then psychoanalysis. Ordination as a cantor came later, fulfilling an almost lifelong dream. All this is to say that my life in the arts was, and is, a comfortable and magical place. Not so much my place in academia, where I never felt as much at home. The world of books, research, critical reading and critical thinking always felt like they belonged to someone else. Working at the Academy, using all my skills, taking on more and varied

portfolios, and meeting Ora and Ayal has brought me to this place where I am both artist and academic, mover and writer.

Movement and dance describe more than things I know how to do. They organize the way I look at the world. They suggest a context in which I view my surroundings. They are the atmosphere I am comfortable thinking in. The Sacred Arts curriculum at AJR offers me a chance to teach in this special way and gives voice to a vision of learning that understands how the body moves and is in movement. That vision helps solidify new ways of learning old material, ancient texts coming alive in modern ways.

A personal sacred arts moment

At a conference workshop with Jewish educators, we led a session that took its jumping-off point from the beloved High Holiday prayer, *Avinu Malkeinu*. We studied the text and then studied source material found in the Talmud (Bavli Ta'anit 25b) which chronicled the positions of Rabbi Akiva and Rabbi Eliezer with regard to *Avinu Malkeinu*'s origins. The Talmudic material was new for each of the participants and showed that the original text came from a prayer for rain during a long and difficult drought. The text conjured images of a community full of anxiety during a time when food was scarce. The participants/dancers were instructed to move in ways that put them in uncomfortable postures, ways that left them feeling they needed a resolution to their discomfort. As the time spent in these positions increased, they each expressed varying levels of need for an immediate resolution. A respite from their troubles seemed necessary in consequential ways, as if their lives depended on it. The experience brought on by the simple dance mirrored the experience of a community pushed to their psychological brink by the specter of drought and hunger.[1]

Ora Horn Prouser's personal statement

My academic background is in the field of Biblical Studies. I have engaged in studying the Bible from the perspectives of ancient Near Eastern languages and literature, literary analysis, Feminist Studies, and Disability Studies. Most of my work in the last two decades has been in the intersection of Disability Studies and Biblical Studies. I have been teaching Bible in seminaries for close to forty years, first at the Jewish Theological Seminary, and then at the Academy for Jewish Religion, where I have found an academic and spiritual home, and where I now serve as CEO and Academic Dean.

My early relationship with the arts was quite negative. I was exposed to and influenced by an overly exacting art teacher, one whom I, with my limited talent

---

[1] Thank you to our colleague, Rabbi Jeff Hoffman, for co-leading this session.

in visual arts, clearly could never satisfy. That led to a fear of the arts, seeing them as a world where I could never fit in or be comfortable. That changed as I became the parent of very artistic children, ones who excelled in visual arts, music, and circus. My world shifted as I became a "circus mom," and saw the beauty, depth, rigor, and clear joy that was part of excelling in an artistic endeavor. My world shifted once again when it became clear, to both Ayal and me, that there was a way to bring together circus and Bible, and, together with my AJR colleagues, that there was a world of Sacred Arts that was rigorous, deep, beautiful, and joyful.

A personal Sacred Arts moment
I have been studying and teaching the Bible for many decades, and for much of that time I paid very close attention to feminist readings of the Bible. I have spent real time on the wife/sister story in which Abraham passes Sarah, his wife, off as his sister in order to protect himself (Genesis 12, 20). I had always read this as Abraham being abusive to his wife, Sarah, by putting her in danger and creating a situation where she was taken into Pharaoh's house to be either potentially or actually subject to sexual violence. During a Sacred Arts circus class, I climbed onto a rolla bolla, a board on top of a cylinder where one stands and strives for balance. While standing on the rolla bolla I then read the wife/sister story again. Because I was feeling unbalanced on the apparatus and concerned about falling, I was suddenly filled with a new empathy for Abraham. I felt his struggle, his fear, and his pain. This is not to say that Abraham was right in his actions, but this new empathy led to a richness in my reading that had not been there before. A very few minutes on the rolla bolla allowed me a new reading of the text.

Ayal Prouser's Personal Statement
There are two tropes surrounding artists that I truly despise: 1. Romanticizing the starving artist; and 2. The "dumb" artist. The first one is easy; pay your artists. The second is trickier. It begins with recognizing multiple manifestations of intelligences from the outside. It also, however, requires teaching artists that well-informed art is good art, whether it be in politics, innovative approaches, intertextual demonstrations, emotional intelligences, etc. This requires artistic forms of learning that are not typically found in school settings, and an appreciation that everything you learn—history, English, science—can inform your art and is therefore part of your art. Studying is artistic practice.

I did not get this for a long time. I was proud of my creative side, but only connected with academics more fully toward the end of high school—and really more fully in higher education. While my high school's structure in no way supported the arts, I had individual teachers who did. I had a Bible instructor who was a theater artist who integrated artistic study and production into her class work. I started to get better grades. I had an English teacher who was a writer and a cinephile. He integrated film study into his curriculum alongside the study of literature; I started to get better grades. I had a rabbinics teacher who had a love for language; he wrote my college recommendation.

In college and graduate school, I focused on Film Studies. In graduate school, however, I focused more closely on the intersection of Film Studies and Circus Studies, integrating my creative practice into my study and my academics into my arts. It was in graduate school where I truly began to further myself academically. The ability to study art, and later, to study with art, made sense to me. I could process thoughts through the art, making me both care about it and understand the concepts more fully. Sacred Arts has been an outlet for sharing this process with others and to practice it myself.

A personal Sacred Arts moment
During an AJR conference on subjects pertaining to gender, participants engaged in some very difficult and complicated conversations leading to tension among participants. For the evening program, as a de-escalation exercise, the entire conference participated in a circus workshop. It started with a short introduction to the role of gender in circus, the importance of reliance on one another, the respect and care needed in working together, and the mutual interdependence of circus performers during their acts. Then the participants simply learned circus moves and had fun. Because of the camaraderie, the trust, the communication, the collaboration, and the fun factor of the circus program, by the end of the evening the mood of the community had fully changed, with participants engaged once again as a community where safety and respect were cherished and promoted. There is a magic to the use of circus in building community, even in difficult circumstances.

Structure of the Book
This book was created out of a love for the Bible, a love of the arts, a love of circus, and a love of creative thought and initiatives. We were delighted and grateful that so many others shared these loves and contributed to this important conversation through their articles and essays.

The book begins with a focus on circus and religious thought. Professor Camilla Damkjær presents an inner dialogue and analysis of her interaction and development as a practitioner of Ashtangi yoga. Calling herself an "Ambivalent Ashtangi," she gives voice to an understanding of the role of movement in personal development. Drawing on her personal experience as a circus artist, philosopher, and academic, she takes us on a journey placing physical practice at the center of her academic, emotional, and spiritual growth.

Jessica Hentoff, a leader in the field of social circus, builds on this theme by putting circus arts at the center of her work toward *tikkun olam*, the desire to do social justice and make a difference in the world. She tells the story of how she built a social circus program in St. Louis, bringing together youth from different communities who never would have interacted if not for their circus work. She then expanded her program to become an international force, joining together with Israeli Jews and Arabs to use circus arts to work for peace and the resolution of conflict.

Understanding that movement has a role in religious thought and growth and in building Jewish community is well documented. Interestingly, the history of circus arts is also deeply intertwined with the Jewish experience. You don't have to dig far to find connections between circus and Jewish life in a historical context.

Juggler and historian Thom Wall starts off this section looking at the history of juggling in antiquity, focusing on ancient Egypt and ancient Babylonia, among other locations. He cites references to juggling in rabbinic literature and explores a possible reference to juggling in the Hebrew Bible itself.

Artist/researcher Stav Meishar investigates the rise of circus in Germany, focusing primarily on Jewish circus artists in the nineteenth and twentieth centuries. The impact of the Holocaust on these circus families was devastating. There are beautiful stories of how circuses saved Jewish artists during the Holocaust, which speaks to the value of community to circus artists.

Artist/educator Roxana Küwen builds on this concept describing the work of the CiNS Collective in Germany, a group that uses circus arts and performance to study and teach circus history and to face and deal with issues such as colonialism, antisemitism, racism, and sexism. They have focused on the fate of Jewish circus families during the Holocaust and have created interdisciplinary performances to tell these important stories.

The history of Jews in circus, however, goes beyond these major historical events. Jews have had a place in circus history starting from the very beginning of "modern circus" in the eighteenth century through to the contemporary period. We share some moments of Jews in circus history to make the point that bringing together circus and sacred literature is very much in keeping with Jewish life.

With this background in circus history, and an understanding of the role of physical movement in personal development, we move on to some theory and practice of the use of movement in study.

Professor Lori Wynters opens up the world of embodiment theory, defining the concept and explaining how the idea that we think with our bodies is a part of our very makeup. She relates it to Jewish life, ritual, and learning and provides a model for bringing embodiment theory into the classroom. We see embodiment theory as, in some ways, the base upon which our work stands. It is this theory—that we think with our bodies—that informs our work in its most basic sense.

The following articles, written by thoughtful educators, all give more specific examples of how they have brought embodiment thinking into Jewish Studies classroom settings of different stages. Shirah Rubin describes the use of movement in language acquisition in preschool settings. Rabba Daniella Pressner gives several examples of the importance of the arts in general in her elementary school in Nashville, Tennessee. She extrapolates from their experience the possibilities inherent in bringing the arts, and especially dance as it relates to Jewish content, into school settings. Professor Ofra Backenroth then discusses her use of dance and dance analysis in college and graduate school classes. She gives examples of using dance as interpretation of text in order to heighten learning.

The next group of articles gives examples of using embodiment theory to teach mathematics and science. Professor Roni Zohar focuses on bringing movement into the study of physics. She goes on to discuss how important movement is to the ability to study and learn over any period of time. Professors Alex Volfson and Yuval Ben Abu specifically use circus to study physics.

The last section of the book is where we explain our method of Sacred Arts. We begin with a review of the importance of movement in Jewish thought and sacred literature, including the Bible and liturgy. We contend that movement is in the Jewish DNA. Our history, from the Exile at the time of the destruction of the Temple through a history of expulsions and longing for Zion, has included travel, the search for home, and a basic sense of transience. The concept is then continued in references to modern Hebrew poetry and Israeli dancing. In this chapter we focus primarily on the more familiar art of dance to demonstrate these ideas. Though less discussed, given the movement basis of circus arts, we see it as equally connected to Jewish communal narratives and ideology as dance.

With that understanding of movement as the underlying structure, we then review our use of both circus and movement to process sacred text, laying out the method with examples of how it has worked. We also explicate the underlying methodology, including Biblical Studies and Circus Studies in our analysis.

In this chapter, we use the less familiar, but deeply compelling, art of circus to demonstrate our theory.

Throughout the book, the role of circus in Jewish life is shown via artwork by Jewish artists.

We invite you to enter this world with us. Run away with us to the circus, and together with us, find a world of religious life, sacred connection, and yet another door to the study of Torah.

Barbette, 1926.
Man Ray, 1926.
Photograph © Man Ray 2015 Trust / Artists Rights Society (ARS), NY / ADAGP, Paris 2023

Extracts from the Autobiography of an Ambivalent Ashtangi: "Acrobatically facilitated modes of consciousness and existential experiences"

The Ambivalent Ashtangi/Camilla Damkjær

Confession

I'm drawn to the acrobatic features of yoga. And I'm drawn to its promise that it may facilitate specific modes of consciousness, existential experiences, and knowledge, though I doubt that I will reach enlightenment. I'm also aware that this may be an illusion, a trick just made to attract me to the practice. A trick intensified by the entry of yoga into capitalist and neo-liberal economies. I have been attracted to other physical practices and disappointed by their tricks, too. Therefore, I am even more reluctant to believe in these tricks now.

As a child in Denmark, I was a practitioner of a specific form of gymnastics. The dopamine kicks of the acrobatic tricks I learned then seem to have predisposed my body to these sensations and, indeed, developed a lack when nothing replaced them. But as an adult I realized to what extent these gymnastic movements carried not only beautiful ideas of democracy and being together, but also imperatives of nation-forming and becoming-alike.

I have also been a ferocious practitioner of circus. I am still fascinated by circus' combination of highly skill-demanding acrobatic tricks, intellectual abstraction and punk courage. But at some distance I wonder what this hormone did to my mind. It was strong enough to make me believe that I could practice Deleuzian philosophy through circus.[1] But even the strongest obsession did not withstand the critical analysis that even the dreams of circus are related to the darker sides of history, imperial pretentions and humans' belief in their own superiority.

Thus, having tried at least twice to let a physical practice be the center of my reflection and being twice more or less disillusioned, I am reluctant to throw myself obsessively into yoga. I already know that yoga is just as tricky a terrain. The history of yoga is just as complex, it is just as involved in the problems of the world. Just as circus, yoga carries the history of imperialism and colonialism,

---

[1] C. Damkjær, *Homemade Academic Circus: Ideosyncratically Embodied Reflections into Research in the Arts and Circus*. Dorset: Iff Books, 2016.

and contains problems of appropriation.[2] Yoga, too, carries histories of abuse.[3] It is just as impossible to believe that yoga may save the world, though it often promises at least to do some good. I'm worried that my analytical capacity for deconstruction may lead to the destruction of the calm of mind that I fool myself to believe that yoga can lead to. Yet, the alternative of not thinking through the body does not exist for me either. And in this no-man's land of reluctant obsession, I try to figure out how the practice of acrobatic movements in yoga may, constructively, be a way of thinking, also for a highly ambivalent ashtanga yoga practitioner.
—A.A./The Ambivalent Ashtangi

Proper introduction
There are many ways in which religious practices are related to corporeal ones. An extreme example of this is when the acrobatic body becomes the vehicle for spiritual experiences or specific modes of consciousness. In this article, I would like to explore an acrobatic practice, adjacent but not identical to circus, and how it is deliberately understood to carry existential experiences and provide the way to specific modes of consciousness.

As critical yoga studies have shown, "transnational postural yoga"[4] is a phenomenon closely related to modern body politics.[5] "Transnational postural yoga" is a term that especially Mark Singleton has used in order to speak of the physical yoga forms practiced in many parts of the world today, stemming from the evolution of yoga into a modern body culture in the late 19th and early 20th centuries. However, in its self-understanding, today's yoga deliberately connects to and transforms historical, pre-modern forms of yoga practice and philosophy. In its modern form, it shares some historical aspects with circus. This can be seen, for instance, through the way it has also been used for display, especially due to the British ban on yoga practices in India.[6]

In this article, I will explore the way Ashtanga yoga specifically (as a form of transnational postural yoga) relates acrobatic bodily practices with expect-

---
[2] Aubrecht, J. F. *Choreographers and Yogis: Untwisting the Politics of Appropriation and Representation in U.S. Concert Dance*. Riverside: Diss: University of California Riverside, 2017.
[3] Remski, M. *Practice and All is Coming: Abuse, Cult Dynamics, and Healing in Yoga and Beyond*. Rangoria: Embodied Wisdom Publishing, 2019.
[4] Singleton, M. *Yoga Body: The Origins of Modern Posture Practice*. Oxford: Oxford University Press, 2010.
[5] See Alter, J. *Yoga in Modern India: The Body between Science and Philosophy*. Princeton: Princeton University Press, 2004; Michelis, E. D. *A History of Modern Yoga: Pantanjali and Western Esotericism*. New York: Continuum, 2005; Singleton.
[6] See Singleton; Pinch, W. R. *Warrior Ascetics and Indian Empires*. Cambridge: Cambridge University Press, 2006.

ed spiritual development and potential modes of consciousness, drawing on, among other things, yoga philosophy and Hindu thinking. Furthermore, I will discuss what it means to these understandings that they also have unfolded and continue to unfold within a transnational, and thus multi-religious, environment.

Taking Ashtanga yoga as an example, I hope to cast light on the potential processes of consciousness that the acrobatic body may carry, and how these are related to, and depend on, not only physiological processes, but also specific cultural understandings that make it possible to tap into modes of embodied being. However, rather than looking at these from a distance, my main question is which modes of knowledge we as practitioners may find in yoga today.

In this work, I will start from the standpoint of the practitioner-researcher, practicing and in and around practice, trying to find strategies to pursue knowledge through yoga. Methodologically, I will take my starting point in post-qualitative practice-based research and auto-ethnography, where I take my own practice as a symptom of a larger cultural question. To structure this symptomatic example, I lead a reflective process with myself as the main character in the "Autobiography of an Ambivalent Ashtangi," exploring the physical road to different states of consciousness, existential experiences, and different forms of knowing.

Thus, I am not pretending to understand the knowledge, the states of mind or the truth of yoga—which most scholars agree do not exist and are impossible to attain. But as Joseph Alter has proposed, we can try to understand what yoga does, how it works performatively.[7] In this case, the main character of the "Autobiography of the Ambivalent Ashtangi" tries to understand which roads to states of consciousness and knowledge contemporary transnational yoga may lead us to tread.

From the "science" of yoga…

First, I was simply fascinated and seduced by a new (to me) physical culture, its physical challenges, its internal rules, and its particular bodily aesthetics. Then I discovered the complexity and richness of the history of yoga as a physical practice. Then I realized that not only did yoga challenge my physical practice in new ways, it also made me question my scholarly understanding of knowledge by proposing another regime of knowledge: the "science" of yoga.

The "science" of yoga takes many shapes and covers many areas—from ethical rules, to dietary recommendations, to physical know-how, to the under-

---

[7] Alter, J. S. "Performativity and the Study of Modern Yoga." In *Yoga in the Modern World: Contemporary Perspectives*, edited by M. &. B. J. Singleton. London: Routledge, 2008, 36-48.

standing of the Absolute. Its discourse seems to be based on the "translation" of Indian concepts of knowledge into a broad and loosely defined, 19th-century-colored version of the understanding of "science." The "science" of yoga evolves, it seems, in the repeated attempts of Western thinkers to find inspiration in Hindu thinking and yoga philosophy, and in the repeated attempts of Indian and other yoga practitioners to explain and promote the benefits of yoga practice and philosophy.[8] In this cultural frame "science" becomes the quality stamp of knowledge.

One part of the "science of yoga" proposes that certain kinds of physical practice, based on yoga postures, may lead to, at least, physical well-being, happiness (hopefully), and ultimately knowledge of the Absolute. Postural yoga today takes many shapes and to different degrees promises a path, if not to enlightenment, then at least to a calm and steady consciousness—referring to the philosophy attributed to the Indian philosopher Patanjali and the often-mentioned yoga sutra stating the purpose of yoga as the stilling of the mind.[9] These promises are based in historically complex discourses, in which ideas of pre-modern yoga practices (real or imagined) have been grafted onto a physical practice that took its modern form in the beginning of the 20th century.[10]

As critical yoga studies have shown, the link between modern and pre-modern forms of yoga is highly contingent. Indeed, modern yoga is not a smooth continuation of pre-modern meditative practices, but a modern invention. These physical practices were coloured also by the development of modern bio-politics and physical culture, finding specific expressions in the Indian context where the hope for an independent nation needed images of strong Indian bodies.[11] Thus, though tempting for an acrobatically inclined human, the idea that it is the acrobatic physical practice that constitutes the way to knowledge is not an ancient, but a modern idea. Indeed, in pre-modern forms of yoga, the postures that were privileged and highlighted seem to have been the sitting postures (sometimes highly challenging for a restless acrobat).

The development of modern physical culture went hand in hand with the modern development of the sciences of biology, physiology and medicine. In the case of yoga, this took the expression of the attempts—starting in the 1920s and 1930s—to try to prove the benefits and effects of yoga practice through the scientific methods of the time.[12] Though these attempts may not seem highly

---

[8] See Michelis.
[9] Bryant, E. F. *The Yoga Sutras of Patanjali*. New York: North Point Press, 2003.
[10] See Alter, 2004; Singleton; Bryant.
[11] See Singleton; Bryant.
[12] See Alter, 2004.

scientific today, this line of thinking continues as contemporary science tries to understand the effects (and bi-effects) of physical yoga practices and meditation, as well as their possible benefits in general and in the treatment or prevention of various conditions such as stress (a condition not unknown to the Ambivalent Ashtangi).[13]

It is into this modern invention of the "science of yoga"—where science may mean anything from knowledge of an unspecified absolute (loosely based in Hindu thinking, only to be interpreted in a trans-religious context) to biomedical research—that the Ambivalent Ashtangi is parachuted. I try to understand how I/the Ambivalent Ashtangi, as a practice-based scholar within the tiny domain of the humanities' tradition of the bodily turn and the attempt to understand embodied knowledge, can possibly come to grasp what kind of knowledge the bodily practice of yoga may provide for its practitioners and how we as researchers can understand this.

... to the A.A.'s version of the balloon theory of knowledge

There is a current anecdote or metaphor that I often return to, though I cannot locate its origin: the idea that knowledge is like the surface of a balloon. The more the balloon grows, the more one's knowledge accumulates, the larger we perceive the balloon's surface toward the exterior areas of ignorance. Though I have worked with physical practices and their modes of knowing in several ways and over many years, I recognize that I am hanging under a large balloon (aerial yoga! The perfect combination of circus and yoga!), whose surface is just growing. As I am not a specialist in Yoga philosophy, Hindu religious thought, or the complex history of the development of Indian culture, I am highly dependent on the fragments of various scholars' knowledge that I have managed to blow into my balloon. I experience more than ever that my knowledge is limited. But, paradoxically, the more I try to fill in the gaps, the more I realize the limits of my own knowledge.

In Yoga discourse, knowledge is supposed to happen through experience. It is not knowing about, but rather, getting to know through, living. Scholars have shown how this idea has evolved in the meeting point between Yoga philosophy, American transcendentalism and other movements of ideas, evolving in the 19th century and continuing into the 20th and 21st centuries.[14] For me, as a researcher-practitioner, this points to one of the sensible joints of my self-understanding.

---

[13] Broad, W. J. *The Science of Yoga—The Risks and the Rewards*. New York: Simon & Schuster, 2012.
[14] See Michelis.

As a scholar, assumed to look at things at a distance, I am not supposed to experience. As a scholar of bodily practices, I know, however, that embodied knowledge—though it can be understood abstractly—appears differently and in more multifaceted ways through experience. But the "knowledge" that Yoga discourse promises, is one that—though often presented as the "science" of Yoga—the academy is reluctant to accept, as it evolves within a discourse that is classified as esoteric and a realm that is, if not religious or spiritual, then at least existential. Thus, it goes beyond even the knowledge that practice-as-research, focusing on the kinds of knowledge developed in and through physical and artistic practices, aims to capture.

However, having experienced how different forms of knowledge are not equally valued within academia, and how academic life—just as any other structure—may lead to the stiffening of our mind, I am curious about how this line of potential knowledge will challenge my self-understanding as a scholar interested in different discourses of knowledge, and especially discourses of knowledge that propose processes of knowledge that pass through physical practices.

My readings into Yoga history make me understand that this particular openness, the idea that Yoga will lead you to enhance "knowledge"—without telling us in which form—is part of the lure of Yoga. By not stating which knowledge we are supposed to find, we can all invest the quest with our specific individual needs, across different temporal and cultural settings.[15]

I recognize that I have been trapped in this lure as well. The lure triggers my ambivalence. And yet I am tempted to see how Yoga may provide ways to knowledge even today. Hoping to fly under a balloon growing with both knowledge and consciousness of my own ignorance, I thus continue on some self-crafted and highly idiosyncratic path of Yoga, as the continuation of—or deviation from—my scholarly quest into the meanders of embodied knowledge. Skeptical as I am, though struggling hard to turn my skepticism into something more constructive, I am not necessarily expecting to find the absolute Knowledge, or the Knowledge of the Absolute (though that is what parts of the Yoga discourse promises). But I do see how Yoga helps me blow air into my own balloon of knowledge—in many different ways.

The transmission of postural know-how
I have recently received and been granted the right to do one more posture in the series of postures I am practicing. In principle, it is not difficult for me to do. I have sufficient strength and flexibility. Nevertheless, there are many details that

---

[15] Koch, M. *Yoga, Une histoire-monde: de Bikram aux Beatles, du LSD à la quête de soi: le récit d'une conquête*. Paris: La Découverte, 2019.

I need to keep track of. Going directly into the posture without any additional, non-necessary movement (it is so easy to let that foot slightly touch the floor first…), grasping the correct wrist with the opposite hand (I keep mixing them up). I know that I will be practicing the posture until the details are sufficiently correct, and my body will display that the posture has been totally integrated into my repertoire. Only then, and that may be in quite a lengthy amount of time, will I be granted the right to try the next posture. Strict measures of progression and acceptance of the authority of the teacher are part of the principles of transmission of postural know-how in the Ashtanga-yoga tradition.

One of the first forms of knowledge that today's practitioner encounters in transnational postural yoga is the elaborate knowledge of the postures. Though many of the basic and reoccurring postures are seductively simple, there is an elaborate culture around every tiny detail: which angles to strive for, which muscles to pull and which to relax. Other figures require a different, more in-depth restructuring of the body before I can pretend that I "know" how to do them. For instance, I may need to gain much more flexibility before my attempts begin to resemble the posture. Yet other postures have elaborate "elite versions" that I do not even try. Thus, Ashtanga yoga culture opens up a possible door to a well of knowledge related to "how to do the postures."

One source of this is the transmission of the details of the postures as they are reported to have been done traditionally—even if this tradition may not reach further back than the beginning of the 20th century and Krishnamacharya's reinterpretation of Hatha yoga.[16] For instance, in Ashtanga yoga there are detailed protocols for when to grab the side of a foot in a posture or when to hold the foot by the big toe. Also, there are protocols (when binding the arms around the body in different ways) when to grab the left or right wrist and in which way—even if the difference may be tiny on a functional level. Diving into yoga is like diving into a well of details, often with no explanation other than "this is the way it is practiced."

Another source in the transmission of the know-how of postures is the anatomical knowledge introduced into yoga slowly by practitioners and teachers over the last century. Many tools and tricks come from physiological and anatomical ideas of how to trigger the opposite muscles, how to release pressure on joints, and how to activate collaborating muscles with more activity. Practicing yoga is, if you care for it, a crash course in practical physiology and anatomy.

Furthermore, knowing the figures is also related to the way these have been explained by a different understanding of the body anchored in Indian history,

---

[16] See Singleton.

describing it in terms of "chakras," "nadis" and other terms referring to specific cultural and historical understandings of the body within pre-modern Hatha yoga—but presented often without further explanation. In this void they keep a mystical ring to them. They are floating somewhere between specific locations in the body and the idea of the energetic body. As a practitioner you may receive the impression that this is the body you will discover, the one you have not located and not experienced yet.

To begin with, I was hesitant toward the disciplined and disciplining form of transmission, wondering if it was superfluous and overly strict. But with time, I acknowledged that it interestingly adds something to the performative experience of yoga. Though it does not change the postures, it changes my relationship to the postures. It makes me fight with some to reach others. It forces me to be patient. And through this fight it forces me to focus on my reactions rather than just the doing. The discussions of what the purpose of this struggle is, if it is old-fashioned discipline or if it has a higher purpose, exists within the environment. It can be a mental steel bath, an ascetic exercise, a testing of your will, commitment and patience. It is one tiny part of the mechanism that transforms the practice of some simple and difficult postures into a mind-puzzling pursuit. Whether or how it is meaningful cannot be answered once and for all, but it can indeed trigger a process of questioning.

By the way—what is Yoga philosophy?

For a year or two I have had a translation of Patanjali's *Yoga Sutras* on my bookshelf: a thick volume including the Sanskrit version of the yoga sutras, translation, commentary, and much more. Though my knowledge of Indian philosophy is limited, I try to see yoga practice as a door that opens a whole world. Realizing that my knowledge of the context is rather limited, I made my way through several introductions to Indian philosophy in my spare time before even opening this volume. Though I am still not an expert, I slowly begin to see some contours of a complexity that I do not master at all.

As a part of the process, I also join the questioning of why the study of philosophy is limited to Western philosophy.[17] Though I do not have philosophical training as such, my studies in Cultural Studies and Performance Studies have included quite a lot of philosophical reading; philosophies that have been transformed to "theories" that I have tried stumblingly to "apply" to the understanding of various performance practices. Having long questioned what this sort of "application" implies, my focus is now redirected toward another problem. The

---

[17] Norden, B. W. *Taking Back Philosophy: A Multicultural Manifesto.* New York: Columbia University Press, 2017.

knowledge I have acquired is limited in a million other ways; for instance, I have never been seriously introduced to ways of performing or thinking outside the Euro-American sphere. I begin to dig into this question, looking into both the historical and philosophical aspects and looking at the colonial processes that have led to the lacuna in the systems of education I have encountered. I realize that I ought to have done something about this before, but rather than regretting it, I throw myself into this new research interest of mine as a way of both acquiring new knowledge and questioning the knowledge I thought I had.

Through my fragmented studies I come to see that even if Patanjali's *Yoga Sutras* seem to be at the center of the yoga tradition, as it is often considered by contemporary yoga practitioners, it is also part of the modern construction of the yoga tradition.[18] The yoga tradition is much more fragmented and multilinear than what the shortcut introduction I have encountered in practice led me to believe. Though the term is practical, it is actually quite hard to delimit the contours of "Yoga philosophy" at the different stages of Indian philosophy, and its overlapping with both Hindu, Buddhist and other forms of thinking. Maybe even this attempt is part of the modern attempt to place yoga as a spiritual, though not necessarily religious, practice. That is convenient for a practice that has been proposed to people of all religious convictions, with the argument that it is a science that can be applied by everyone.[19] Today, this tendency continues with the ways in which, for instance, mindfulness is proposed as a health-related practice, and where meditation is independent of any kind of conviction.

I am partly out of my bounds here, as I am not a specialist of the trajectories of transnational religious thinking. In addition, the terminology "philosophy" and "religion" is problematic when talking about yoga and Indian religion and philosophy. Though I begin to glimpse the complexity, the balloon that I am flying under is only half full of air. Nevertheless, the door that was opened gives me a glimpse of a part of world history of which I have too little knowledge. Though this may be an illusion and though I still have a lot to discover, I imagine that with a little bit of effort I can slowly get to know some parts of this world a little better. I see it as part of possible paths leading toward, if not knowledge of the Absolute, then at least some knowledge of different ways of thinking about the Absolute.

Sanskrit—practicing linguistic postures

One of the keys that I am lacking to properly enter the world of Yoga philosophy, and thus let the physical practice open up into more dimensions of thinking, is

---
[18] See Bryant; Singleton.
[19] See Michelis; Koch.

language. Most of the important texts that the Yoga tradition refers to are in Sanskrit. Even in the physical tradition, all postures have names in Sanskrit. Though some of these names may be modern constructions, they give the impression of a long tradition. They blend corporeal and natural vocabularies, giving the postures a half scientific, half nature-cult glow. Having no prior knowledge of Sanskrit, they are difficult to memorize as the words are long and the postures often have composite names.

My curiosity is awakened, I begin to wonder how this language is structured, what its components are. Sanskrit is a primarily liturgical language transmitted in the Brahman tradition. How it came to be the lingua franca of these acrobatic figures triggers my curiosity. My urge is to know more, to let the words open up, bit by bit, a world that is closed to me as long as I understand nothing. As a present I receive a textbook of Sanskrit, and I begin learning on my own. I quickly realize that, just as in the expansion of my knowledge of the body, and my knowledge of Indian philosophy, it may take me forever to have a minimal understanding of this language. But I find the elementary pleasure of learning—character by character, word by word, verb by verb. My mind responds to it as a puzzle or a crossword; I cannot "read," but I can spend hours deciphering a simple sentence of an exercise. The brain slowly masters linguistic postures. At the most intensive moments, I even imagine that I can sense how matter is redisposed in my brain to make space for this new language.

Though it is obviously a kind of complementary information that is necessary, this kind of effort does not easily enter into the strategic planning of a contemporary scholar. The strategic scholar is supposed to dig deeper and deeper into the same area of knowledge, and here I am, going further and further away from the place that I started from, to the extent of learning languages that it may take me years to decipher.

Yet it makes sense. As a scholar, I have an obligation not only to specialize, but also, when necessary, to amend the most flagrant areas of my ignorance—even if it places me, as many times before, in the situation of the beginner. Also, it makes sense for my practice-based, auto-ethnographic exploration of yoga's different forms of knowledge. If I think of my own case as a symptom of contemporary, transnational yoga practice, I am not a special case either. Many practitioners try to memorize at least some of the Sanskrit terms. These terms circulate in a transnational environment, floating in the midst of other languages, shared by non-specialists, invested and reinvested with contemporary meanings, probably displacing everything, but in the hopeful attempt to understand something. We may not know what we understand or not, but the quest is also part of the contemporary journey.

Experiencing the stilling of the mind—
the non-thematic content of yoga knowledge

At certain moments, when the practice of yoga seems to do something, I am almost frightened: the calm of mind that I sense is almost like a void. Thoughts circulate so much more slowly, as if there is no thinking at all. What if yoga does not promote thinking, but stops it?

When practicing the yoga postures, I am practicing the physical know-how of semi-acrobatic or acrobatic movement. When exploring the history of yoga, the philosophy of yoga or the languages that have carried it, I am focusing on a specific thematic content. But an important part of the practice of yogic knowledge is not about physical know-how or accumulation of content, but rather about practicing specific methods for obtaining non-thematic states of mind. To a large extent, at least if the discourse of yoga makes sense to us and the practice convinces us, the knowledge of yoga does not lie in the accumulation of knowledge, but in the methods to train certain states of mind.

The thinking process of yoga is not thought to function as, let's say, academia's idea of bending ideas and fighting over them with others. The idea of yoga, if one can believe the common discourse, is the idea of stilling the mind (with reference to Patanjali's famous *Yoga Sutra*), and through this stilling, perhaps opening the mind to another level of understanding. Socialized into academia's imperative to always think about something, it is almost frightening to just let the thoughts pass, not try to make them go faster or multiply them to make them all the more complex.

Yoga practice contains many different methods for obtaining this stilling of the mind, training the capacity to let consciousness be and observe it. Some of those that are currently practiced in transnational postural yoga are of course the yoga postures, as well as breathing exercises. But in the yoga tradition, these ideas are also related to other practices, such as ethical and devotional practices and different kinds of meditation. In the Ashtanga tradition, the "eight limbs" of yoga—ranging from ethical principles to advanced states of meditation—are often mentioned, though in contemporary yoga the practice of "asanas" and breathing exercises are the most current—though often interpreted in the light of the other "limbs."

In the physical practice some of the methods that—performatively—seem to foster the stilling of the mind are, for instance, combinations of breath and movement, repetitions that allow your mind to rest on the well-known and acknowledged sensation and specific focus points of your gaze, thus limiting your impressions. But also, the physical sensations of stretching/effort or difficulty that forces you to be attentive to the here-and-now seem to "do" something.

Some of these methods seem to be enhanced by slowness. For instance, one of the strongest experiences I have had of something that I would perceive as a "stilling of the mind" occurred at a moment when we were asked to perform the postures half as slowly as usual, or when having very long sessions of breathing exercises. Though Ashtanga yoga seems highly acrobatic, some of its methods lie in its extreme repetitiveness and slowness. It leads us back to the meditative yoga's seated positions. It is in the stillness of the body that the stillness of the mind occurs—even if it may happen after extreme physical exercise.

If we think about knowledge as content, then we miss a large part of the states of consciousness and existential experiences that yoga can provide us. The question is not whether yoga makes us stop thinking, but what happens in our consciousness in the moments that we experience as a kind of stopping or stilling of the mind. This is what scholars in the cognitive sciences have tried to figure out when studying the neurological aspects of meditative states. What they see so far is that these meditative states do seem to do something to our minds—to the extent that they influence the body physiologically and the mind neurologically; though much remains unknown from a scientific vantage point.[20]

Maybe one way of seeing these states and their relation to thinking is to think of them as a kind of prerequisite. Just as our brains need sleep to function, maybe our minds, at times, need stillness to function. Being so used to environments where one is constantly supposed to "think," this state of mind can be both frightening at the same time as it is relieving. Perhaps one of the things yoga can teach us is to see these states of resting of the mind as important, and to remember that thinking is not only about content, but also about the concentrated forms in which the thinking occurs. Yoga is one way of training those forms.

The mind of the acrobat
Of all the possible kinds of knowledge to which yoga can open a door, one may wonder if there is one in which the acrobatic aspect of yoga is essential. One may wonder if the acrobatic element is simply a fancy surplus added at a moment of modern body cult and nationalism, or if it is just the "circus" of yoga that lures hyper-active souls into the practice of yoga.

Yoga practitioners and teachers have been fast to refuse yoga as circus, and it is a recurring trope in yoga discourse to underline that yoga is not circus, as one sees, for instance, in the repeated comments on this in the Ashtanga tradition. This trope, however, needs to be seen in a certain context. Indeed, since the

---

[20] Goleman, D. & R. D. Davidson. *Altered Traits: Science Reveals How Meditation Changes Your Mind.* New York: Penguin Publishing Group, 2017.

17th-century itinerant yogis in India were compared to traveling acrobats, and when the British banned yogis—due to the fact that they considered them dangerous, as some of them were yogic warriors—the yogis indeed had to present their skills in the streets to earn a living.[21] When modern yoga formed itself, it did all it could to escape this image and instead presented a yoga turned toward devotional practices and health. However, focusing on contemporary practice, it is perhaps possible to reconsider this refusal of "circus," and instead focus on the performative effects of acrobatic movements on processes of consciousness. Maybe there are other parallels to be found and processes of the mind to be deciphered.

For the last couple of years, due to a coincidence of circumstances, I have been practicing yoga focusing mostly on the meditative aspects, accepting my physical limits, seeing it as an exercise of humility. It allowed me to explore more deeply how the use of minimum body strength affects flexibility. It allowed me to experience moments of calm and rest. And yet, when coming back to more acrobatic movement, I realized that something had been missing. Something that may be alluring but perhaps not essential (given that it is not always physically possible), but something that does "do" something to the mind.

Coming back to the acrobatic figures, to the necessity of using and building strength, I returned to the momentary experiences of pleasure and heightened self-confidence. You may say the experience of what contemporary science of exercise also points to: that exercise (and preferably strenuous exercise) triggers a chemical bath that is beneficial even for the mind: a dopamine bath. Sweaty exercise is supposed to help relieve stress, prevent or ease depression, and increase cognitive capacities. At these moments of flying high on the effects of strenuous acrobatic efforts, I am willing to believe this.

Paradoxically, two seemingly opposed states of mind meet in the experience of yoga: the state of mind obtained through slow movement, breathing and sitting still, and the state of mind obtained through advanced acrobatic figures, dedicated concentration combined with acrobatic difficulty. In both cases a certain stilling of the mind occurs. The number of thoughts unrelated to the movement itself decrease, and a heightened awareness of the present, a certain feeling of pleasure, occurs.

In both cases, it is maybe not so much the content of the thinking which is important, but how these states of mind function as the prerequisite for thinking, as the prerequisite for concentration as such. If thinking is based on a focused mind with the capacity for concentration, then acrobatic movement—in

---

[21] See Singleton; Pinch.

yogic or other forms—may be a way to train it. Though highly acrobatic movements are not necessarily the way to understanding the Absolute, they may be a way to train the brain's ability to concentrate; an ability that we need in any effort of thinking.

Knowledge of life
To an academically trained Ambivalent Ashtangi, the first thing to get used to and figure out how to relate to is the fact that the "science" of yoga provides knowledge of life through life. In this respect, the knowledge of yoga is an existential knowledge. It is not a knowledge about the world or about life, but a knowledge of life in the world. It is full of guidelines and suggestions for how to lead life—and promises of what happens next. These are the kinds of knowledge that in the academic world are easily degraded to lifestyle and self-help literature—discourses that academia is happy to analyze, but without entering into the argument: how are we then supposed to lead meaningful lives?

Though academia and yoga may provide different paths to knowledge, both fields and discourses agree on the importance of knowledge in some way. As a scholar who is growing slightly older, no longer tempted by knowledge as competition, frequently annoyed by the fights over status and power loosely disguised under the headline of "knowledge," a last resort to save my illusions is to think: What do we actually need knowledge for? What good may it provide in our lives? Though it may not be scientifically valid, there is an experiential and existential value to knowledge that helps us live. "Research"—though constantly touching on such areas—is reluctant to openly provide such knowledge. We have to craft it as individuals. This is where experiential, existential knowledge comes into the picture. This is where we need to construct practices and paths that pursue knowledge as a tool for both physical and mental survival. And though it may not seem obvious at first glance, acrobatic movement can be an important companion on this path.

Some conclusions
We live in a society focused on knowledge as content, as propositional knowledge or as know-how that can be used for the purpose of economic productivity. But the forms of thinking present in highly acrobatic movement in yoga (and, I would assert, also in circus) point to other equally important aspects of thinking. The kind of thinking we train in acrobatic movement is not so much focused on content—though there is one and it is important—as it is focused on the prerequisite for and form of the thinking: a clear mind and the capacity for concentration.

Just as knowledge as content needs to be practiced, knowledge as method for obtaining concentrated states of mind needs to be trained. This is especially true in a time where we are constantly disturbed by an excess of digital information ready to invade our awareness at any moment. Paradoxically, both extreme bodily stillness and extreme bodily effort seem to be capable of providing this kind of training.

In the case of postural yoga, those two modes are at the extreme of different ways of practicing—slowly or vigorously. These approaches may seem opposite, but they meet. Similarly, postural yoga and circus may not be as contradictory as certain practitioners have tried to imply, when underlining the devotional, meditative aspect of yoga. Their common points lie not so much in the acrobatic figures used, but in the fact that they provide a training of the forms of concentration. Acrobatic movement provides many other forms of knowledge—movement-based know-how, knowledge of context, knowledge of history, and the opening of worlds. But in terms of what kinds of thinking acrobatic movements provide, this is maybe where the promise lies. At least, that is the temporary conclusion of the limited experience of the Ambivalent Ashtangi.

—A.A./The Ambivalent Ashtangi.

References

Alter, J. *Yoga in Modern India: The Body between Science and Philosophy*. Princeton: Princeton University Press, 2004.

Alter, J. S. "Performativity and the Study of Modern Yoga." In *Yoga in the Modern World: Contemporary Perspectives*, edited by M. &. B. J. Singleton. London: Routledge, 2008, pp. 36-48.

Aubrecht, J. F. *Choreographers and Yogis: Untwisting the Politics of Appropriation and Representation in U.S. Concert Dance*. Riverside: Diss: University of California Riverside, 2017.

Broad, W. J. *The Science of Yoga: The Risks and the Rewards*. New York: Simon & Schuster, 2012.

Bryant, E. F. *The Yoga Sutras of Patanjali*. New York: North Point Press, 2003.

Damkjær, C. *Homemade Academic Circus: Ideosyncratically Embodied Reflections into Research in the Arts and Circus*. Dorset: Iff Books, 2016.

Goleman, D. & R. D. Davidson. *Altered Traits: Science Reveals How Meditation Changes Your Mind*. New York: Penguin Publishing Group, 2017.

Koch, M. *Yoga, Une histoire-monde: de Bikram aux Beatles, du LSD à la quête de soi: le récit d'une conquête*. Paris: La Découverte, 2019.

Michelis, E. D. *A History of Modern Yoga: Pantanjali and Western Esotericism*. New York: Continuum, 2005.

Norden, B. W. *Taking Back Philosophy: A Multicultural Manifesto*. New York: Columbia University Press, 2017.

Pinch, W. R. *Warrior Ascetics and Indian Empires*. Cambridge: Cambridge University Press, 2006.

Remski, M. *Practice and All is Coming: Abuse, Cult Dynamics, and Healing in Yoga and Beyond*. Rangoria: Embodied Wisdom Publishing, 2019.

Singleton, M. *Yoga Body: The Origins of Modern Posture Practice*. Oxford: Oxford University Press, 2010.

Circus A, Zamy Steynovitz.
All rights are reserved to the Steynovitz Estate, www.steynovitz.info.

Circus, *Tzedek*, and *Tikkun Olam*

Jessica Hentoff

"Would you be interested in bringing your circus group to Israel to work with us?" Rabbi Marc Rosenstein asked me via email. My instant response was, "Absolutely not! It's too dangerous!"

This was the fall of 2006. I was already the Artistic/Executive Director of Circus Harmony, a social circus school in St. Louis, Missouri. My personal definition of social circus is "the teaching and performing of circus arts to motivate social change by building character in individuals and bridges between communities."

Rabbi Marc Rosenstein was an American who had made *Aliyah* to Israel. He had helped start the Galilee Foundation for Value Education to help bring Israeli Arabs and Jews together. The Galilee Foundation had the first online Jewish/Arab newsletter. They did extensive educational programming for visiting Americans. But they were just starting a program to bring together Jewish and Arab young people. They had planned to do a theater company but then they chose circus because, in Rabbi Marc's words,

> First of all, you don't need a language, and it doesn't matter if they speak Arabic or Hebrew. Second of all, they need to trust each other. When one young person jumps the second one must catch him, and they have to trust each other completely. The third and most important advantage, which affects all areas of life, is the need to overcome fear. This isn't something natural, something you can take for granted when you're talking about circus exercises, and certainly not when you're talking about the fear of other people.[1]

I had been doing social circus work since founding the St. Louis Arches youth circus troupe in the late 1980s. I did not know it was "social circus" work. I taught circus arts because I had fallen in love with it at 18 years old and when I asked my circus teacher, Warren Bacon, how I could thank him for introducing me to circus, he said, "I'll tell you what my teacher, Fay Alexander, told me: 'Pass it on.'" So, I did. I just happened to be passing it on to a group of children, poor and rich, Black and white, from different St. Louis neighborhoods.

At that time, I had 15 children in my advanced youth circus performance

---

[1] Ahiyah Reved, "'Trusting Each Other' A Jewish Arab Circus" July, 2007. https://www.ynetnews.com/articles/0,7340,L-3426415,00.html.

troupe, the St. Louis Arches. They ranged in age from 10 to 16 years old and were from different cultural and socioeconomic backgrounds. I was also a Jewish mother of three children. As members of St. Louis' Central Reform Congregation, like all American Jewish children, they were offered a trip to Israel through Taglit Birthright Israel which would have helped pay for them to go to Israel when they were 17. I had not signed them up. My impression of Israel, at the time, was that it was a very dangerous place. At the same time, St. Louis had surpassed Detroit as the most dangerous city in America.[2]

I was also teaching a soon-to-be 80-year-old woman how to do an aerial act. She had actually joined the circus as a showgirl when she was a teenager. When her parents went to bring her home, she talked them into letting her stay with the promise that she would not do any aerial work. She came to me at 79, saying, "I promised my parents I wouldn't do aerial work, but they are gone now; do you think it is too late?" I said, "No," and she started training to do an aerial act for her eightieth birthday. This woman had a tattoo on her ankle that said, *Esse quam videri*—Latin for "To be rather than to seem."[3]

Right after I emailed Rabbi Marc that I thought it would be too dangerous for me to bring my students to Israel, I left to attend the American Youth Circus Organization's Educators Conference, which was in Chicago that year. The focus of the conference was on social circus. As the director of one of the foremost social circuses in America, I was one of the speakers. I was also one of the people involved in a very emotional discussion about the definition of social circus. There were some who believed that it meant only working with marginalized youth. I argued that the definition of "social circus" is found in the intention of the work. Part of the power of Circus Harmony's work is bringing together children from different backgrounds, specifically, children who are of means and children who are not of means, children who are Black and children who are white, children who are Christian and children who are Jewish; all children, really. We show them that they have more in common than not and that when they focus on what connects them instead of what divides them, they can create something amazing!

When I came home from the conference, there was an email waiting for me from Rabbi Marc. "I understand you think it is too dangerous," he said. "Would you happen to know another group of children from mixed backgrounds who might be willing to come to Israel?" *To be rather than to seem*, I thought. "We will come," I responded. And so it began. It was the beginning of a partnership

---

[2] CNN: Best of the Best and Worst of the Worst, 2021. https://money.cnn.com/popups/2006/real_estate/best_worst/2.html.

[3] Interestingly, this phrase was also the motto of the family of Raoul Wallenberg, the Swedish diplomat who saved thousands of Jews during the Holocaust.

that lasted more than a decade between Circus Harmony in St. Louis and the Galilee Circus. This partnership became the subject of a movie by Alexander Lipsitz called *Circus Kids* and of a book by Cynthia Levinson called *Watch Out for Flying Kids*. It also became a life-changing experience for many of the people who were part of it, and continues to change lives today.

In addition to being the mother of three biological children, and circus mother of numerous circus children, I am also the daughter of the writer and social justice warrior, Nat Hentoff, of blessed memory. He defined himself as "a stiff-necked Jewish atheist" but took the Jewish focus on social justice beyond seriously. My father wrote about his own father, my grandfather, Simon Hentoff, who had emigrated to the United States from Russia, "My father, without sloganeering, believed that the essence of Judaism was to lead a just life. He despised racial or any other form of discrimination. I was not raised as a religious Jew but I was raised with the religion of social justice."[4] And that is how my father raised me.

My father was a man who made a difference. He taught me telling stories was important; saying your truth out loud was imperative; standing up for others had to happen; maintaining integrity was seamless; and that words that lead to actions matter. His life bridged many interests that intertwined. Bridge is the operative word. He was a bridge between people, between ideas and ideals. To him it all connected. His life and work also had a profound influence on many people and I am certainly one of them. I was raised quite conscious that I was Jewish but with no religious education.

As is often the case with children raised as secular Jews, I joined a Jewish congregation when I myself had children. It was summer when I decided to do so. None of the other synagogues in St. Louis had summer programs for children and, in fact, did not seem very welcoming of children at all. The only one I found where God did not seem to take a vacation (or go to Jewish summer camp), was Central Reform Congregation. It was also the only Jewish congregation in the city of St. Louis. The CRC website states:

> Our core values are central to everything we do and serve as guideposts for prioritizing our activities. **A deep sense of community** where we, in part, draw strength from each other by connecting both in crisis and in celebration. It is a community that strives to make Judaism relevant and meaningful in the lives of its members. **A respect for diversity** including the valuing and sharing between generations and inclusiveness of

---

[4] Nat Hentoff, "Civil Liberties War Among Jews," *Village Voice*, January, 2002. https://www.villagevoice.com/2002/01/08/civil-liberties-war-among-jews/.

all who seek to be a part of our community. **A focus on others** through commitment to social issues and a reaching out to the broader community. This is further supported by a deep belief in the possibilities of Tikkun Olam—the repair of the world.⁵

Even though I was a lifelong Jew, it was at the Central Reform Congregation that I first heard the age-old concept of *Tikkun Olam* that my father had modeled for me his whole life but I had not known had a name. The term *Tikkun Olam* is often interpreted to mean "repairing the world." Circus arts have long been recognized as a tool for making the world a better place. In Judaism, there is an oft-repeated talmudic story about Rabbi Broka asking the prophet Elijah if anybody in a marketplace would have a share in the World to Come. At first, there was no one in the marketplace who seemed to fit the description, until two men entered. And Elijah said, "Those two would have a place." When the rabbi asked them their occupation, they replied "We are clowns. When we see someone who is sad, we cheer them up. When we see people quarreling, we try to make peace between them" (Taanit 22a). Similarly, in a 1953 Ringling Brothers and Barnum & Bailey Circus program, Ernest Hemingway wrote, "Everything else is supposed to be bad for you. But the circus is good for you. It is the only spectacle I know that, while you watch it, gives the quality of a truly happy dream."⁶

So, 15 St. Louis kids flew a quarter of the way around the world for this Peace Through Pyramids partnership. The flight to Israel was over 12 hours long. Some of the children were awake the whole time, fascinated by the seat-back entertainment center. Rabbi Marc Rosenstein, who had invited us, met us at the airport. We took a bus for an hour and a half to a parking lot in Karmiel, a Jewish town in the Galilee. The bus pulled into the parking lot and we could see a group of kids waiting for us. The Israeli kids ranged in coloring from light-skinned, blue-eyed and blonde to dark tanned skin with dark eyes and black hair. As we got off the bus, one of my students asked me, "How will we tell who's Jewish and who's Arab?" In America, it is generally easy to tell who is Black and who is white. It often amused me that people in America often assumed that all of the African American children in our troupe were poor, though that was not the case.

Part of the reason Rabbi Marc was bringing us to Israel was to show the Galilee Circus children that it really was not about some of them being Arab

---

⁵ Central Reform Congregation. "About CRC." 2023. https://www.centralreform.org/about/.
⁶ "Nowhere Left To Run Away To: The Circus' Final Days," Penn Live Patriot-News, January, 2017. https://www.pennlive.com/entertainment/2017/01/nowhere_left_to_run_away_to_th.html.

and some being Jewish; what mattered was that all the children were *circus*. The kids lined up and stared at each other as if they were at a middle school dance. Then one of the Israelis, a boy named Shai, took five balls out of his backpack and started juggling. Circus Harmony's Lemond did a five ball take-away. Everyone applauded and the ice was broken. More people started juggling and then talking, and the adventure truly began. Not all the Arabs spoke Hebrew and not all the Jews spoke English—but all these young people spoke *circus*. And over the next two weeks, they managed to create a show and forge friendships, some of which last to this day!

These young people, who spoke three different languages, created a show in two days and then performed it throughout Israel. There was also something that happened that had never occurred with the Galilee Circus before. Because we were there, Jewish children stayed with the American children in homes in the Arab village, and Arab children stayed in Jewish homes. Something so small and everyday—a child's sleepover—happened because a youth circus was involved. The next year, the Galilee Circus came to the United States and performed around the St. Louis metropolitan area. After that, the troupe reunited every two years, alternating between Israel and America. The last time we were in Israel, the Jewish and Arab families were having picnics and gathering in each others' homes on a regular basis.

There was also the impact on the people who saw the shows of the combined troupes. Rabbi Marc observed, "I think many who saw the shows felt the same tears in their eyes, maybe out of the feeling one is seeing a vision of something that we all long for... the total obliteration of barriers, whether social, economic or gravitational."

One night, near the end of that first journey to Israel, we stood around watching my students do somersaults over a campfire. Rabbi Marc turned to me and said, "When I first invited you to Israel, you said it was too dangerous. I'm watching this and I have to ask you, 'What is your definition of danger?'"

I told him that it was when I felt we were not in control of a situation. I knew my flying children could safely leap over a campfire. I didn't know that we would be safe in Israel. But we took the risk anyway and it became the beginning of a great social circus adventure that has rippled out into the world and continues to do so via the movie *Circus Kid*s, the book *Watch Out for Flying Kids*, and the children whose lives were changed by being part of this captivating collaboration. Most importantly, students from both countries are performing, living, and working all over the world. Some remain in touch with each other and are still inspiring people wherever they go! They took control of their lives and are showing the world that anything is possible. *Esse quam videri.*

Our Peace Through Pyramids partnership found our beautifully blended troupe of acrobats performing in very interesting places, times and situations. In Israel in 2010, we were performing in a town square where there were posters still up from the 2009 election where the slogans for one of the political parties was a promise that they would not allow Arabs to live in that town. There we were, Jews and Arabs, Blacks and whites, performing together and holding each other up in their town square.

In St. Louis, on August 5, 2016, an Israeli Jewish circus boy on a unicycle carried the torch for the Maccabee Games (Jewish Olympics). He was part of a 21-person troupe that consisted of Israeli Jews and Arabs along with St. Louis city and suburban children who together performed breathtaking acrobatics and other circus arts at the Jewish Community Center on the very day the Jewish Federation of St. Louis denounced the Black Lives Matter platform plank that said America should no longer aid Israel. Many times we were in places where we were modeling one way of being and in the same time and space, the opposite was being presented. In 2010, at an Israeli water park where we performed during the day, and then were sleeping on the grounds at night, we heard yelling and cheering later in the evening. We went to see what it was, only to find out it was an Arab political rally that was anti-Jews.

Rabbi Marc was under no illusion. On the Galilee Circus website, he acknowledged that "Circus will not bring peace to the Middle East. But it can help to make dialogue possible by reducing fears, lowering barriers, and building trust. It can provide a model of a shared loyalty that transcends ethnic identities. It can teach the art of taking risks for the common good. It can demonstrate, to a wide audience, that what appears to be impossible is indeed possible." He added, "The circus is a drop in the bucket. But we hope the drops will accumulate."

The last year that we went to Israel, in 2014, we almost didn't go. The night before we were to leave, Gaza started bombing Israel. We spent the night in America, before we left, scanning the news and talking to people in Israel and to all of our families. In the end, we decided to go. Only one family pulled out. They thought it was too dangerous. I understood.

While we were there this time, our schedule was constantly changing to avoid places where there was active, violent conflict. We were staying in different houses in both Jewish and Arab villages. All the houses had the TV on constantly; in the corner of the screen on every station was the death toll and a list of where the bombings were. Over 2,000 people were killed between July and August of that year in the conflict. Most of them were Arabs.

Whenever we traveled to Israel, we saw soldiers everywhere and they were usually armed. But in 2014, it was different. At dusk, there was an armed military presence at the entrance to every Arab village. Within days of our return to St. Louis, the suburb of Ferguson erupted in violence after a white police officer shot and killed an African American teenager named Michael Brown. With Circus Harmony's office being in the nearby community of Florissant, we were actually closer to the violence at home than when we were in Israel. Circus Harmony believes the path to peace is one of cooperation and communication. Teaching children from different neighborhoods how to stand on each other's shoulders may seem like a strange way to take this path, but it works for us! So, we started Peace Through Pyramids: Ferguson. This expanded into a Peace Through Pyramids partnership with children from Ferguson and children from the Saul Mirowitz Jewish Day School just a few towns away. To celebrate Martin Luther King, Jr. Day in 2016, we presented a Peace Through Pyramids show with these partners in Ferguson and in the well-to-do suburb of Creve Coeur, where the Saul Mirowitz school is located. Parents of the children went to both shows in both places.

The last year that the Galilee Circus came to St. Louis, we performed at the Ferguson Community Center. Sadly, the Galilee Foundation for Value Education folded after that year and the Galilee Circus never found a foothold in a new home. However, some of the Arab children (now adults), who were part of the very first partnership with Circus Harmony, continue to offer classes in the Arab village of Deir al Asad.

Back in St. Louis, the first partnership between children from Ferguson and children from Saul Mirowitz spread to Peace Through Pyramids partnerships between other schools in different neighborhoods. When it became clear that there was no Galilee Circus to continue the partnership with, Circus Harmony started a new Peace Through Pyramids partnership with a social circus in Puerto Rico. In 2018, our troupe joined the Puerto Rican troupe which called themselves the Revolution Circus and we co-created the Revolution for Harmony Circus Tour to bring the joy and excitement of circus to places in Puerto Rico that were recovering from the destruction of Hurricane Maria.

In the isolated town of Comerio, high up in the mountains of Puerto Rico, an artist-activist named Edgardo Larregui Rodriguez told us that he believed that public art experiences, like us bringing the art of circus into neighborhoods, are a necessary part of building community. "Art is what unites us in our community," he said. "It is an activation of the abandoned spaces. It's an action of reclaiming community. It's not just drawing, or painting, or making sculptures, but a vision of community, of uniting people to make public spaces better."[7]

A number of the early members of the first Peace Through Pyramids part-

---

[7] Sophie Hurwitz, "Youth Circus Brings Joy to Puerto Rico A Year After Maria," *Huffpost* August, 2018. https://www.huffpost.com/entry/circus-puerto-rico-hurricane-maria_b_5b6daf30e4b-002bcfeab61d0.

nership with Israel have gone on to become professional circus performers and toured around the world. Many of them have been American but some have also been Israeli. One night several years ago, one of my biological sons sent me a photo of him with another young man. It looked like the Israeli boy, Shai, who had broken the ice by juggling when we all first met. I thought my son was in Europe touring with a circus at the time. "Where are you?" I asked. "In Brussels," my son answered. "My plane got delayed but I remembered Shai is here, so I am staying with him." Circus means having family all over the world. We have had Israeli and Puerto Rican students come and spend a year with us.

Why does social circus work to change lives while it builds capacity in individuals and bridges between communities... and how does this relate to Judaism? Let's go back even further than our first invitation to Israel. I started the youth circus troupe, the St. Louis Arches, in 1989, because the professional show I was working with, Circus Flora, wanted to do circus work in the community of the city of St. Louis. Along with some other performers, we started teaching in the city's public schools. From these early classes, we chose 10 children and started the St. Louis Arches. Because we were teaching in low-income, inner-city neighborhoods, those are the children who comprised the original Arches troupe. I was just sharing something I loved. I did not know that what I was doing had a special name until a man that many call the grandfather of social circus, Reg Bolton, came to visit around 2003. Reg was an Irishman who lived in Australia. He had used circus to connect Catholic and Protestant youth in Ireland. Reg worked with aboriginal children in Australia. I had never even heard of the term *social circus* until, over a cup of tea, Reg asked what I thought of the term. At that point, it had edged out the term *community circus* to refer to the sort of work Reg and I both did—which went beyond just teaching children to flip, fling and fly. When he came to visit me in St. Louis, I had already started Circus Salaam Shalom to bring together children from a Jewish temple and Muslim mosque. While the two places of worship were only blocks away, the children never crossed paths until they joined the circus. This program showed everyone—including me—how much more we have in common than what is different about us.

Still, what is social circus? Cirque du Soleil's *Cirque du Monde* program defined it as:

> ...an innovative social intervention approach, which uses the circus arts as a tool for fostering the personal and social development of at-risk individuals. It targets various at-risk groups living in precarious personal and social situations, including street or detained youth and female survivors of

violence. The primary goal of this approach is not merely to learn circus arts. Rather, it's designed to help participants achieve personal and social development by nurturing their self-esteem and trust in others, teaching them social skills, inspiring them to become active citizens, and helping them to express their creativity and explore their potential. Social circus is a powerful catalyst for creating social change, because it helps marginalized people to assume citizenship within a community and enrich that community with their talents.[8]

While I still maintain that social circus work does not mean ONLY working with marginalized youth, that viewpoint may make the connections to Judaism a little more obvious.

The ancient Jewish call *"Tzedek, tzedek tirdof!"* or "Justice, justice you shall pursue!" from Deuteronomy 16:20 has been a cornerstone of Reform Judaism and its focus on political activism.[9] Social Circus uses circus to pursue social justice. Even as a secular Jew, I was raised with the concept that while Passover celebrates the Jews' exodus from being slaves in Egypt, none of us is truly free until everyone in the world is free.

The American Circus Educators Association believes that

> Social Circus refers to the use of circus arts as a medium for social justice and individual wellness and uplifts the role of art and culture as powerful agents for change. Social Circus practitioners support participants as creative change makers through the collective development of self-esteem, solidarity, and trust.[10]

The concepts of *Tzedek*/Justice and *Tikkun Olam*/Repairing the World are central tenets of Judaism. The construct of *mitzvot* is the covenant between Jews and the Almighty. It seems to me that Judaism is about keeping God's laws, living life with those laws in mind, and arguing about what it all means. I believe that justice means that everyone should have equal power, opportunity, and control of their own lives.

Whether you feel you have this covenant to uphold or you just feel it is the

---

[8] Michel Lafortune, *Social Circus Trainer's Guide: Basic Training.* Canada: Cirque Du Soleil, 2012.
[9] Rabbi Marla Feldman, "Why Advocacy is Central to Reform Judaism," 2023. https://urj.org/what-we-do/social-justice/why-advocacy-is-central-to-reform-judaism.
[10] American Circus Educators, "Social Circus." https://www.americancircuseducators.org/overview/.

right thing to do, the work is the same. Biblically, the command to help others is repeated over and over again. The Torah claims "there will never cease to be needy ones in your land" (Deuteronomy 15:11). To me, this does not mean just people who are poor. There are a lot of needs and many ways children are underserved besides being poor; many social issues derive from the inequality between those who have and those who have not. In fact, the problems often seem to stem from the viewpoint of there being an *us* and an *other*. What can we do to eradicate this gap? We are back to the Passover exhortation that no one is free until we are all free. Helping others is not limited to Judaism, but it is commanded there. It is a tremendous responsibility to feel it is your job to try to save the world—or at least make it a better palace. Yet, we are all called to do so. I think the *mitzvah* of *Tikkun Olam* can be done using any sort of glue—music, medicine, law, or whatever you choose. I chose to use circus arts as my way to repair little pieces of this broken world.

My father's father passed this on to him and he passed it on to me. I recognize how much of my work and style is connected to the values I was raised on through my father's life—the stubbornness/tenacity (depending on your point of view!), bridge-building, and even the extremism and activism. The way my father used writing, I use circus arts to motivate social change.

My responsibility as a human is the same as my job as director of the social circus, Circus Harmony: to give young people abilities and opportunities. My father's work was about telling the stories of individuals. My work is about helping individuals write their own stories. More profoundly, the circus work I do pursues the very ideals that were at the heart of my father's work—*Tzedek* and *Tikkun Olam*. I have found that Social Circus is about helping young people overcome not only gravity but labels and other limitations placed on them by society. It is about giving children the power to define themselves. Beyond that, I want my children—both biological and circus—to find their strengths, realize their creativity, and learn to accept and encourage themselves and others to be the best they can be, both in and out of the circus ring. My hope is that they will be the ones to ensure a more inclusive world by finding a place for everyone, connecting people from different communities, and helping to find creative solutions to real-world issues.

References

Central Reform Congregation. "About CRC," 2023. https://www.centralreform.org/about/.

CNN: Best of the Best and Worst of the Worst. 2021. https://money.cnn.com/popups/2006/real_estate/best_worst/2.html.

Feldman, Rabbi Marla. "Why Advocacy is Central to Reform Judaism." Union for Reform Judaism, 2023. https://urj.org/what-we-do/social-justice/why-advocacy-is-central-to-reform-judaism.

Hentoff, Nat. "Civil Liberties War Among Jews." *Village Voice*. January 2002. https://www.villagevoice.com/2002/01/08/civil-liberties-war-among-jews/.

Hurwitz, Sophie. "Youth Circus Brings Joy to Puerto Rico A Year After Maria," *Huffpost*, August, 2018. https://www.huffpost.com/entry/circus-puerto-rico-hurricane-maria_b_5b-6daf30e4b002bcfeab61d0.

Lafortune, Michel. *Social Circus Trainer's Guide: Basic Training*, Canada: Cirque Du Soleil, 2012.

"Nowhere Left To Run Away To: The Circus' Final Days." Penn Live Patriot-News. January, 2017. https://www.pennlive.com/entertainment/2017/01/nowhere_left_to_run_away_to_th.html.

Reved, Ahiyah. "'Trusting Each Other' A Jewish Arab Circus." July, 2007. https://www.ynetnews.com/articles/0,7340,L-3426415,00.html.

Seated Clown, Irene Aronson.
Photo © The Israel Museum, Jerusalem by Zohar Shemesh.

Juggling Across the Ancient World

Thom Wall

As with dance, so with juggling: the moment that the performer finishes their routine, the act ceases to exist beyond the memory of the audience. There is no permanent record of what transpired, so studying the ancient roots of juggling—that skill of throwing and catching objects—is fraught with difficulty.

Using the records that do exist, juggling appears to have emerged around the world in cultures independent of one another in the ancient past. Paintings in Egypt from 2000 BCE show jugglers engaged in performance. Oral histories from across the South Pacific place the activity with their goddess of the underworld—a figure who has guarded volcanic caves since time immemorial. Games and rituals that utilize juggling skills are pervasive in isolated Inuit cultures in northern Canada and Greenland, as well as across indigenous cultures throughout North America. Though the earliest representation of juggling is 4,000 years old, the practice is surely much older—in the same way that humans were doubtlessly singing and dancing long before the first bone flute was created.

Today, the English word *juggling* conjures images of clowns, circus tents, and buskers on the street. The story, however, doesn't begin with these modern associations. In 21st century English, *juggling* refers to the skill of throwing and catching multiple objects in repetition—with no undertone of trickery, magic, or deception. This limited use of the word was entered into the *Oxford English Dictionary* in 1897. Before this point, *juggling* referred to any number of entertainments including musicianship, animal training, tumbling, sleight of hand, tossing and catching, and more. It wasn't until the end of the 20th century that our modern, semantically-exclusive use of the word took shape. Similar shifts and splits have occurred in languages all over the world—some of which add granularity, such as the Latin *pilarii* (those who throw balls) and *ventilatores* (those who throw knives, among other objects)—and others which don't, such as the Japanese *Daikagura* (which refers to a religious form of object manipulation that a Westerner would understand immediately to be "juggling") and *Juggling* (the English loan-word in Japanese that captures the Western notion of throwing and catching and uploading videos of yourself to the Internet—a very different thing, indeed). This complicates the task of exploring the ancient roots of today's jugglers and their practices through language alone. By examining material evidence, however, the story begins to take shape.

The following is an attempt to catalog the earliest traces of juggling across Egypt, Israel, and the surrounding lands.

34 · Under One Tent: Circus, Judaism and Bible

Figure 1 Jugglers in Theban Tomb no. 15 at Beni-Hassan. This illustration erroneously includes a fourth juggler catching a ball. This person is not actually represented in the frieze at Beni Hasan. From *Manners and Customs of the Ancient Egyptians* (Volume 2, pp. 66-67) by J. G. Wilkinson, 1837, London.

Ancient Egypt

Our story begins on the walls of the 15th tomb at Beni Hasan (fig. 1). This particular grave in the 4,000-year-old cemetery holds Baqt III, governor of an area known as Oryx Nome.[1]

Likely referred to as *jmd*[2] in its time, the Egyptian practice of skillful throwing and catching was documented for the first time in 1837 by John Gardner Wilkinson in the second book of his five-volume work *The Manners and Customs of the Ancient Egyptians*. He noted:

> The game of ball was not confined to children or to either sex, though the mere amusement of throwing and catching it appears to have been considered more partially adapted to

---

[1] Newberry, P. E. *Beni Hasan* (Vol. II). London: Egypt Exploration Society, 1893. http://digi.ub.uni-heidelberg.de/diglit/newberry1893bd2/0061.

[2] Decker, W. *Sports and Games of Ancient Egypt*. (A. Guttmann, Trans.) New Haven and London: Yale University Press, 1992. Much like modern Arabic and Hebrew, words in the ancient Egyptian language are formed from roots. Tri-consonantal clusters are placed into fixed patterns with prefixes, infixes, and suffixes, along with unwritten vowels that speakers can intuit while reading. Since no speakers of ancient Egyptian remained when the Rosetta Stone was discovered and the Egyptian language was deciphered at the turn of the nineteenth century, the pronunciation of the language remains a mystery. In our case here, we know that the root of the word for this Egyptian ballgame was jmd, but any pronunciation of the word would be conjecture. See Gadalla, M. *The Musical Aspects of The Ancient Egyptian Vocalic Language*. Greensboro, NC: Tehuti Research Foundation, 2016.

Figure 2 Girls playing with the ball - 15th Tomb of Beni Hasan. From *Beni Hasan* (Volume II) by P. E. Newberry. London: Egypt Exploration Society, 1893.

females. They had different methods of playing… sometimes they showed their skill in catching three or more balls in succession, the hands occasionally crossed over the breast.[3]

Interestingly, this isn't the only representation of ball playing in the tombs at Beni Hasan. In Tomb No. 17 of that same complex—the tomb of Kheti, an 11th-dynasty provincial governor or "nomarch"[4]—there are paintings of women in similar scenes, playing with balls and performing acrobatics (fig. 2).[5]

Wilkinson infers from the dress and hairstyles of the women depicted in the Beni Hasan paintings, however, that these are not mere hobbyists. Rather, he claims that "…it is evident that they were professional dancers or jugglers." Decker suggests that juggling and playing ball sports were women's games, since they "…appear in connection with exclusively female occupations." Though children of either sex "played with the ball," it appears that only women could take it on as a profession (fig. 3,4,5).

According to Wilkinson, the Ancient Egyptians' juggling balls were made of sewn leather and stuffed with bran or corn husks, or made of braided reeds covered in leather (fig. 6). He suggests their balls may even have been made in multiple colors, similar to today's classic juggling beanbags: "covered, like many of our own, with slips of leather of a rhomboidal shape, sewed together longitudinally, and meeting in a common point at both ends, each alternate slip being of a different color." Though he points out that we only know this from illustrations on pottery, which doesn't give us enough information as to exactly how they were constructed.

---

[3] Wilkinson, J. G. *Manners and Customs of the Ancient Egyptians* (Vol. 2). London, 1837. Though some scholars have speculated about a connection between Greco-Roman and Egyptian ball games and juggling, Egyptologist Wolfgang Decker refutes that claim in his definitive book *Sports and Games of Ancient Egypt* (1992).
[4] Decker.
[5] Newberry. The ball games that are often depicted have sophisticated sets of rules. If a player dropped the ball, that person would be "…obliged to suffer another to ride on her back, who continued to enjoy this post until she also missed it: the ball being thrown by an opposite party, mounted in the same manner, and placed at a certain distance, according to the space previously fixed by the players; and, from the position and office of the person who had failed, it is not improbable that the same name was applied to her as those in the Greek game, who were called… 'asses,' and were obliged to submit to the commands of the victor" (Wilkinson, 1837).

Figure 3 Girls playing with the ball – 17th Tomb of Beni Hasan. From *Beni Hasan* (Volume II) by P. E. Newberry. London: Egypt Exploration Society, 1893.

Figure 4 Female acrobats and girls playing with the ball – 15th Tomb of Beni Hasan. Adapted from "BH 4," by Cairo Info, 2009.
(https://www.flickr.com/photos/manna4u/4127122259/)

Juggling Across the Ancient World · 37

Figure 5 Entrances to the rock-cut tombs at Beni Hasan. From "Pharaonic Monuments at Minya," Egyptian State Information Service, 2017. (http://sis.gov.eg/Story/116395/Pharaonic-monuments-in-Minya).

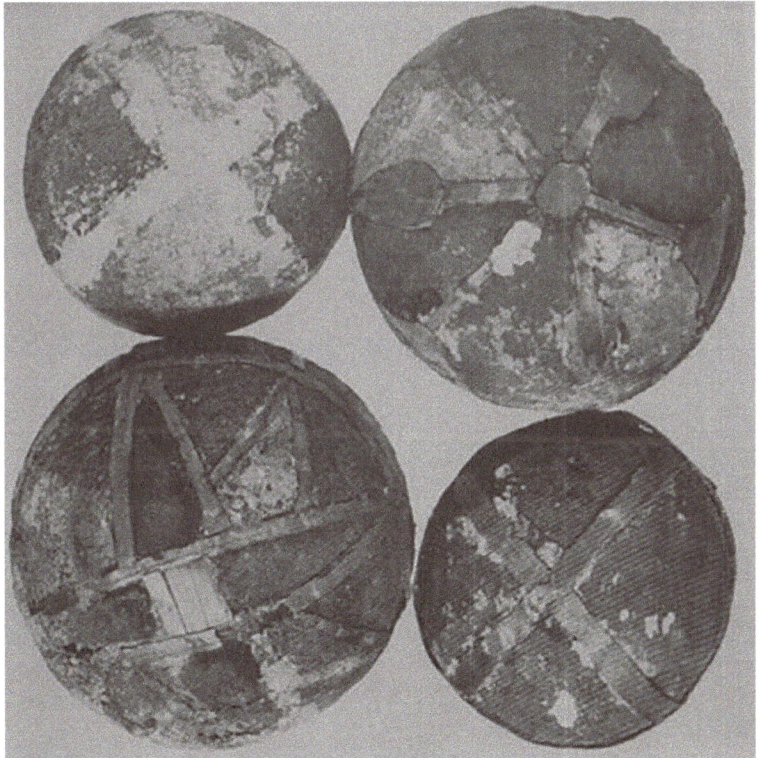

Figure 6 Linen ball from Grave 518 at Tarkhan, Egypt; a bag of rocks, or the first-ever juggling ball? From "Ancient Egyptian Parents Put This in Their Child's Grave to Play with in the Afterlife," by Sue Giles, 2018. (https://museumcrush.org/ancient-egyptian-parents-put-this-in-their-childs-grave-to-play-with-in-the-afterlife/).

J. G. Wilkinson was the first to publish a survey of the tombs at Beni Hasan, including a depiction of the juggling women from Tomb No. 15. However, Wilkinson's illustration with the juggling women had an error—a fourth woman throwing and catching a ball was added to the group.

Historian Sonja Boeckmann believes that this was a simple error in publication—that the woman is actually a member of a group of six ball-players from elsewhere in the frieze, inserted and reflected into the group as a byproduct of the printing methods used to create the book's illustration plates.[6]

Although the wall painting was more faithfully copied and published by Newberry's illustrator in 1893, Wilkinson's illustration from a half-century prior is the one that has found a home in popular culture.

One of the earliest and most popular trade juggling books to include an illustration of these juggling women was Ziethen and Allen's 1985 work *Juggling: The Art and Its Artists,* which used Wilkinson's image of four women.[7] Since this was the first pictorial representation of juggling in ancient Egypt that the juggling community had access to, it spread like wildfire across the early Internet. As a result, Wilkinson's erroneous "fourth woman" has been found on T-shirts, tea towels, and tattoos all around the world for decades.

Ancient Babylonia

In Babylon and Assyria, jugglers and bear tamers were known by the Sumerian word *u-da-tuš*. Primary-source texts from the provinces of Ĝirsu and Drehem give accounts of these performers and allude to their roles within society. Although these texts are undated, linguists have concluded through a study of the ancient Sumerian and Babylonian languages that this word was in common use until around 1000 BCE.

The *u-da-tuš* traveled throughout the region, perhaps performing as part of religious ceremonies. It seems that about 120 *u-da-tuš* resided in the temple of Sulgi, located in the capital city Ĝirsu-Lagaš, and received a weekly ration of barley as part of an arrangement related to their activities within the temple. Two male performers, Hu-wa-wa and Ze-bi, lived at the temple and were mentioned in these texts in a ledger accounting for their barley rations. This ledger is interesting because it includes an official seal that scholar Franco D'Agostino says definitively links the profession of juggling and bear taming with religious ceremony.[8]

---

[6] Boeckmann, S. (11/1/2018). (T. Wall, Interviewer).

[7] Boeckmann, S. *"Es fliegt was in der Luft" – Kulturgeschichtliche Aspekte des Jonglierens.* Carl von Ossietzky Universität Oldenburg, 2003.

[8] D'Agostino, F. "Some Considerations on U-da-tuš (Bear Tamer) and Jugglery in Ur III." *His-*

Another document demonstrates the "contiguity of the professional spheres" of singers with jugglers and bear tamers, where the singer Ur-niĝar is given a bear cub "for the craftsmanship of the juggler/bear tamer." One can imagine this gift was made to allow the performer to expand their repertoire.

Unfortunately for juggling historians, the only references to the *u-da-tuš* exist in these ancient administrative ledgers and not in literature or folklore (see D'Agostino). This does not, however, preclude other words that may have been used to refer to these people or their profession; there are likely other words for "juggler" that appear in other genres of texts.

This tradition of skillful entertainment seems to have carried long into the future, as evidenced in the 19th dissertation of Maximus of Tyre (~100 CE). This text records the story of an Ionian juggler who performed for an unnamed Babylonian king.[9] This entertainer performed a "wonderful feat" in which he fixed a long steel point on the wall, then walked back a considerable distance and threw a succession of balls of dough at the spike. His aim was apparently so perfect that each ball was impaled onto the spike, lining up along its shaft. The final ball was thrown with such force and accuracy that it drove all of the dough balls flat against the wall.[10]

Ancient Rome

In Ancient Rome, jugglers practiced their skills with knives, balls, and rings. Those who played with knives were called *ventilatores,* and those who used

---

toriques, Philologiques et Epigraphiques en L'Honneur de Paolo Matthiae, (2012): 89-99. www.jstor.org/stable/42771745.

[9] Unfortunately, given the limited textual references to this story, it is impossible to know when it would have taken place. Assuming the reference to a Babylonian king is correct (meaning that the king in question reigned over the Babylonian Empire, and not referring to a king of another empire in the geographic region often referred to as Babylon), this would have taken place sometime between 1595 and 1160 BCE.

The story of the dough-thrower has remarkable similarities to a tale referred to in the exhibition catalog of *The Art of the Juggler,* which accompanied a 1929 exhibit about juggling at the Museum of Circus and Variety Arts in Leningrad. According to the booklet, which cites Alexander the Great's historian Quintus Curtius Rufus as its source, when Alexander campaigned in India he saw a similar performance. Alexander "was shown a juggler who had perfected his art to such an extent that he could throw peas onto sharp distance [sic] needles without missing the target" (Gershuni, 2018). Your author could not find Quintus' words pertaining to this remarkable feat, however.

[10] St John, J. A. *The History of the Manners and Customs of Ancient Greece* (Vol. 1). London: S & J Bentley, Wilson, and Fley, 1842. https://books.google.es/books?id=w8A_AQAAIAAJ&pg=PA146&lpg=PA146&dq=babylonian++dough+juggler&source=bl&ots=9YicPzRgzW&sig=oa81U_kHJHRvO6x3sXODj268zp0&hl=en&sa=X&ved=0ahUKEwjVkNHn9LLaAhUJSBQKHbVgAisQ6AEIRzAJ#v=onepage&q=babylonian%20%20dough%20juggler&f=f.

balls or rings were referred to as *pilarii*.[11] These Roman juggling practitioners are seen in numerous statues and reliefs around their former empire (fig.7).

The number of examples of juggling on ancient vases shows that it was a favorite recreation of women. "A woman seated is shown as playing with two balls on a vase from Nola in the British Museum, and the date assigned to it is 430 BCE... [it also]includes an illustration of a woman seated playing with three balls." The author goes on to explain that these juggling games were extremely popular, and practiced "especially in the baths. Even Julius Caesar, Marcus Aurelius and Alexander Severus are said not to have disdained to take part in them."[12]

A terra-cotta statue of a *pilarius* was discovered in Thebes dating to the Hellenistic period of Egypt's history (323-31 BCE), when Rome annexed the country. This statue depicts a man—likely a slave, as evidenced by his race, neck collar, and loincloth—who balances balls on various parts of his body.[13]

We know that some military officers juggled as a pastime, thanks to letters written by Sidonius Apollinaris, where he briefly reports on his unique hobby. Though he wasn't a professional entertainer, this military man liked to entertain his troops through juggling tricks with three and four balls.[14]

The Romans also played a kind of three-man juggling game called *trigon* (fig. 8). In this game, which was usually played in a sandy court at the baths, three players standing in a triangle would toss glass balls to one another. Missed catches would be tallied, so the quick return of a caught ball was the mark of an expert player.[15] In this fast-paced game, sometimes players have two or three balls thrown to them at the same time, requiring quick reflexes and a keen eye.[16] Some scholars suggest that balls were caught with one hand, then returned with the other.[17] Whichever player dropped the fewest balls would be declared the

---

[11] Chambers. *Chambers's new handy volume American encyclopædia* 7. Hurst, (1891).

[12] Allen, J. R., & Cox, J. C. "Jugglers." *The Reliquary & Illustrated Archaeologist*, 1907. http://dev.juggle.org/history/archives/jugmags/37-1/37-1,p34.htm.

[13] Juggling historian Karl Heinz Ziethen notes in his beautifully updated work, *Juggling: The Past and Future*, that the legendary performer Enrico Rastelli (1896-1931) began his routine in a similar pose, and wonders if that was a coincidence (Ziethen, *Juggling: The Past and Future*, 2017). Academics from other fields wonder if this is a balance trick at all, or rather an attempt by the sculptor to portray a performer executing a three-ball pattern where balls are bounced from the knee to the head and back to the hand (See Mendner, 1956).

[14] Sagemüller, H. *Michael Kara: König der Jongleure: Jongleur der Koenige*, Baldingen, 1973.

[15] McDaniel, W. B. "Some Passages Concerning Ball Games." *Transactions and Proceedings of the American Philological Association, 37* (1906): 121-134. https://archive.org/details/jstor-282704.

[16] Smith, WLLD, Wayte, Marindin. *A Dictionary of Greek and Roman Antiquities, 1890*. http://www.perseus.tufts.edu/hopper/text?doc=Perseus:text:1999.04.0063:entry=pila-cn.

[17] White, D. "The Game of Trigon." *Expedition Magazine*, 27(2) (1985). https://www.penn.museum/sites/expedition/the-game-of-trigon/. This style of juggling play is similar to that of the women of the Polynesian island of Tonga. There they practice *hiko*, a game that involves

Juggling Across the Ancient World · 41

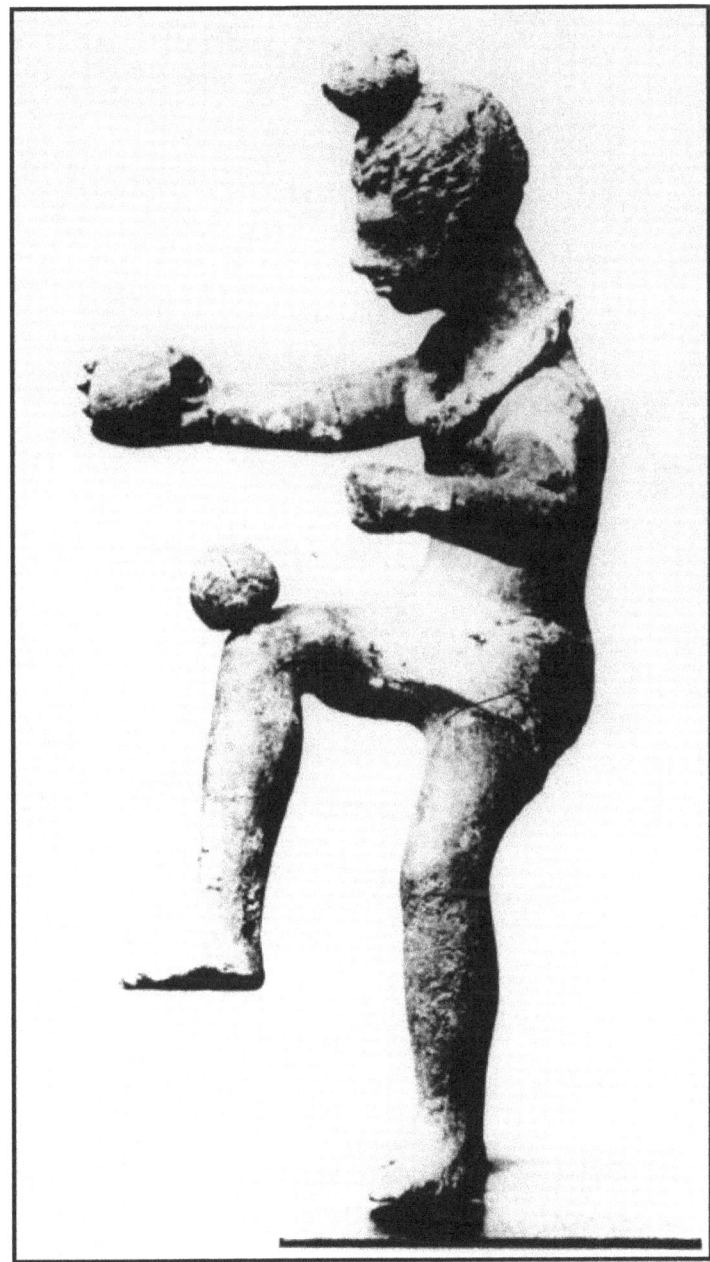

Figure 7 A Roman slave juggles balls
in this terra-cotta statue from 200 BCE.
From *4,000 Years of Juggling* (cover illustration), by K. H. Ziethen, 1981, M. Poignant.

Figure 8 Sketch of a now-destroyed wall painting portraying a trigon game at the Baths of Trajan in Rome. Three boys learn to play the game under the supervision of an older man, either a noble or a slave. From "The Game of Trigon," by D. White, 1985, *Expedition Magazine*, Volume 27, Issue 2.

winner. Surviving examples of these balls are around 55 millimeters in diameter, slightly smaller than a modern juggling ball (fig. 9,10).[18]

A large marble tablet from the second century CE, discovered in Rome in 1592, is inscribed with a description of a master "player of the ball" named Ursus Togatus (fig. 11).[19] This is one of the first jugglers whose name we know through

---

throwing *tui-tui* nuts (candlenuts) in a tall circle for as long as possible while singing songs (See Williams).

[18] McClellan, M. C. "To Play Properly With A Glass Ball." *Expedition Magazine, Vol. 27*, No. 2 (1985). https://www.penn.museum/sites/expedition/to-play-properly-with-a-glass-ball/.

[19] Bang, M. *Corpus Inscriptonum Latinarum* (Vol. VI). Rome: Berolini, 1933. http://arachne.uni-koeln.de/arachne/index.php?view%5blayout%5d=buch_item&search%5bconstraints%5d%5b-buch%5d%5balias%5d=CILv6p4fIII1933&search%5bmatch%5d=exact. "Togatus" isn't Ursus's last name. Rather, it refers to his social standing—that he was esteemed enough to be allowed to wear the toga.

Juggling Across the Ancient World · 43

Figure 9 A marble statue, found in Cyprus, perhaps of a trigon player holding three balls (circa 365 CE). From "To Play Properly With a Glass Ball," by M. C. McClellan, 1985, *Expedition Magazine*, Volume 27 Issue 2.

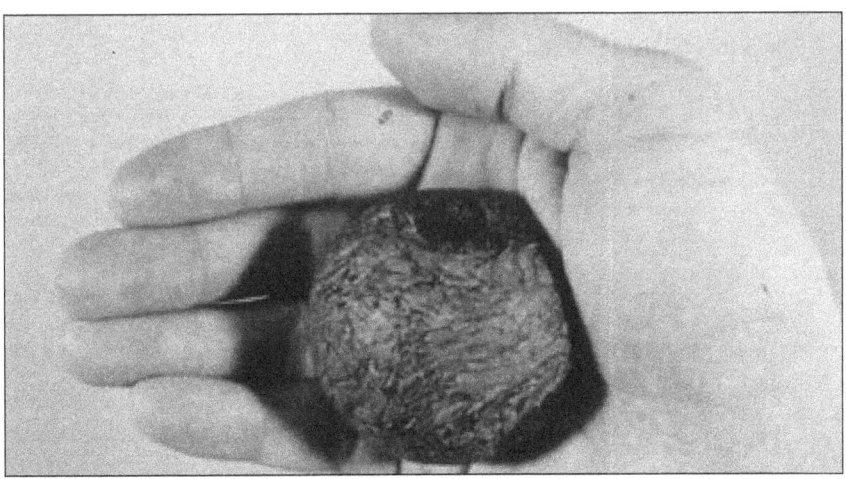

Figure 10 A glass ball, likely used to play trigon, from the collections of the Penn Museum. From "To Play Properly With a Glass Ball," by M. C. McClellan, 1985, *Expedition Magazine*, v.27 i.2.

Figure 11 The inscription with Ursus Togatus' epitaph. From "Inscription in verse 'in honour' of Ursus Togatus" by Musei Vaticani, n.d.

http://www.museivaticani.va/content/museivaticani/en/collezioni/musei/galleria-lapidaria/sezione-xi--iscrizioni-di-vario-contenuto--ultime-acquisizioni/iscrizione-in-versi-in-onore-di-ursus-togatus.html.

written record rather than myths and oral histories. The inscription reads:

> I am Ursus Togatus. I was the first to show skill in playing with balls of glass among my players, to the great applause of the people in the baths of Trajan, Agrippa, and Titus, and very often in those of Nero. Yes, you may be assured that I am Ursus Togatus. Approach, you handlers of balls, strew on the statue of your friend flowers, violets, leaves, and essence of perfume. Pour out the dark Falernian wine, the wine of Setia and of Coecubum,[20] taken from the cellar of my master. Vie with one another in celebrating with accord the old man Ursus, merry, full of jests, a master in handling balls, who excelled all of his predecessors in taste, in grace, and in the subtleties of the art. Nevertheless, to speak the truth in my old age, I confess that not once but often I was surpassed by my patron, thrice consul, and willingly do I call myself his buffoon.[21]

---

[20] These are the "choice cellars of the emperor"—a bold demand from fair Ursus! Champlin, E. "The Glass Ball Game." *Zeitschrift für Papyrologie und Epigraphik, 60* (1985): 159-163. www.jstor.org/stable/20184295.

[21] Your author humbly reminds his readers that this inscription is written in the first person, and that anyone in showbiz knows that it's important not to believe what a performer says about themselves (especially when they're asking you to pour wine and perfume on their statue in effigy!). Was Ursus the first *pilari* to juggle balls? We can't say for sure. Is this the first record we have of a juggler referring to themselves as such? It seems that way. That's what's so interesting

Figure 12 A woman juggles apples on a Roman vase. "Woman Juggling Apples. Attic Red Figure, White Ground Pyxis, ca. 470-460 BCE."
Photo: M. Daniels, Toledo Museum of Art.

Ursus, according to scholars, was a *pilicrepus*—someone who manufactured the glass balls used in the game of *trigon* and also acted as a referee of some kind. Allen and Cox assert that he was also a juggler who "performed alone the feat of keeping several balls in motion," and they assert that the "play" with glass balls mentioned in the above inscription refers to this form of juggling, not to the game of *trigon*.[22] Allen and Cox also insist that the use of glass balls was to add a sense of danger to the game, as they might smash on a hard floor when dropped. Other scholars maintain that the game was played only on sandy courts in the baths.[23]

Latin scholar Edward Champlin argues that "the glass ball game" has roots in the Byzantine Empire and was, perhaps, imported to Rome at some point in history. He further argues that the Ursus Togatus inscription is *not* actually about a real person, and rather uses the "game of the glass ball" as an allegory for political maneuvering. In any event, the game of *trigon* was popular enough to be a cultural reference point—whether the inscription is a clever joke about politics or actually an homage to a great player is a question for another scholar.[24]

The *Ursus* inscription isn't the only written record describing *trigon*, of course. An undated graffito scratched onto a wall of the basilica of Pompeii

about this passage!

[22] Allen, J. R., & Cox, J. C. "Jugglers." *The Reliquary & Illustrated Archaeologist*, 1907. http://dev.juggle.org/history/archives/jugmags/37-1/37-1,p34.htm.

[23] White, D. "The Game of Trigon." *Expedition Magazine*, 27(2) (1985). https://www.penn.museum/sites/expedition/the-game-of-trigon/.

[24] Champlin.

gives the lineup of an impromptu game, likely played by a group of a noble's slaves. This inscription reads: "Let Amianthus, Epaphra, [and] Tertius play, along with Hedystus. Iucundus from Nola is to go after [the balls], Citus is to keep score—as is Stacus."[25] The passage describes a simple game of pickup *trigon*, complete with scorekeepers and people fielding dropped balls.

Pilarii, the art of throwing and catching balls, is used as an allegory in Quintilian's *Institutio Oratoria*, a textbook from around 95 CE that describes the theory and practice of speech and rhetoric. In the book's tenth volume, Quintilian compares the skilled public speaker reading aloud from a page to the skills of a juggler on stage. "...A certain mechanical knack... [allows the speaker to] see what is coming before the reader has articulated to himself what precedes. It is a similar knack which makes possible those miraculous tricks which we can see jugglers and masters of sleight of hand perform upon the stage, in such a manner that the spectator can scarcely help believing that the objects which they throw into the air come to hand of their own accord, and run where they are bidden"[26] (fig.12).

Though this allegory doesn't describe an actual juggling act, it does serve as evidence that *pilarii* and *ventilatores* engaged in skillful throwing and catching frequently enough that it served as a meaningful analogy for Quintilian's first-century Roman readership—and that these performers were so remarkable in their precision that they defied their audience's belief.

A *pilarius* also makes an appearance in Manilus's five-volume poem *Astronomica*, which discusses astrological phenomena. The work was written around 10 CE and states that the *pilarius* "...is skilled in scattering a number of balls over his limbs and in passing his hands up and down over the whole of his body, so that he may grasp so many spheres, set them in movement again, and bid them to flit around him at his pleasure."[27] Some scholars assert that the seven objects manipulated by this *pilarius* are a reference to the seven planets. Symbolic or not, the description of this performer's routine is certainly evidence of mastery in skillful throwing and catching—and of rolling balanced objects on the body.

An ivory carving, documented in Maffei's *Museum Veronense,* a collection of engravings illustrating antiquities housed in a museum in Verona, depicts a figure giving the signal for a Roman circus to begin.[28] In the panels below him,

---

[25] Benefiel, R. R. "Amianth, a Ball-Game, and Making One's Mark" CIL IV 1936 and 1936a. *Zeitschrift für Papyrologie und Epigraphik,* 167 (2008): 193-200. www.jstor.org/stable/20476576.
[26] Quintilian. *Institutio Oratoria* (Vol. 10, 95). (H. E. Butler, Trans.), 95. http://www.perseus.tufts.edu/hopper/text?doc=Quint.%20Inst.%2010.7&lang=original.
[27] Allen & Cox.
[28] Roman circuses, named for the circular shape of the arenas, were large, outdoor entertainment venues used "...first and foremost for races with four-horse or two-horse chariots.... [that] also

Figure 13 Panels from Maffei's Museum Veronense. From Museum Veronense, S. M. Maffei, 1749, Verona.

horses are led forth, and a young boy tosses and balances seven balls (perhaps in the way Milanus describes), accompanied by pipes and a kind of rudimentary organ (fig.13).

A similar juggling feat is depicted on a Roman monument to Septuma Spica. On one side, a *pilarius* keeps five balls in the air while two extra balls are manipulated with his feet. On the other side, a *pilarius* performs a similar trick with four balls in the air.[29]

---

served as the venue for other events. They included ridden horse races, races by horseback riders who dismounted to complete the race on foot, athletics (chiefly boxing, wrestling, and long-distance running), the Troy Game (maneuvers performed on horseback by young boys of noble birth), wild beast hunts, gladiatorial combats, stage battles between opposing armies, and a variety of other entertainments" (Humphrey, 1986). The Roman circus's circular format would later be drawn upon—and standardized—by Philip Astley in the late 1700s when he created the entertainment format with acrobatic entertainment and horsemanship that we recognize as "modern" traditional circus (Jando, 2018). Astley established the 42-foot-diameter circus ring, dimensions that "...[create] the steadiest speed and the optimum balance between centrifugal and centripetal forces for a man attempting to maintain balance on the back of a galloping horse." Astley's creation itself wasn't referred to as "circus," however. His company was called the "New British Riding School" or "Amphitheatre Riding Ring" (Burgess, 1974).

[29] Allen & Cox. Historian Giovanni Labus believed that a seventh ball was once depicted on the

Figure 14 Monument to Septuma Spica at the Royal Museum in Mantua.
From "Jugglers," by J.R. Allen and J.C. Cox, 1903, *The Reliquary & Illustrated Archaeologist*, pp. 1-16.

There are also indications that a number of juggling entertainers from the Far East appeared in Rome around the year 1 CE. In A. T. Sinclair's 1907 article "Gypsy and Oriental Music," the author reports that a number of Oriental "musicians, singers, dancers, jugglers, tumblers, knife and ball tossers,[30] tight-rope performers, and other showmen" arrived in Rome at this time, where they made a living. It's unknown, however, whether they integrated into Roman society or simply banded together and formed their own communities.

Music historian Emil Naumann reports that though these foreign entertainers lived in Rome, they were not permitted any civil rights: "Their existence was tolerated, but all real protection of the law was withdrawn from them. Indeed, to such an extent was this carried that a strolling player might suffer bodily injury, even by the sword of his assailant, and yet have no claim for redress... thus this remarkable people unwittingly possessed of a romantic spirit remained throughout the Middle Ages honorless and homeless outcasts" (fig. 14).

Likewise, many Roman jugglers traveled to the Far East to perform during the Han Dynasty (206 BCE-220 CE), when Emperor Wu Di sent diplomat Zhang Quian westward, opening the Silk Road. This trade route went as far as the Roman Empire, and was used not only for economic trade but also for cultural exchange. Acrobatics—including stagings of the "Hundred Enter-

---

left side of this relief when it was in better condition. See also Labus, G. *Museo della Reale Accademia di Mantova*. Mantova, 1883. http://arachne.uni-koeln.de/arachne/index.php?view%5blayout%5d=buch_item&search%5bconstraints%5d%5bbuch%5d%5balias%5d=Labus1833Vol2&search%5bmatch%5d=exact.

[30] Sinclair, A. T. "Gypsy and Oriental Music." *The Journal of American Folklore*, 1-3 (1907): 16-32. www.jstor.org/stable/534723. Observant readers might notice that both "jugglers" and "knife and ball tossers" are listed here. Remember that the word "juggling" when this was written could also refer to magic, animal training, and a number of other entertainment disciplines.

Figure 15 A pilarius, engaged in a juggling act.
From *Harpers Dictionary of Classical Antiques* by Peck. New York: Harper and Brothers, 1898.

tainments" (a traditional spectacle that could be considered an ancient form of Chinese "circus" or acrobatic theater)[31]—were used as a form of political diplomacy along the trade route as well.[32]

Alex Scobie, scholar of storytelling in Greco-Roman antiquity, mentions that "...some of these [variety entertainers] not only traveled extensively within the Roman world, but are known to have journeyed as far as China. Such is the case with jugglers from Roman Syria who were prized at the court of a Chinese emperor in early imperial times."[33] This group of jugglers performed in China at the beginning of Chinese-Western relations (approximately 200 BCE), and were said to "...conjure, spit fire, bind and release their limbs without assistance, interchange the heads of cows and horses, and dance cleverly with up to a thousand balls."[34]

However, not all of these performers traveled voluntarily. There was a darker side as well, as historians tell us that jugglers and acrobats were often purchased

---

[31] Quiyu, Y., Dongsheng, H., Wichmann, E., & Richardson, G. "Some Observations on the Aesthetics of Primitive Chinese Theatre." *Asian Theatre Journal,* 6(1) (1989): 12-30. www.jstor.org/stable/1124287.

[32] Fu, Q. *Chinese Acrobatics through the Ages.* Beijing: Foreign Languages Press, 1985. Some readers may appreciate the "echo" that seems to have happened in the mid-20th century, when the Chinese government once more began using the export of circus performances as a political strategy. See Ala-Rashi, M. *China's Bending Bodies: Contortionists and Politics in China.* Philadelphia: Modern Vaudeville Press, 2022.

[33] Scobie, A. "Storytellers, Storytelling, and the Novel in Graeco-Roman Antiquity." *Rheinisches Museum fur Philologie, 122*(3/4), (1979): 229-259. www.jstor.org/stable/41244988.

[34] Needham, J. *Science and Civilisation in China* (Vol. 1). Cambridge: Cambridge University Press, 1954. This must certainly be an exaggeration. If not, today's jugglers may as well hang up their props and call it a day. Those Syrian-Roman jugglers who juggled a thousand balls were more skilled than anyone else in history!

as slaves in Persia and the Roman Empire. These entertainers were brought back to China to perform for the Emperor and his subjects in courts and city squares across his domain.[35] This practice was documented in the *Ch'ien Han-shu,* a Chinese historical text from the 1st century, CE. The document describes a diplomat sent from Rome to China to deliver "ostrich eggs and Lee-keen [Roman] jugglers, which he presented as offerings, and with which the Emperor was greatly delighted."[36]

The cross-cultural exchange facilitated by the Silk Road had an immense impact on the art and culture of communities along its route. Scholars assert that the route led to a period of renaissance in art, music, religion, and poetry—not to mention the variety arts—in Chinese and other cultures.[37]

Judaism In Late Antiquity
Juggling also appears in the Near East and along the Eastern Mediterranean coast. In the Babylonian Talmud, Tractate Sukkah 53a, there are passages about rabbis and other holy men celebrating festivals with incredible feats of dexterity:

> They said about Rabban Shimon ben Gamliel that when he would rejoice at the Celebration of the Place of the Drawing [of the Water], he would take eight flaming torches and toss one and catch another, [juggling them,] and, [though they were all in the air at the same time,] they would not touch each other... (b. Sukkah 53a, Koren Talmud Bavli, The Noé Edition)[38]

The story about Rabban Shimon ben Gamliel is found not only in the Babylonian Talmud, but also in the Tosefta (3rd century CE) and the Jerusalem Talmud (also known as the Palestinian Talmud, edited in either the 4th or 5th century CE). The Mishnah, Tractate Sukkah, gives us some additional information about the way these torches were constructed:

---

[35] Wood, F. *The Silk Road: Two Thousand Years in the Heart of Asia.* Berkeley: University of California Press, 2004, 53.
[36] Dorn'Eich, C. *Ban Gu - Annalen der Aelteren Han - Die Westlaender.* Universitaet. Stuttgart: Berlin, 2003.
[37] Chang, L.H. "Cross-Cultural Musical Processes and Results: Music along the Silk Road (from the second century B.C. to the tenth century A.D." *Revista de Musicologia,* v.16 n.4 (1993): 1888-1895.
[38] A note about these passages from the Talmud—bracketed text indicates that it is not part of the literal translation, but rather context added by the translator. This is important to note when considering the roots which are explained below.

From the worn-out pants of the priests and from their [worn-out] belts they would tear [pieces], and they would [use them as wicks to] light with them. And there was not a courtyard in Jerusalem that was not illuminated by the light of the place of [water] drawing. Pious people and men of [great] deeds would dance before them with lit torches in their hands, and say before them words of song and praise." (Mishnah Sukkah 5:3-4, Koren Talmud Bavli, The Noé Edition)

In conversations with Matthew Goldstone, Ph.D. in Hebrew and Judaic Studies, he notes that in Tosefta Sukkah 4:3, Rabban Shimon ben Gamliel is said to have been *dancing* with eight torches (using the Hebrew root of "to dance" [r.q.d.] in this text)—while the version in the Babylonian Talmud literally says that he would take them, throw one, and then take another (using the Hebrew roots for "to throw" [z.r.q.] and "to take" [n.ṭ.l.]). This discrepancy could be the result of a number of things. It's possible that the Talmud's authors actively changed the text of the original version. It's also possible that the Talmud simply used a different version of the Tosefta, as there are numerous differences between similar *baraitot* (early rabbinic traditions) preserved in the Tosefta and in the Babylonian Talmud. However unlikely, it's also possible that the Talmud was working with a different source than the passage found in the Tosefta entirely.[39]

Interestingly, the Jerusalem Talmud offers a slightly different version of the story of Rabban Shimon ben Gamliel, giving us a clue as to what these torches might have looked like: "They say about Rabbi Shimon ben Gamliel that he would dance with eight torches of gold and one would not touch the other" (y. Sukkah 5:4 55c).

The Leiden manuscript of the Jerusalem Talmud gives us an insight into the way these passages were revised throughout time. It originally read "...and one would not touch *the ground.*" The word was changed, either by the same scribe or a different one,[40] to read "...and one would not touch the other" instead (fig. 16). Goldstone believes this might have been done to bring the text more in line with the Babylonian Talmud's version of the story, as it focuses on Gamliel's great skill at keeping the torches in the air rather than simply not dropping them.

The passage in b. Sukkah 53a continues, describing more juggling feats:

---

[39] Goldstone, M. (August, 2018). Personal correspondence with T. Wall.
[40] A professional paleographer, versed in the study of ancient handwriting, could probably answer this question. However interesting, this matter is beyond the scope of our inquiry into the history of juggling.

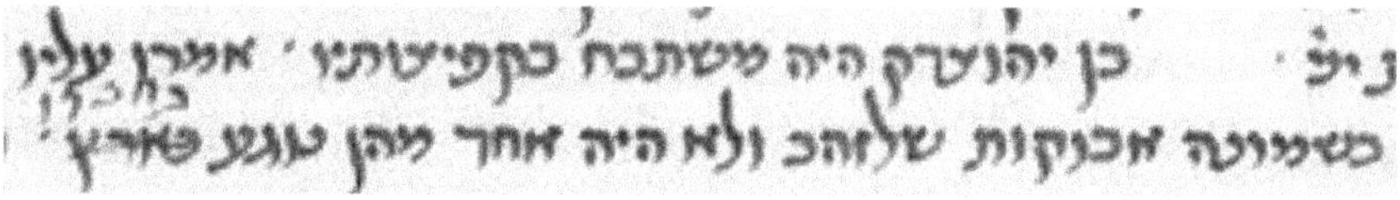

נב׳ · כן יהודה היה משתבח בקפיצותו ' אמרן עליו
כשמונה אבוקות של זהב ולא היה מהן אחד נוגע בארץ

Figure 16 Notice the revision in the lower left hand corner of this image, taken from the Leiden manuscript of the Jerusalem Talmud, completed in 1298 CE. Adapted from MS Leiden, Scaliger 3, Bibliothek der Rijksuniversiteit, n.d.
http://dlib.nli.org.il/webclient/StreamGate?folder_id=0&dvs=1534530472008~840.

> [Apropos the rejoicing of Rabban Shimon ben Gamliel at the Celebration of the Place of the Drawing of the Water, the Gemara recounts:] Levi would walk before Rabbi [Yehuda Ha-Nasi juggling] with eight knives. Shmuel would juggle before King Shapur with eight[41] glasses of wine [without spilling].[42] Abaye [would juggle] before Rabba with eight eggs. Some say [he did so] with four eggs. (b Sukkah 53a, Koren Talmud Bavli, The Noé Edition)

Scholars have cast doubt on the possibility that this ever actually took place. It's possible that the reference to King Shapur in the story of Shmuel's juggling serves a purpose other than simple narrative storytelling. Invoking King Shapur could also serve as a kind of boast about the influence of this juggling sage, as the king was an impressively wise and powerful figure. It is also possible that "King Shapur" in the text is a reference to Jewish scholars from ancient Babylonia and Israel who were associated with the King in other stories.[43]

There is one other passage that may refer to toss juggling in the Babylonian Talmud, found in Tractate Ketubot 17a:

> [With regard to the mitzvah of bringing joy to the bride and groom, the Gemara relates: The Sages] said about Rabbi Yehuda bar Elai that he would take a myrtle branch and

---

[41] Clever readers will have doubtlessly noticed a theme—the number eight comes up in these juggling references several times. Although the number eight has a symbolic meaning in Judaism, Goldstone reminds readers that other numbers hold much more traditional importance. He is unconvinced that the symbolic value of the number eight would have influenced these descriptions of juggling in the Talmud (Goldstone, 2018).

[42] King Shapur reigned the Sasanian Empire from 240-270 CE. (Sasania is the empire that inhabited the same geographic region as the Babylonian Empire some eight hundred years after Babylon fell.) Juggling with cups comes up frequently in middle-Persian literature discussing court entertainment in Sasania (Mokhtarian, 2012). The artistic discipline was known as *tās-bāzi* or *kāsa-bāzi*, and the juggler was called *tās bāz* (Morgenstierne, 1982).

[43] Secunda, S. The Iranian Talmud, 105. Philadelphia: University of Pennsylvania Press, 2013.

dance before the bride, and say: A fair and attractive bride. Rav Shmuel bar Rav Yitzhak would [base his] dance on three [myrtle branches that he would juggle]. (b. Ketubot 17a, Koren Talmud Bavli, The Noé Edition)

The word "juggle" here was added by a translator. This was likely taken from the comments of Rashi, a famous medieval Jewish commentator on the Talmud, who interpreted the phrase "on three" to mean "[with] three branches; throwing one and receiving another."[44]

Goldstone cautions readers that these sources shouldn't necessarily be taken at face value and that these stories don't necessarily mean that these rabbis were able to juggle even two or three objects. He writes, "It could just be an exaggeration created by later rabbis in order to imagine what the scene was like. But while it's not necessarily historically accurate for what the rabbis could do, it is helpful for recognizing that the rabbis were aware of juggling and that juggling eight objects was seen as a difficult or near-impossible feat."[45]

Scholars suggest that these juggling feats likely took place at the water-drawing festival—known in Hebrew as *Simchat Beit HaShoeva*—but they can't be certain, given the limited references in the Talmud (Goldstone, 2018). *Simchat Beit HaShoeva* is the culminating feature of *Sukkot*, a weeklong festival in the fall that follows Rosh Hashanah (the Jewish New Year) and Yom Kippur (the Day of Atonement). *Sukkot* is mandated in the Torah as "a time of year singularly dedicated to the expression of joy."[46]

According to the early rabbis, "One who did not see the joy of the water-drawing celebrations has not seen joy in his life" (Mishnah Sukkah 5:1). Perhaps I speak for all modern jugglers when I say it'd be a joyful day to see someone juggle eight glasses of wine without spilling a drop!

After all of this rejoicing, it should be noted that in the Babylonian Talmud, it states:

---

[44] Goldstone.
[45] Goldstone.
[46] Vernoff, C.E. "Feast of Redemption." *Tradition: A Journal of Orthodox Jewish Thought,* 33(4) (1999). https://www.jstor.org/stable/23262257. See Deuteronomy 16:13-5: "After the ingathering from your threshing floor and your vat, you shall hold the Feast of Booths [Sukkot] for seven days. You shall rejoice in your festival, with your son and daughter, your male and female slave, the Levite, the stranger, the fatherless, and the widow in your communities. You shall hold a festival for the LORD your God seven days, in the place that the LORD will choose; for the LORD your God will bless all your crops and all your undertakings, and you shall have nothing but joy" (NJPS translation).

Interestingly, the Hebrew root word for "joy" and "rejoice" in this passage is the same root word used for Rabban Shimon ben Gamliel when he "rejoiced" at the "celebration."

"Happy is the man that hath not walked"... to theaters and circuses of idolaters "nor stood in the way of sinners"—that is he who does not attend contests of wild beasts; "nor sat in the seat of the scornful." ('Abodah Zarah 18b)

Some scholars have interpreted this to be "admonishing Jews not to attend games and performances, even of jugglers,"[47] but this statement seems to rest on a misconception surrounding the word "circus." The Roman circus focused on gladiatorial combat and blood sport, not the tricks of dexterity found in the modern circus.[48] The Roman circus often featured idol worship and was considered "distinctive institutions of pagan Rome" that should, therefore, be avoided.[49] These institutions often started their proceedings with animal sacrifices to the gods. The events themselves often featured mockery of the Jewish people—or worse—the literal torture and killing of the religion's followers.[50]

However, the rabbis would have likely endorsed juggling in Jewish contexts such as *Simchat Beit HaShoevah* in order to properly rejoice (b. Sukkah 53a) or a wedding in order to fulfill the commandment of bringing joy to the bride and groom (b. Ketubot 17a).

Juggling possibly makes an appearance in the Hebrew Bible, as well. In 2 Samuel 6, King David brings the ark to Jerusalem. "And David and all the house of Israel played before the LORD on all manner of instruments made of fir wood, even on harps, and on psalteries, and on timbrels, and on cornets, and on cymbals" (2 Samuel 6:5 King James Version). In the original Hebrew, the word *broshim* (here, translated as "instruments made of fir wood") does not actually imply that all of the objects were musical instruments. It is entirely possible jugglers performed tricks with sticks or clubs made of cypress or fir wood in celebration of the ark's arrival.[51]

---

[47] Simmonds, Andrew. "Mark's and Matthew's Sub Rosa Message in the Scene of Pilate and the Crowd." *Journal of Biblical Literature*. 131 (2012): 733-754. 10.1353/jbl.2012.0028.

[48] That's not to say that Roman circuses and theaters were devoid of wholesome fun. Mimes and clowns, though sometimes present, just weren't the main attraction. Yehuda HaNasi, the 2nd-century rabbi, looked for some good in the circus, writing "We must thank the heathens that they let mimes appear in the theaters and circuses, and thus find innocent amusement for themselves" (Gottheil & Krauss, 1906). (See Genesis Rabbah 80:1 for more on this.) There are records attributed to Pompey in 61 BCE of a circus advertised as being "interspersed with... acrobatic feats of great daring and dexterity" as well (May, 1932).

[49] Gottheil, Richard; Samuel Krauss. "Xystus." In Singer, Isidore; et al. (eds.). *The Jewish Encyclopedia*. New York: Funk & Wagnalls, 1906. There is one notable exception to this rule, however. Under this law, Jewish people were allowed to attend gladiatorial combat if their intent was "to yell out that the loser be spared" (Simmonds, 2012).

[50] Bloch, R. "Part of the Scene: Jewish Theater in Antiquity." *Journal of Ancient Judaism*, 8 (2018): 150-169. Goettingen: Vandenhoeck & Ruprecht GmbH.

[51] Prouser, Ora H. Personal interview. August 2021. Commentators and translators have difficulty

So What Does It All Mean?

The desire to master the limits of gravity through dexterity must be part of the human condition ... but without the work of jugglers of the past, the practice of throwing and catching would not have advanced to the point it has reached today—an unbroken chain of people throwing and catching from ancient times until this very moment. Jugglers stand on the shoulders of giants—and if you're inspired to learn the skill, you soon will, too!

In his presentation titled *La Evolucion del Arte Circense in Mexico* (The Evolution of the Circus Arts in Mexico) at the Mexican National Anthropology Museum, director of the college of circus arts in Puebla, Julio Revolledo Cardenas,[52] put it succinctly:

> [Circus] is the art of marveling, astonishing, and surprising. The more feelings of danger and anguish the arts provoke [in their audiences,] the more impact the show will have. It's the fight of the human being trapped within himself, demonstrating that he can transcend the supposed limits of his natural condition.[53]

The practice that we call *juggling* arose in cultures across the world in antiquity, in places so disparate they didn't know of one another—much less communicate and share the idea of this wonderful craft. Traditions arose, skills developed, and audiences welcomed the practice as part of their culture—all because people around the world began throwing objects into the air thanks to some shared instinct. Juggling, it seems, is inside all of us.

---

with this clause, and this line is often emended—as was done in Robert Alter's work *The David Story*: "The translation reads here [with all their might in song] *bekhol 'oz uveshirim* with 1 Chronicles 13:8. The Masoretic text has *bekhol 'atsey beroshim*, 'with all cypress woods,' which only by a long interpretive stretch has been made to refer to percussion instruments." As the biblical text is somewhat unclear, there is room for an interpretation which includes juggling. Adding to this (admittedly aspirational!) interpretation, the line in question also includes the conjunction *vav*, which can be seen as a separation between musical instruments and juggling sticks—perhaps there *was* juggling when the Ark arrived?

[52] Nephew of the great Mexican juggler Rudy Cardenas—the "Rastelli of Mexico" and Richard Nixon's favorite juggler (Giduz, 1995).
[53] Instituto Nacional de Antropologia e Historia. *Acrobacia Prehispanica. 2, 10* (2008).

References

Ala-Rashi, M. *China's Bending Bodies: Contortionists and Politics in China*. Philadelphia: Modern Vaudeville Press, 2022.

Allen, J. R., & Cox, J. C. "Jugglers." *The Reliquary & Illustrated Archaeologist*, 1907. http://dev.juggle.org/history/archives/jugmags/37-1/37-1,p34.htm.

Alter, Robert. *The David Story: A Translation with Commentary of 1 and 2 Samuel*. New York: W. W. Norton and Company, Inc., 1999.

Bang, M. *Corpus Inscriptonum Latinarum* (Vol. VI). Rome: Berolini, 1933. http://arachne.uni-koeln.de/arachne/index.php?view%5blayout%5d=buch_item&search%5bconstraints%5d%5bbuch%5d%5balias%5d=CILv6p4fIII1933&search%5bmatch%5d=exact.

Benefiel, R. R. "Amianth, a Ball-Game, and Making One's Mark" CIL IV 1936 and 1936a. *Zeitschrift für Papyrologie und Epigraphik, 167* (2008): 193-200. www.jstor.org/stable/20476576.

Bloch, R. "Part of the Scene: Jewish Theater in Antiquity." *Journal of Ancient Judaism*, 8 (2018): 150-169. Goettingen: Vandenhoeck & Ruprecht GmbH

Boeckmann, S. *"Es fliegt was in der Luft" – Kulturgeschichtliche Aspekte des Jonglierens*. Carl von Ossietzky Universität Oldenburg, 2003.

Boeckmann, S. (11/1/2018). (T. Wall, Interviewer).

Burgess, H. "The Classification of Circus Techniques." *The Drama Review: TDR, Vol. 18 No. 1* (1974): 65-70. www.jstor.org/stable/1144863.

Chambers. *Chambers's new handy volume American encyclopædia 7*. Hurst, (1891).

Champlin, E. "The Glass Ball Game." *Zeitschrift für Papyrologie und Epigraphik, 60* (1985): 159-163. www.jstor.org/stable/20184295.

Chang, L.H. "Cross-Cultural Musical Processes and Results: Music along the Silk Road (from the second century B.C. to the tenth century A.D." *Revista de Musicologia*, v.16 n.4 (1993): 1888-1895.

D'Agostino, F. "Some Considerations on U-da-tuš (Bear Tamer) and Jugglery in Ur III." *Historiques, Philologiques et Epigraphiques en L'Honneur de Paolo Matthiae*, (2012): 89-99. www.jstor.org/stable/42771745.

Decker, W. *Sports and Games of Ancient Egypt*. (A. Guttmann, Trans.) New Haven and London: Yale University Press, 1992.

Dorn'Eich, C. *Ban Gu - Annalen der Aelteren Han - Die Westlaender*. Universitaet. Stuttgart: Berlin, 2003.

Fu, Q. *Chinese Acrobatics through the Ages*. Beijing: Foreign Languages Press, 1985.

Gadalla, M. *The Musical Aspects of The Ancient Egyptian Vocalic Language*. Greensboro, NC: Tehuti Research Foundation, 2016.

Gershuni, E.P. *The Art of the Juggler*. (Helena K., Trans.) Createspace.com, 2018.

Giduz, B. "Starting Young, Staying Strong." *Jugglers World* (p. 22). International Jugglers' Association, 1995.

Goldstone, M. (August, 2018). Personal correspondence with T. Wall.

Gottheil, Richard; Samuel Krauss. "Xystus." In Singer, Isidore; et al. (eds.). *The Jewish Encyclopedia*. New York: Funk & Wagnalls, 1906.
Halakhah.com, The Babylonian Talmud: Tractate 'Abodah Zarah. http://halakhah.com/zarah/zarah_18.html.
Humphrey, J. H. *Roman Circuses: Arenas for Chariot Racing.* Los Angeles: University of California Press, 1986. https://books.google.es/books?id=couetXBQO9AC&printsec=frontcover&dq=roman+circus&hl=en&sa=X&ved=0ahUKEwid6-j6k9jaAhVC6RQKHYXSCswQ6AEIKTAA#v=onepage&q=roman%20circus&f=false.
Instituto Nacional de Antropologia e Historia. *Acrobacia Prehispanica.* 2, 10 (2008).
Jando, D. *Philip Astley & The Horsemen who invented the Circus.* Createspace, 2018.
Koren Noe Talmud - William Davidson Edition. https://www.sefaria.org/Sukkah?lang=bi&p2=Sukkah.53a.10&lang2=en.
Labus, G. *Museo della Reale Accademia di Mantova.* Mantova, 1883. http://arachne.uni-koeln.de/arachne/index.php?view%5blayout%5d=buch_item&search%5bconstraints%5d%5b-buch%5d%5balias%5d=Labus1833Vol2&search%5bmatch%5d=exact.
May, E. C. *The Circus: From Rome to Ringling.* Cornwall: Duffield & Green, 1932, 1.
McClellan, M. C. "To Play Properly With A Glass Ball." *Expedition Magazine, Vol. 27*, No. 2 (1985). https://www.penn.museum/sites/expedition/to-play-properly-with-a-glass-ball/.
McDaniel, W. B. "Some Passages Concerning Ball Games." *Transactions and Proceedings of the American Philological Association, 37* (1906): 121-134. https://archive.org/details/jstor-282704.
Mendner, S. *Das Ballspiel im Leben der Völker.* Muenster: Aschendorff, 1956.
Mokhtarian, J.S. "Empire and Authority in Sasanian Babylonia: The Rabbis and King Shapur in Dialogue." *Jewish Studies Quarterly*, Vol. 19, No. 2 (2012): 148-180. https://www.jstor.org/stable/41681771.
Morganstierne, G. *Monumentum Georg Morgenstierne: Vol 2 (Acta Iranica),* 76. Leiden: Brill, 1982.
Naumann, E. *The History of Music.* London: Cassel & Company Ltd., 1886. https://archive.org/details/historyofmusic01naum.
Needham, J. *Science and Civilisation in China* (Vol. 1). Cambridge: Cambridge University Press, 1954.
Newberry, P. E. *Beni Hasan* (Vol. II). London: Egypt Exploration Society, 1893. http://digi.ub.uni-heidelberg.de/diglit/newberry1893bd2/0061.
Oxford English Dictionary. *"juggle,"* v. OED.com.
Prouser, Ora H. Personal interview. August 2021.
Quintilian. *Institutio Oratoria* (Vol. 10, 95). (H. E. Butler, Trans.). http://www.perseus.tufts.edu/hopper/text?doc=Quint.%20Inst.%2010.7&lang=original.
Quiyu, Y., Dongsheng, H., Wichmann, E., & Richardson, G. "Some Observations on the Aesthetics of Primitive Chinese Theatre." *Asian Theatre Journal,* 6(1) (1989): 12-30. www.jstor.org/stable/1124287.

Sagemüller, H. *Michael Kara: König der Jongleure: Jongleur der Koenige,* Baldingen, 1973.

Schreier, R. J., ed. Koren Talmud Bavli (The Noé Edition, Vol. 10: The Tractate Sukka). Jerusalem: Shefa Foundation; Koren Publishers Jerusalem, 2013.

Scobie, A. "Storytellers, Storytelling, and the Novel in Graeco-Roman Antiquity." *Rheinisches Museum fur Philologie, 122*(3/4), (1979): 229-259. www.jstor.org/stable/41244988.

Secunda, S. The Iranian Talmud, 105. Philadelphia: University of Pennsylvania Press, 2013.

Simmonds, Andrew. "Mark's and Matthew's Sub Rosa Message in the Scene of Pilate and the Crowd." *Journal of Biblical Literature.* 131 (2012): 733-754. 10.1353/jbl.2012.0028.

Sinclair, A. T. "Gypsy and Oriental Music." *The Journal of American Folklore*, 1-3 (1907): 16-32. www.jstor.org/stable/534723.

Smith, WLLD, Wayte, Marindin. *A Dictionary of Greek and Roman Antiquities, 1890.* http://www.perseus.tufts.edu/hopper/text?doc=Perseus:text:1999.04.0063:entry=pila-cn.

St John, J. A. *The History of the Manners and Customs of Ancient Greece* (Vol. 1). London: S & J Bentley, Wilson, and Fley, 1842. https://books.google.es/books?id=w8A_AQAAIAAJ&pg=PA146&lpg=PA146&dq=babylonian++dough+juggler&source=bl&ots=9YicPzRgzW&sig=oa81U_kHJHRvO6x3sXODj268zp0&hl=en&sa=X&ved=0ahUKEwjVkNHn-9LLaAhUJSBQKHbVgAisQ6AEIRzAJ#v=onepage&q=babylonian%20%20dough%20juggler&f=f.

Vernoff, C.E. "Feast of Redemption." *Tradition: A Journal of Orthodox Jewish Thought,* 33(4) (1999). https://www.jstor.org/stable/23262257.

White, D. "The Game of Trigon." *Expedition Magazine, 27*(2) (1985). https://www.penn.museum/sites/expedition/the-game-of-trigon/.

Wilkinson, J. G. *Manners and Customs of the Ancient Egyptians* (Vol. 2). London, 1837.

Williams, H.W. *Dictionary of the Maori Language.* Wellington: Government Printer, 1975, 50.

Wood, F. *The Silk Road: Two Thousand Years in the Heart of Asia.* Berkeley: University of California Press, 2004, 53.

Ziethen, K. H. *Juggling: the Past and Future.* Lulu.com, 2017.

Ringling Brothers: The Lorch Family, 1909. Ink on paper.

Circus Jews Under National Socialism: The Rise and Fall of German-Jewish Circus Dynasties

STAV MEISHAR

Over the past few years I have given talks about Jewish circuses in Nazi Germany many times, in a wide variety of settings: Jewish museums, synagogues, and conventions where the audience was primarily Jewish; but also academic conferences where most attendees were non-Jews. No matter where I speak or who the audience is, without fail, a variation on the same theme always comes up at the closing Q&A session: An audience member will raise their hand with less of a question, more of a bewildered statement: "Jews and circus, what an unlikely pairing!" In my reply, I frequently cite the trope of the Wandering Jew, or the stereotype of Jews in show business, or both—Why should Jews in circus be so surprising when we've been displaced and traveling for millennia? Why is it unlikely, when there are so many Jews in Hollywood, Jews in comedy, and in other strands of show business?

Usually this catches people off guard, confused, unable to explain their own bewilderment at the concept; but in the cases they do reply, it's always countering with another stereotype: that of the weak, awkward, helpless Jew; a nebbish Woody-Allen-esque figure with bad physique and even worse coordination. They hit the nail right on the head: "Jews and Sports?" opens the introduction to the book *Emancipation Through Muscles: Jews and Sports in Europe*. "Do the two really go together? Just as one knows that all Jews are smart and business-minded, one is certain of the fact that they are inept in sports."[1] It seems that people (maybe even Jews in particular) think of a typical Jew as a clumsy weakling. Hardly an ideal candidate for a circus career, one which requires physical prowess, highly developed motor skills, balance, strength, flexibility, grace...

But this weakling image, though steeped in antisemitic thought, has never reflected a comprehensive reality of the Jewish experience.[2] During the turn of the century and early 20th century in central Europe, there lived a variety of strong, accomplished Jewish athletes, and successful Jewish sports teams in the fields of soccer, wrestling, water polo, and more, who won trophies and reaped

---

[1] Brenner, Michael, and Gideon Reuveni. *Emancipation Through Muscles: Jews and Sports in Europe*. University of Nebraska Press, 2006.
[2] Editor's Note: An interesting analysis of the weakling Jew historically and as a long-time antisemitic trope is Ehud Luz, *Wrestling with an Angel*, New Haven: Yale University Press, 2008, 42-65.

acclaim for their countries.³ For example, in the field of athletic performance, Siegmund (Zishe) Breitbart was a major star of the period—a Jewish strongman who bent iron with his bare hands and pulled wagons full of people by his teeth—and was contracted by Circus Busch, a major Berlin circus.⁴

The concept of Jewish circus artists and Jewish circuses might seem unexpected to present-day audiences, but Jews were prominent figures in German popular entertainment for many generations. Circus exists at the intersections of sports and entertainment, of show and business. To run a successful circus company, one must be a keen businessperson, cultivate a creative eye, and be a great showperson—qualities exhibited by Jewish circus people of the era. In this paper I will offer a wide-lens view on Jews in German circus, starting by tracing the roots of German circus through the Golden Age of Circus in Germany, and the place Jews held within it. I will focus on three of the most prominent Jewish circus families in early 20th-century Germany: the Blumenfeld, Strassburger and Lorch families. I will establish what made them unique in the landscape of German circus as enterprises, and map their fates under the Nazi regime, both as businesses and as individuals.

Early history of German circus

Let us first trace a quick timeline of circus in Germany. Long before the foundation of the German state in 1871, circus had its roots in the sideshows at regional trading fairs. Trading fairs were a common element of German life from the time of the Middle Ages, steadily increasing in importance well into the 19th century. These crowded, noisy markets were at the beating heart of the German economy. At first they were the place for local merchants to offer their wares. Over the centuries, as these markets grew and expanded, they attracted foreign traders who brought their merchandise from all corners of the world. The German people would flock to these fairs to procure goods unavailable to them locally, such as spices, lace and silk, precious metals, and many other products, both luxuries and necessities.⁵ It was a ripe environment for traveling

---

³ Editor's Note: The image of the *sabra* and Israeli *chalutz* as the "New Jew," first proposed by Max Nordau at the Second Zionist Congress in 1898, is another area where the trope of the weakling Jew was drastically changed. See, e.g., Gdalit Neuman, "Dancing Between Old Worlds and New" *Performance Matters* 2.2 (2016): 11-24; Arye Naor, "Jabotinsky's New Jew: Concept and Models," *Journal of Israeli History*, 30:2 (2011): 141-159. DOI: 10.1080/13531042.2011.610120

For another approach to the trope, see also, Gavin Schaffer, "Unmasking the 'muscle Jew': the Jewish soldier in British war service, 1899–1945," *Patterns of Prejudice*, 46:3-4 (2012): 375-396, DOI: 10.1080/0031322X.2012.701809.

⁴ For more on Breitbart, see Gillerman, Sharon. "Samson in Vienna: The Theatrics of Jewish Masculinity," *Jewish Social Studies*, vol. 9 no. 2 (2003): 65-98. Project MUSE, doi:10.1353/jss.2003.0012.

⁵ Otte, Marline. *Jewish Identities in German Popular Entertainment, 1890-1933*. Cambridge

showmen to attract attention. In between bargaining and arguing, buying and selling, fair visitors encountered a myriad of entertainers: jugglers, puppeteers, dancers, clowns, animal trainers, and more. These traveling entertainers offered their audiences a respite from everyday life, joyful moments of escapism filled with jokes, tricks, stories, and magic. But the life of a traveler was not an easy one; often law enforcement and locals alike were distrustful of them. Their welcome was frequently more suspicious than warm, and sometimes downright hostile. Circus historian Dominique Jando writes:

> [Itinerant entertainers] protected each other, which was vital when traveling between tightly knit, sedentary communities. They were foreign intruders whose "unearthly" talents were sometimes perceived as disturbing or dangerous [...] and they were often the object of harassment and persecution. Many gypsies and Jews joined their ranks and created their own performance dynasties.[6]

We can trace the roots of the Jewish Lorch, Strassburger and Blumenfeld dynasties to the trading fairs of the era: The Blumenfelds traveled as early as the 17th century, performing as acrobats and tightrope walkers; the Lorches traveled with horse-drawn caravans, equipment vehicles, and animals, touring the villages of the Upper Rhine from the 17th century onward;[7] and the Strassburgers' horse-riding traditions go back to the early 19th century,[8] though it is likely they were traveling performers even earlier than has been documented.

The Golden Age of Circus[9]

By the mid 19th century, rapid urbanization and industrial development in various European regions led to the slow decline of trading fairs. The German railway networks were developing rapidly, and their growth enabled traveling

---

University Press, 2011, 36.
[6] Jando, Dominique, Noel Daniel, Linda Granfield, and Fred Dahlinger. *The Circus: 1870-1950.* Taschen, 2010, 72.
[7] Merschroth, Hermann. *Circus Lorch Eschollbrücken.* Eschollbrücken/Eich: Verein Für Heimatgeschichte, 1989.
[8] Holler, Martin. "Hugo Strassburger (1880-1942) and Family—the Fatal Return from South America." *Diverging Fates*, November 20, 2018, www.divergingfates.eu/index.php/2018/11/20/hugo-strassburger-1880-1942-and-family-the-fatal-return-from-south-america/.
[9] The term "Golden Age" ("Blütezeit des Zirkus") was first used by Joseph Halperson, *Das Buch vom Zirkus* (Düsseidorf, 1926), 127. Cited in Otte, 37.

circuses[10] to stretch their tours farther than ever before.[11] It was now possible to reach both new and old audiences in less time and at lesser expense. During this period, electricity became a common feature and for the first time circuses could extend their work day and perform after dark. Artificial illumination meant that the entire population could visit the circus, even on work nights. In 1872, the first American circus came to Europe and introduced the chapiteau[12]—the mobile, canvas tent that nowadays is synonymous with circus. Up until that point, traveling circus companies performed under the sky or in temporary wooden structures. The former was too much at the mercy of weather conditions, the latter was often hastily built, clunky and unsafe. Chapiteaux were more cost-effective and offered a higher degree of mobility; they completely revolutionized European circuses.[13] With better railroads and a highly mobile venue, traveling circuses were now able to both cut expenses and increase their profits, and circus was flourishing.

Alongside traveling circuses, which still visited towns and rural areas all over Germany, some circuses were now able to make a permanent home for themselves in the bigger cities where the population was dense enough. For cities, having their own circus was a status symbol, the same way that today cities might have their own sports teams. All the stationary circuses of that period were owned by non-Jews. The Jewish-owned circuses, however, were all of the traveling kind, owned by families who ran every aspect of the business—onstage and backstage. Historians look back at this moment in time and define this era as the Golden Age of Circus. Between the 1870s and the First World War, circus became the main form of mass entertainment in Germany.

Circus Lorch and Other Jewish Circuses

A case in point of a prominent Jewish circus of the period is Circus Lorch. Founded by Hirsch Lorch in the mid 19th century (though Hirsch is quoted as saying that his own grandfather was constantly "on the road," stretching the

---

[10] Editor's Note: The timeline that distinguishes fairground itinerant acrobatic family performances from circus, as well as that which differentiates between global acrobatic performances and circus (e.g., Chinese acrobatic theatre, South American ritual aerial performances, and African religious stilt dancing) is somewhat blurry. That said, there are tropes, symbols, aesthetics, and specific acts that came to be understood as "circus" in the eighteenth century. Even with all the debate around what should be defined as the beginning of circus, of course the term is older than the "Golden Age of Circus." Philip Astley, who is often cited as the grandfather of circus, opened his first circus show on Easter of 1768, in England.
[11] Sheehan, James J. *German History, 1770-1866*. Oxford, 1989, 485. Cited in Otte, 37.
[12] Otte, 37.
[13] Wittman, Matthew. "The Transnational History of the Early American Circus." *The American Circus*, edited by Susan Weber and Rachel Adams, Bard Graduate Center, 2012, 55–86.

family's entertainment roots as early as 1750),[14] Hirsch's sons Adolph and Louis inherited their father's circus in 1873, when this Golden Age of Circus was just beginning. Their personal history reflects those bigger changes in circus history: That same year they acquired a proper tent,[15] a stepping stone in their journey as circus professionals.[16]

Circus Lorch, now managed by the brothers, toured Europe with a comprehensive program, showcasing their families and other dedicated, renowned artists as well as many animals. They were well known for their equestrian acts, large displays of dressage and horse riding tricks. In September 1887 their circus burned down—no one was hurt, yet the damage to property was severe. Nevertheless, they got back on their feet and, in true circus spirit, put up a show only two days later, and recovered quickly.[17]

Circus Lorch was particularly successful in Southern Germany, Austria and Switzerland.[18] Adolph was regarded as the executive director and was both the ringmaster and the animal trainer, while Louis fulfilled the role of artistic director.[19] Circus Lorch had a regular schedule: they would practice at their quarters in Eschollbrücken during the winter months, give local performances before the season began, then go on tour for the summer in various European cities.

In 1903 Louis branched away from the family's circus to create his own acrobatic Risley troupe, made up mostly of his own children.[20] The Lorches' Risley act was one of the world's biggest—and indeed one of the best—Risley acts:

---

[14] Merschroth.

[15] Merschroth says 1860, but Prior and Kober say 1873. Cross-referencing different accounts, it is most likely that the first tent was acquired in 1860 but it was faulty and insufficient, and a better tent was acquired in 1873.

[16] It was an important change not only because performances could now take place in most weather conditions, but more so because it meant a major shift in how they earned their living: When the show performed in open arenas, tickets could not be pre-sold. Money was collected from spectators voluntarily, by circulating a plate, and there was no option to monitor the audience so that only paying customers could watch the show. A circus tent changed how they managed their finances; it was finally possible to sell tickets in advance.

[17] An inventory issued in 1888 gives a detailed picture of the Lorches' wealth at the time: They owned real estate, stocks and fixed-interest securities, and made several loans to townsfolk and colleagues. Their business assets consisted of 8 ponies, 17 horses, 2 elephants and a camel, as well as tents, sleeping wagons, baggage and other vehicles and carts, plus costumes and a stables tent for traveling.

[18] Kober, A. H. *Star Turns*. Translated by G. J. Renier, Noel Douglas, 1928.

[19] Merschroth.

[20] The troupe went on to be booked by some of Europe's leading impresarios, and did not often perform at their own family circus. The act was composed of up to 11 performers—Lorch family members as well as partners or apprentices—and at times horses. Risley, also known as Icarian Games, is a circus discipline owing its name to the American showman Professor Risley, who developed the act as early as 1840-1841. Traditionally presented by members of the same family, it is an acrobatic display of human juggling where bodies become both catapult and catcher. Louis's eldest son, Julius, trained and led the troupe.

> They make their entrance, all eleven of them in order of size, dressed in Spanish bull-fighters' costumes, and start by executing a whirlwind of jumps, tumbles and somersaults. Then the three "throwers" lie down on the red velvet cushions with their legs in the air, and throw the three smallest members of the company from foot to foot, passing them across to one another and catching them again. [...] Julius Lorch is called the King of Icarians because he is able to throw his son three times into the air and make him execute a double somersault each time.[21]

The Lorch Risley troupe was a true star attraction and very much sought after, traveling all over the world, including with the Ringling Bros. Circus in the United States, with Circus Sarrasani in South America, and in many circuses and music halls throughout the United Kingdom.

Circus Strassburger also enjoyed unprecedented success during this time. In addition to their original circus,[22] two of the Strassburgers—Adolf and Leopold—opened an additional circus under the Strassburger name at the turn of the century.[23] The "Circus Brothers Strassburger" performed mainly in Germany, but also in Sweden, England, the Netherlands and Belgium. The circus had a big tent with three rings and owned more than 100 horses; the family was known for their horse riding skills.[24]

Circus Blumenfeld enjoyed an even bigger success during this Golden Age of Circus, with various family members running multiple traveling circuses simultaneously under the Blumenfeld name:

> By 1900, the Blumenfeld circus managed to visit 120 cities in one season and twenty-four locations in one month. This was all the more remarkable in that the circus traveled at this time with six tents in addition to the chapiteau, 28 wagons, 130 horses, a huge collection of electrical equipment, and its own string orchestra.[25]

---

[21] Kober.
[22] The circus was run by the family's patriarch Salomon, and then transferred to his son Hugo.
[23] "Ehepaar Straßburger Und Seine Tochter Henriette." *Die Ottostadt Magdeburg*, Aug. 2017, www.magdeburg.de/media/custom/37_27034_1.PDF.
[24] Van Dixhoorn, Frits. "Strassburger, Wilhelmine Sophia Eleonora (1910-1988)." *Biografisch Woordenboek Van Nederland*, Instituut Voor Nederlandse Geschiedenis, 11 Dec. 2013. resources.huygens.knaw.nl/bwn1880-2000/lemmata/bwn5/strassbu.
[25] Otte, 84-85.

By the time World War I broke out, the Golden Age of Circus in Europe was on the decline. Two hundred circuses traveled Europe in 1900, yet only 70 remained by 1912, the eve of the war. One of the circuses that was shut down was the original Strassburger Circus, which was sold to Lorenz Hagenbeck of the Hagenbeck Circus in 1916.[26] Post-war, Germany was suffering from a financial crisis, and circus continued to be affected. The number of German traveling circuses dwindled from 43 in 1918 to 30 in 1924.[27]

This, however, was in no way the end of the Strassburger Circus. The brothers Adolf and Leopold decided to continue running the "Circus Brothers Strassburger"[28] jointly, with their brother Hugo as the head stableman. It was a prosperous time for the Strassburger Circus, and they now had a large, modernly-equipped tent with space for well over 3,000 spectators, and a large number of dressage animals.

Amidst all the hardships, circuses survived and found enthusiastic audiences to attend their shows. The Strassburger, Lorch and Blumenfeld families led successful traveling circuses in pre-World War II Germany and the non-Jewish circuses frequently employed Jewish talent.[29]

While non-Jewish circuses catered more toward the bourgeoisie, the Jewish circuses were more modest in their aspiration and shaped their reputation and shows around different concepts. The Blumenfeld Circus, for example, sought to forge an image of middle-class respectability. They wanted to brand themselves as honorable and honest businessmen and as romanticized idealizations of artists. Their tours frequented the same stops year after year, hoping to create a loyal crowd of regulars who would return to see them, thus minimizing their economic risk. They also emphasized their resistance to the Americanization of German circuses in both marketing materials and artistic content, attempting to arouse a sense of patriotism in their audience and to draw them to the performances by creating a feeling of nostalgia.[30]

Partnerships between artistic families were commonplace among traveling artists. This allowed for resources to be pooled together, for skills to be shared and for fending off competition. Oftentimes these partnerships were solidified

---

[26] Hagenbeck, Lorenz. *Animals Are My Life*. London: The Bodley Head, 1956.
[27] Arnold, Herman. *Fahrends Volk: Randgruppen des Zigeunervolkes*. Landau, Pfalz, 1983, 165. Cited in Otte, 50.
[28] The names "Strassburger Circus" and "Strassburger Brothers Circus" seem to have often been used interchangeably, as was the case with the Lorch Circus. It appears that the families weren't too particular about the business name (as used in advertisements) as long as it had their family name in it.
[29] Such talent includes the Konyot family trick riders and the Lorch family Risley act.
[30] Otte, 70, 96.

by marriage. The non-Jewish Althoff Circus, for example, had members marrying into two Jewish circus families—the Lorches and the Blumenfelds—thus keeping circus in the family even when religions mixed.

Not only was it common for circus members to marry within the business, but Jews at the time also tended to marry other Jews. And so it was only natural that many Jewish circus artists ended up associated by blood, business, or both. For example, over four generations the Blumenfelds married into the Konyot, Lorch, Strassburger and Goldkette families, mostly arranged marriages which were meant to fortify each family's circus and increase their financial stability and artistic offerings.[31]

There is very little information about the religious practices of these families, so it is difficult to gauge what kind of relationship they had with Judaism, if at all. The Lorch family home provides a silent testimony: every door in the house holds a *mezuzah*—a small capsule containing a scroll of the *Shema* prayer, and a staple of Jewish homes.[32]

According to Irene Danner-Bento, a descendant of the Lorch family,[33] the family kept Shabbat.[34] Irene described her grandfather as taking these practices very seriously, and remembered a specific incident when this respect was put to the test:

> My sister Gerda was never able to stay serious when grandfather blessed us. She giggled and chuckled and made me do so, too. One day we imitated our grandpa in the kitchen. We nodded our heads and mumbled some prayer words that we had picked up from him but didn't understand. In that very moment he came in through the door. We received a hailstorm of blows! In this matter he knew no jokes.[35]

---

[31] For more on marriages in Jewish and gentile German circus families, see Otte.

[32] During World War II, when a house was inhabited by a non-Jewish family, they painted over *mezuzahs* but did not remove them. The great-great-grandchild of Adolphe and Louis, Mary Bento, lives in the home built by her ancestors. The *mezuzahs* they placed are still nailed to every doorpost.

[33] Prior, 21-23.

[34] No sewing, washing, cleaning or any other work was done, though she and her sister were still required to do their homework. Together the family lit the Shabbat candles, and their grandmother, Sessie, would bake challah. Irene's grandfather, Julius, seems to have been the most observant of the family. Whenever he wasn't touring he required his wife to cook according to Jewish law, and Irene would be sent to buy meat from the nearest kosher butcher. He was a heavy smoker, but come Shabbat he would extinguish his cigarillo and refrain from smoking until Shabbat was over. On Shabbat he would go to the nearest synagogue, in the neighboring town of Pfungstadt, to pray.

[35] Prior, Ingeborg. *Der Clown Und Die Zirkus Reiterin*. München: C Piper Verlag, 1997.

The Nazi Era

Jewish circuses in pre-WWII Germany provided a display of diversity that was sadly soon to be extinguished from the German landscape; it was a world populated by an exceptional variety of artists representing vastly different racial, religious, and national identities. All of this changed with the rise of the Nazis, and one by one all the Jewish circuses were forced to close: Circus Blumenfeld collapsed in 1928 due to financial hardships; Circus Lorch was forced into bankruptcy in 1930 as rising antisemitism led to dwindling attendance; and in 1935, the Strassburgers withdrew from managing their circus and were pressured to sell it. The tents, the lights, the seats, the caravans, the trapezes—everything these families owned was dismantled and auctioned off. These Jewish circuses, as enterprises, did not survive Hitler. As for their members, it is hard to trace what exactly became of each of them; but the overall picture is of nearly complete annihilation of the German-Jewish circus royalty.

So what did become of the three Jewish circus giants? The Blumenfelds, who had been the most renowned of all Jewish circus families, owned multiple traveling circuses which figured among Germany's ten leading circus enterprises, winning both national and international fame. They were so successful that, in the 1920s, they became the only Jewish circus to have a permanent home,[36] situated in the city of Magdeburg.[37] But the global economic crisis, unemployment and the incipient political radicalization eventually led the Blumenfelds to go bankrupt in 1928.[38] After they closed, they struggled to find work all over Europe, as it had been forbidden to employ Jews.

A personal letter written by Alfons Blumenfeld, dated January 1939, was preserved by a descendant of the family, Professor Ron Beadle, and reveals the family's distress and helplessness. Alfons had fled Germany to Paris two months earlier, following Kristallnacht, along with his wife Olympia (who was a descendant of the Konyot circus family, who were also Jewish) and their daughter Ruth. In this letter, Alfons is writing to his brother-in-law, who was still in Germany, to thank him for some money he had sent them. Here are translated excerpts from the letter:

---

[36] The stationary circus building was owned by three of the Blumenfeld brothers—Alex, Alfons and Arthur—although they preferred to rent the building to other companies and tour with their family's traveling circus. The three brothers held important roles in the program of their family circus: Alex performed a dressage act with his horse "Puppchen" (Little Doll), dancing to operetta melodies; Alfons had a liberty horse act; and Arthur had two trained bulls.
[37] "Circus Blumenfeld: Overview & General History." Circus Blennow & Blumenfeld Genealogy, 15 Feb. 2016. blennowgenealogy.wordpress.com/circus-blumenfeld-overview-general-history/.
[38] Winkler, Gisela, and Dietmar Winkler. *Die Blumenfelds Schicksale Einer jüdischen Zirkusfamilie*; Eine Dokumentation. Ed. Schwarzdruck, 2012.

> My Darlings, we received your lovely letter and the money and would like to thank you from the bottom of our hearts. We were really happy about your quick response and help. However, if we knew about your own struggle with such big difficulties and illness, we would not have mentioned the money. Now we hope that you get the contract and have enough money for the journey. We understand how hard it must be for you too with such a large troupe when not continuously working. It is a hard life that we have to struggle through and believe us that it is difficult for us to ask for support, especially as we have always been in the position to help ourselves and for the first time we cannot. [...] Do you by any chance have an acquaintance in America who could possibly make an affidavit for us so that we can go there? Everything is so difficult and one gets sick from all the worrying. We often heard that you have a beautiful routine and it is a pity that such beautiful routines are not booked; My brother Arthur's horse-riding act is really beautiful and the poor guy is also never contracted. Now he is in Riga and he also tried very hard for us, but he unfortunately could not do anything either...[39]

Alfons, Olympia, and Ruth never made it to America; they were murdered in Auschwitz. Alfons' brother Alex, who dazzled audiences with his operetta-dancing horse, emigrated multiple times—to Denmark, Belgium and France—in an attempt to escape the Nazis. The French Police eventually caught and deported him to a work camp, and he was murdered in Auschwitz.[40]

The building where the Blumenfeld Circus once stood was bombed in 1945 and was completely destroyed. All that remains there today are stumbling stones[41] commemorating the names of the Blumenfelds who did not survive the Holocaust. Immediately after the war, in 1945, Arthur tried to reestablish his family's circus and held performances for American G.I.s and children from

---

[39] From the personal family archives of Professor Ron Beadle, Olympia's great-nephew.
[40] Holler, Martin. "Brothers Blumenfeld jun.—the Fall of a Jewish Horse Circus Dynasty." *Diverging Fates*, April 26, 2018.
[41] Stumbling stones, or *Stolperstein*, are four-inch-square, brass-capped bricks commemorating victims of the Holocaust and Nazi persecution. The brainchild of German artist Gunter Demnig, each stone is inscribed with the name and details about the death of each victim, and installed outside the person's former home or workplace. More than 90,000 commemorative stones have been installed in more than 600 sites across Europe since 1992.

displaced persons camps. He was not very successful and ended up selling his circus to Paula Busch in 1949. He died only two years later.[42]

The Strassburger family, related to the Blumenfelds by marriage, for the most part faced a better fate. Theirs was the last Jewish circus to remain under Jewish ownership. They were under attack as early as 1933, with SA squads (the Nazi Party's original paramilitary wing) posted outside their venue, chanting to passersby, "Germans, do not visit the Jew circus!"[43] For a while they managed to get by, surviving under the protection of their general manager Emil Wacker, who was personal friends with Hitler's deputy, Rudolf Hess. Wacker persuaded Hess to give the Strassburger Circus special treatment, and the circus was given temporary easing of ordinances and provisions. However, it did not last, and eventually they were forced to close. In 1935 they sold their circus to Paula Busch. At the time, the Strassburger Circus was the biggest German circus company under Jewish ownership, since the Blumenfelds had closed down almost a decade earlier, and in fact the fourth largest traveling circus in Germany. Busch bought their circus for 200,000 *Reichsmarks*, far below its real value.

Paula Busch, a non-Jewish circus owner, plays a notable role in the history of Jewish circuses in Germany. Busch was "the only female directress of a circus in the Weimar Republic and the Third Reich… One of the most glamorous women of her time."[44] In a field dominated by men, she stood out as a highly regarded circus manager. When observing her relationship with Jewish circus artists, it is unclear whether she acted out of concern or out of economic opportunity, or both.[45] Like many German circus owners of the time, Busch joined the Nazi party—whether in true support of their cause or simply to stay afloat and be allowed to conduct business, is impossible to tell.

Busch's circuses suffered greatly during those difficult years, and buying the Strassburger Circus was a wise investment that helped her fortify her business. When Busch bought the Strassburger Circus, she made their old manager, Wacker (who was also her son-in-law, and a member of the Nazi party like her),

---

[42] "Circus Blumenfeld: Overview & General History." Circus Blennow & Blumenfeld Genealogy, Feb. 15, 2016. blennowgenealogy.wordpress.com/circus-blumenfeld-overview-general-history/.
[43] *Circus. Freedom. Enforced Alignment.* CiNS, 2017. roxanacircusartist.com/wp-content/uploads/2018/03/BROSCHUERE-CiNS.pdf.
[44] Otte, 53.
[45] Under Busch's leadership, the Busch Circus reached such levels of success that they had permanent buildings in Hamburg, Vienna (which closed in 1920), Berlin and Breslau. Her father, Jakob Busch, employed the Lorch Family Risley act. Paula herself was the first to bet on Zishe Breitbart, who would later become a legendary circus strongman, and gave him his first major performance engagement at her circus in 1919.

the co-owner. The sale of the Strassburger Circus to Paula Busch was received favorably in German media: "The circus company is now in pure Aryan hands," reported the *Geraer Observer*.[46]

After selling their circus, the Strassburgers were left with 10,000 *Reichsmarks* each, and were allowed to keep a few mobile homes, training horses and two working elephants. They took all they had and emigrated to the Netherlands, where they took refuge during the war and founded the new Circus Strassburger, in partnership with impresario Frans Mikkenie. During WWII, Circus Mikkenie-Strassburger was able to tour the Netherlands, Belgium, Denmark and Sweden. Post-war, throughout the 1950s, theirs was the leading Dutch circus, and they became the National Circus of the Netherlands. Even Queen Wilhelmina and Queen Juliana and her daughters enjoyed attending the performances.[47] The new Strassburger Circus, however, never returned to Germany. It closed in 1963; some of the Strassburgers' descendants are still in the circus business to this day.

Many of the Strassburger family members survived, including brothers Adolf and Leopold and their children. But their sibling, Hugo, faced a worse fate. Hugo, his wife Karolina and their three children were not in Germany when their family circus was sold. Like the Lorch family a decade before them, the Strassburgers had an engagement on the South American tour of the Sarrasani Circus starting in 1934. Eight Jewish circus staff members used the two-year journey for emigration, but Hugo Strassburger decided—despite all warnings—to return with his family to Germany. When he was interrogated by the Gestapo in May 1936, Hugo realized the danger they were in and vowed to make all efforts to emigrate as soon as possible. The family then arranged for an engagement with Cirque Amar in France, and they moved to the French town of Blois at the beginning of July 1936. There, Hugo's youngest daughter Bella married the Belgian clown Eugène Babusiau, became Catholic, and moved with him to Brussels, where she survived the war.

Hugo, Karolina, and their older children, Adolph and Henriette, remained with Cirque Amar and enjoyed relative security for the following three years. In September 1939, however, with the beginning of the Second World War, the French police arrested Hugo and his son and sent them to the internment camp Gurs as "enemy aliens." Adolph was released on restrictive conditions and returned to Blois where Shérif Amar helped him hide, first in a circus depot in Blois, later in changing apartments in Paris and Aubervilliers. Employees and relatives of Amar provided Adolf with food; he survived the war.

---

[46] "Ehepaar Straßburger Und Seine Tochter Henriette." *Die Ottostadt Magdeburg*, Aug. 2017, www.magdeburg.de/media/custom/37_27034_1.PDF.

[47] Van Dixhoorn.

Hugo remained interned even after the Franco-German ceasefire. At the beginning of August 1942, he was transferred to Drancy and from there deported to the Auschwitz concentration camp where he was murdered in the gas chambers. His daughter Henriette had been deported to Auschwitz two months earlier, in June; his wife Karolina was deported there the following February. Both women perished in Auschwitz.[48]

The Lorch family faced a fate similar to the Blumenfelds. They too were forced to close as the increase in antisemitism made their circus drop in popularity and fail financially by 1930. After the Nazis rose to power in 1933 the Lorches found themselves unwelcome in their own hometown of Eschollbrücken, which had been their winter quarters for decades. As the situation for Jews in Germany continued to worsen, a branch of the family—siblings Rudolph, Arthur, Julius, and Jeanette Lorch—managed to escape Germany to Belgium. When Belgium fell under the Nazi regime in May 1940, Rudolph and Arthur were captured by the Gestapo and deported to the work camp Gurs; the brothers eventually died in Auschwitz.[49]

Julius and Jeannette managed to avoid deportation—Jeanette was not home at the time the Nazis came, and Julius was deemed unfit for work having had his leg amputated two years earlier due to blood poisoning. Understanding they were no longer safe, Jeanette and Julius hid in an attic in Brussels. In December 1941, Julius's granddaughter, Irene, was smuggled across the border from Germany to secretly visit her grandfather and great-aunt. As she was in danger since she had a Jewish parent, the Busch Circus helped her by allowing her to hide in their train car as they traveled to Brussels for a six-week work engagement:

> We hugged and burst out in tears. This was the first time I saw my grandfather crippled. It hurt my heart. My proud Grandfather, the honorable Circus Director—so miserable, so pitiful! His hands, which were holding the wooden crutches, were busted and bloodied from the cold. He didn't have a pair of gloves. He couldn't say anything for a long time and the tears were running down his face.[50]

For six weeks Irene stayed with her family in their secret attic and worked at the Busch Circus in the box office and as an usher. She wore a disguise—a wig

---

[48] Holler, Martin. "Hugo Strassburger (1880-1942) and Family—the Fatal Return from South America."
[49] Lorch, Arthur, and Rudolph Lorch. *Briefe aus den Lagern: Briefe der Brüder Arthur und Rudi Lorch aus Gurs, Noé und anderen Lagern in Südfrankreich*. Edited by Renate Dreesen. Pfungstadt: Arbeitskreis Ehemalige Synagoge, 2014.
[50] Prior, 75-76.

and a Rococo costume—so that none of her old colleagues would recognize her (she had performed with the Busch Circus from 1935-1938). The Italian horse-riding troupe The Carolis, who had trained Irene and made her part of their act, recognized her but did not report her, protecting her due to their friendship; they all pretended to be strangers.

She gave her grandfather and great-aunt her small salary every day. A friend from the Busch Circus gave her a bit of chocolate, wine or cigarettes for her grandfather—small treats that used to be common but were now items of luxury. She slept on the floor of the attic, covered in her winter coat to protect from the bitter cold. On Shabbat, she watched her grandfather put on his best clothes and pray. Eventually it was time for the Busch Circus to return to Germany, and Irene said goodbye to her family. Six months later Julius died at age 67, his already ailing body succumbing to a combination of cold, malnutrition, and illness. Jeanette survived the war and was eventually buried alongside her father, Louis, at the Darmstadt Jewish cemetery. Julius's wife Sessie was killed in Auschwitz, and so was his brother Eugen. Other siblings emigrated to England, Italy and America.

Circus Righteous Gentiles
One branch of the Lorch family survived in Germany by a combination of luck and kindness. Sessie and Julius's 19-year-old granddaughter Irene fell in love with Peter Bento, the non-Jewish clown of the Althoff Circus.[51] Irene persuaded the owner, Adolf Althoff, to give her a job despite the strict laws on employing Jews.[52] As the war progressed and more and more Jews were being deported, Irene and Peter persuaded the Althoffs to shelter Irene's family—her mother Alice, her father Hans, and her sister Gerda. They spent the remainder of the war hiding in plain sight at the Althoff Circus, working and performing in its shows. They were assisted by Mohamed Sahraoui, a Moroccan acrobat who became their best friend. Whenever the Nazis came for inspection Mohamed would hide Irene and her family in a secret corridor built especially for them in one of the circus trailers.[53] Adolf described how he distracted the Nazis during their visits:

> When the Nazi gentlemen came to check on us [...] they wanted to know about my opinions. I kept telling them that I was a circus man, and that circus people live in the entire world

---

[51] Coincidentally, Peter Bento is a relative of the Belgian clown Babusiau, whom Bella Strassburger married.
[52] "Adolf and Maria Althoff." Yadvashem.org, Yad Vashem The World Holocaust Remembrance Center, www.yadvashem.org/righteous/stories/althoff.html.
[53] Mohamed Sahraoui, in-person interview by author, June 2018.

and of the entire world. We couldn't exist only in Germany, where there were many other circuses. We therefore had to adjust and behave in every country that we visited as if we were at home, that is—be well behaved. I was always especially kind, gave them free tickets for the extended family, generously poured cognac, told them stories from my past. [...] When they wanted to check the premises, I usually was able to divert them. I told them that I had a meeting with one of their superiors, but that my wife Maria would take care of them. By that time she had set the table in our wagon, and offered them coffee. She never forgot the bottle of cognac. Our hospitality became famous.[54]

For saving the Lorches' lives, Adolf and his wife Maria received the honorable title of "Righteous Among the Nations" from the Yad Vashem Museum in Jerusalem. The families remained friends until their last days. While Irene's story of rescue became the most well-known, The Althoffs were hardly the only non-Jewish circus people to have saved Jewish lives: Cirque Amar helped save members of the Strassburger family; Adolf Althoff's sister, Carola Williams, hid a member of the Blumenfeld family at her circus (who happened to be married to her aunt), and supported the Blumenfeld brothers in the work camps with packages of food, clothing, cigarettes, and medicine;[55] Rosa Bouglione and her family, a Sinti (Romani) family who managed the Cirque d'Hiver building in Paris, hid a number of Jewish artists, including the Pauwels, a family of Jewish-Belgian clowns.[56] Who knows how many other Jews, circus or otherwise, were saved thanks to the generosity of circus people whose stories remain untold.

These days, when I give talks about Jewish circuses in Nazi Germany, it is rare for any audience member to have heard of these families. The Nazis not only destroyed lives, they tore down entire dynasties and eradicated much of their legacies. But these families changed the landscape of German circus, and their descendants—through generations of family bonds—are still involved in circuses today. These Jewish giants left their mark, and their stories are not forgotten.

---

[54] "From the Testimony of Adolf Althoff." Yadvashem.org, Yad Vashem The World Holocaust Remembrance Center, www.yadvashem.org/righteous/stories/althoff/althoff-testimony.html.
[55] Jeanette Williams, phone interview by author, August 2020.
[56] Gasche, Malte. "Rosa Bouglione (1910-2018), in a Parisian Circus under German Occupation." Diverging Fates, 31 Mar. 2017, www.divergingfates.eu/index.php/2017/03/31/rosa-bouglione-1910-in-a-parisian-circus-under-german-occupation/.

References

Arnold, Herman. *Fahrends Volk: Randgruppen des Zigeunervolkes*. Landau, Pfalz, 1983.
Brenner, Michael, and Gideon Reuveni. *Emancipation Through Muscles: Jews and Sports in Europe*. University of Nebraska Press, 2006.
"Ehepaar Straßburger Und Seine Tochter Henriette." *Die Ottostadt Magdeburg*, Aug. 2017, www.magdeburg.de/media/custom/37_27034_1.PDF.
Gillerman, Sharon. "Samson in Vienna: The Theatrics of Jewish Masculinity." *Jewish Social Studies*, vol. 9 no. 2, (2003): 65-98. Project MUSE, doi:10.1353/jss.2003.0012.
Hagenbeck, Lorenz. *Animals Are My Life*. London: The Bodley Head, 1956.
Halperson, Joseph, *Das Buch vom Zirkus*. Düsseidorf, 1926.
Holler, Martin. "Brothers Blumenfeld jun.—the Fall of a Jewish Horse Circus Dynasty." *Diverging Fates*. April 26, 2018.
Holler, Martin. "Carl Strassburger (1899-1953)—From a Boycotted 'Jewish Circus' to a Successful Dutch Company." *Diverging Fates*, October 29, 2018, www.divergingfates.eu/index.php/2018/10/29/carl-strassburger-1899-1953-from-a-boycotted-jewish-circus-to-a-successful-dutch-company/.
Holler, Martin. "Hugo Strassburger (1880-1942) and Family—the Fatal Return from South America." *Diverging Fates*, November 20, 2018. www.divergingfates.eu/index.php/2018/11/20/hugo-strassburger-1880-1942-and-family-the-fatal-return-from-south-america/.
Jando, Dominique, Noel Daniel, Linda Granfield, and Fred Dahlinger. *The Circus: 1870-1950*. Taschen, 2010.
Kober, A. H. *Star Turns*. Translated by G. J. Renier, Noel Douglas, 1928.
Lorch, Arthur, and Rudolph Lorch. *Briefe aus den Lagern: Briefe der Brüder Arthur und Rudi Lorch aus Gurs, Noé und anderen Lagern in Südfrankreich*. Edited by Renate Dreesen. Pfungstadt: Arbeitskreis Ehemalige Synagoge, 2014.
Luz, Ehud, *Wrestling with an Angel*, New Haven: Yale University Press, 2008.
Merschroth, Hermann. *Circus Lorch Eschollbrücken*. Eschollbrücken/Eich: Verein Für Heimatgeschichte, 1989.
Naor, Arye. "Jabotinsky's New Jew: Concept and Models," *Journal of Israeli History*, 30:2 (2011):141-159. DOI: 10.1080/13531042.2011.610120 .
Neuman, Gdalit. "Dancing Between Old Worlds and New" *Performance Matters* 2.2 (2016):11-24.
Otte, Marline. *Jewish Identities in German Popular Entertainment, 1890-1933*. Cambridge University Press, 2011.
Prior, Ingeborg. *Der Clown Und Die Zirkus Reiterin*. München: C Piper Verlag, 1997.
Schaffer, Gavin. "Unmasking the 'muscle Jew': the Jewish soldier in British war service, 1899–1945," *Patterns of Prejudice*, 46:3-4 (2012):375-396. DOI: 10.1080/0031322X.2012.701809.
Sheehan, James J. *German History, 1770-1866*. Oxford, 1989.
Van Dixhoorn, Frits. "Strassburger, Wilhelmine Sophia Eleonora (1910-1988)." *Biografisch Woordenboek Van Nederland*, Instituut Voor Nederlandse Geschiedenis, 11 Dec. 2013. resources.huygens.knaw.nl/bwn1880-2000/lemmata/bwn5/strassbu.

Winkler, Gisela, and Dietmar Winkler. *Die Blumenfelds Schicksale Einer jüdischen Zirkusfamilie*; Eine Dokumentation. Ed. Schwarzdruck, 2012.

Wittman, Matthew. "The Transnational History of the Early American Circus." *The American Circus*, edited by Susan Weber and Rachel Adams, Bard Graduate Center, 2012, 55–86.

The Lorch Family. Ink on Paper. Date unknown.

Following up on the previous chapter, this short piece, written by German circus artist Roxana Küwen, reflects further current artistic and research-oriented work on the subject of Jewish circus families under National Socialism.

Circus.Freiheit.Fleichschaltung.
Insights Into the Interdisciplinary and Challenging Work of the CiNS Collective
Roxana Küwen

The CiNS Collective is a heterogeneous project group from Germany that deals with circus history and the potential of (circus) arts to create awareness of political topics amongst diverse audiences using a multidisciplinary approach. Many of us come from different backgrounds and currently work as circus pedagogues, professional circus artists, political activists, filmmakers and academic researchers, and many of us are former travelers in traditional circuses.

Our work originally started with a focus on the history of circus in Germany during National Socialism and World War II and the impact of that time on Jewish and other persecuted circus artists. The specific theme of circus under fascism is very much neglected in the discussions and the discourses of *Aufarbeitung*—usually referred to as coming to terms with the past in Germany—especially compared to other art forms like theater or dance. Our basic motivation to research this topic was to learn about it and to make it public in order to contribute to a commemoration of the victims amongst circus artists.

The fates of many individual circus artists have remained obscure until the present. Until today there have hardly been any so-called "compensation payments" to the artists or circuses in question. This is partly due to the fact that circus in Germany has never been acknowledged as a cultural asset and the circus companies thus have never been entitled to subsidies, nor has academic research been supported

The starting point: exposition
We created "CIRCUS.FREIHEIT.GLEICHSCHALTUNG" [Circus-Freedom-Enforced Alignment] in 2011. It is a traveling exposition which allows us to reach as many different people as possible. We present it at circus festivals, circus pedagogic conferences, in established theaters, alternative arts festivals, political anti-racist festivals, libraries, schools, and the like. Realizing that the

structure of the exposition excludes people with less interest or a lack of ability to read long texts, we started working on a performance that would transmit information on a more accessible level. That performance became a play reading that includes elements of lecture, reading, acting, circus arts and live music.

The program consists of fragments of the life experience of Irene Bento, a circus artist from the famous Jewish Lorch circus family. She saved herself and parts of her family from the Nazis by hiding in Althoff Circus. Seeing how much our audience was touched by our performance, we understood how performing arts are a very important element to transmit both academic knowledge and emotional experience. The fact that so few survivors and witnesses of the time are still alive today to share their stories makes this even more relevant and important. We continue to adapt and critically reflect on our performance, taking into consideration new aspects of historical research and contemporary issues of discrimination and persecution. Throughout the years during which we performed the piece, we found it was very important to us to find a language to transfer emotional knowledge without making the audience feel numb or helpless in regard to the suffering caused by the *Shoah*. We believe that the will to fight discrimination and persecution these days needs to be encouraged by a feeling of hope. Therefore our performance's dramaturgy shifts between very painful scenes to lighter scenes in which we make use of inherent circus metaphors such as joy, collaboration, and community.

From 2017-2020 we toured our performance and exposition together with the band Bejarano & Microphone Mafia, consisting of the famous musician and Auschwitz survivor Esther Bejarano, her son Yoram Bejarano and the hip-hop artist, pedagogue, and activist Kutlu Yurtseven. Esther passed away in July 2021; we continue touring with the duo, always searching for new ways to keep Esther's and other survivors' stories and messages alive for the next generations. Therefore we also do pedagogical project weeks in schools in which we encourage students to choose relevant aspects from history and work in artistic ways on themes of discrimination and exclusion.

We are continuing our research by visiting different archives, connecting to other researchers, and speaking with the few witnesses of the time who are still alive today. In that context, our encounter with the family of Irene Bento was very important and touching. We interviewed her children, Mary and Jano Bento, twice, as well as speaking with an old friend of their family. Hearing their stories and learning about the remaining trauma in the families that continued well after the war meant a lot to us. We realized that many historians and journalists who aim to work in support of the witnesses often reinforced those traumas by using insensitive styles of interviewing or by commercializing their stories. Therefore one of our principles is to pay attention to this particular danger of instrumentalizing remembrance.

The acknowledgment of our work by the Bento family was of great personal meaning to all of us. But as our resources are limited, our research has not reached out as far as it could. We think that circus history needs more interdisciplinary exchange and international networking, regardless of whether it is researched by scientists, historians, circus artists themselves, or an interdisciplinary group like us. We see a great necessity for circus to critically deal with its history with regard to different aspects, including colonialism, antisemitism, racism, sexism and more. We hope this work will find its translation into artistic expression as well as academic research and production.

Roxana Küwen, CiNS Project
https://www.projekt-cins.de/

Purim Box.
Photo © Collection of the Mishkan Museum of Art, Ein Harod, Israel by Ran Arda.

Jewish Circus History

AYAL PROUSER, ORA HORN PROUSER, AND MICHAEL KASPER

The history of circus arts is deeply intertwined with the Jewish experience. Many don't realize that you do not have to dig far to find connections between circus and Jewish life in a historical context. However, the relationship between Judaism and circus arts is somewhat complex.[1] On the one hand, the rabbis shunned participation in the Roman circus because it advanced values contrary to their vision of Judaism, such as idolatry, idleness, drinking, and harm to people and animals.[2] On the other hand, the rabbis describe their colleagues as engaging in performative and ritual contortion and juggling.[3] There is even a reference to trained monkeys and elephants.[4] Jewish skepticism and antagonism toward the circus continued through the medieval and modern period. Given that much of this demonization of the circus revolves around casting it as the antithesis of Torah study and Jewish values, the present volume serves as an important intervention towards cultivating a successful synthesis between study of sacred Jewish text and circus arts.

In many books about Jewish thought, you read about the "chain of tradition," the generations of rabbis debating Jewish jurisprudence. Below are brief write-ups of what we have cheekily referred to as the (circus) "train of tradition," generations of Jews partaking in the circus, some of whom are also part of the standard chain of tradition. We have provided sources at the bottom if you are interested in learning more.

Please enjoy.

Resh Lakish
Shimon ben Lakish, better known as Resh Lakish, lived c. 200 CE–275 CE After a financial setback, he sold himself to a gladiator circus where, thanks to his great strength, he fought with animals and entertained the audience (Gittin 46b). The gladiators fought at Circus Maximus, ancient Rome's largest arena, where there were a variety of chariot races, fights, and other entertainment.

---

[1] Thank you to Rabbi Matthew Goldstone, Ph.D. for assistance with these insights.
[2] See, e.g., Jerusalem Talmud Berachot 4:2; Mishnah Berurah 307:59. Note also the modern moderate Israeli *posek* R. Eliezer Melamed who writes in his *Peninei Halakhah* (Kashrut 15:12:3) a prohibition of circus attendance based on danger to humans and the harsh treatment of animals.
[3] See, e.g. Sukkah 51b including Rashi on "flaming torches," 53a.
[4] See Eiruvin 31b.

Circus Maximus, as photographed in 2022 by Ora Horn Prouser and as illustrated by Luisa Vallon Fumillus.

Jacob DeCastro

Jacob DeCastro (1758-1824), the son of the rabbi of London's Portuguese synagogue, first experienced theater in the form of Purim plays. While many expected him to become a rabbi like his father, he instead chose to work in theater. For 38 years he worked with Philip Astley (1742-1814), who is often called the father of modern circus. While Astley himself was not Jewish, he hired many Jewish performers who were known as "Astley's Jews," and DeCastro was undoubtedly the one responsible for introducing so many of them to Astley in the first place (Burnam, 73)[5]

Jacob de Castro, by R. Humphreys. Published by Sherwood, Jones, and Co., London, 1824.

Andrew Levi

Andrew Levi, a Jewish circus artist, performed as an equestrian in Cirque Olympique in the early 19th century. The circus toured throughout the United States, the Caribbean, and the West Indies. Benjamin Brown, who managed the show, described Andrew Levi's intricate and elaborate act:

---

[5] For discussion of the position of Jews at Astley's and in the theatergoing public in general, see below, DeCastro, Dibdin, Rubens, and Wolf.

Jewish Circus History · 89

Cirque Olympique by Jacques-Alphonse Testard, 1837. Ink and gouache drawing, Théâtre National.

The biggest card in my show was a boy named Levi, a Jew. He was a wonderful rider. We had a piece of canvas twelve feet wide, then a hoop eighteen inches in diameter covered with paper, a balloon it was called, and Levi held in his hand a hoop nine and a half inches in diameter. He'd jump over that banner, through the balloon and through the little hoop, all at the same time. That was called a big feat in those days. (Wittman)

Albert Salamonsky

Albert Salamonsky (1839-1913) was descended from a family of Jewish equestrians. Despite coming to Moscow relatively penniless, he was able to fulfill his vision of founding Circus Salamonsky, which became a very prominent circus in Moscow. The circus, at its opening, included tightrope walkers, jugglers, equestrians, clowns, and acrobats. Before that time, circuses were considered adult-only entertainment, but Salamonsky changed the approach by creating shows specifically for children. He also performed equestrian acts in the circus himself. (Jando)

Albert Salamonsky (ca.1875).
Circopedia Archive

Zishe Breitpart.
From the promotional pamphlet "Muscular Power" promoting his course.

Zishe Siegmund Breitbart

Siegmund Breitbart (1883-1925) was known as the "Iron King... the world's strongest man." His acts included bending iron bars, tearing horseshoes apart, and pulling in a tug-of-war against two horses (see Obituary in *The New York Times*, October 13, 1925). He'd lay on his back with a bridge-like construction leaning on him, upon which people, horses, and elephants walked. His father was a blacksmith, so he grew up around iron bars and other metal products, all of which became part of his act. Though his act was not itself Jewish, he highlighted his Jewishness in other ways, such as entering the arena in a horse-drawn chariot with Stars of David on the side while music from the operetta *Bar Kokhba* played.

He fought for the Russians in World War I and was taken prisoner by the Germans. After the war he stayed in Germany performing feats of strength. Circus Busch found him and he became part of their troupe. He performed throughout Europe and the United States, becoming famous enough that two German films and a Yiddish screenplay were written about him.[6] His strength

---

[6] These films include *Invincible* (2001) and *Der Eisenkönig* (1973).

"Yidn in Tsirk Arena." Article in *Idishe Bilder*, 1937.

Zoltan Hirsch.
Courtesy Szilaghi Gyorgy, Budapest.

"Roly Zoli."
Courtesy of Eitan Prouser.

was inspirational to Jews who felt oppressed and a popular Yiddish saying maintained, "If a thousand Breitbarts were to arise among the Jews, the Jewish people would cease being persecuted." In 1925 he returned to Poland to visit his ancestors' graves and promote physical culture in the Jewish community, performing his feats and highlighting his Jewish bona fides. (Meishar, 2018; Portnoy, 135)

Pese and Leah Rosenzweig

In the early 1930s, Pese and Leah Rosenzweig, sisters from Mohilev-Podolsk, were tightrope walkers. They married two other Jewish circus performers: Yamkev Birnboym, a tightrope walker and acrobat, and Itsik Gaylor, a clown. They all continued performing together in the same circuses. During each performance, the women's mother used to sit backstage and recite Psalms while they performed, praying for their safety. They would not go on until they saw her swaying in prayer. (Portnoy, 127)

Zoltan Hirsch

Zoltan Hirsch (1885-1944), whose stage name was Zoli Hirsch, was a Hungarian Jew of short stature who performed as a clown and acrobat in circus and vaudeville shows. He was well known as a clown who performed in a variety of circuses, and in many famous acts. In 1944 he was deported to Auschwitz where he perished. A toy, *Roli Zoli*, was created in the 1970s to memorialize Hirsch in the form of a clown on a red scooter. (Meishar, 2019; Asso)

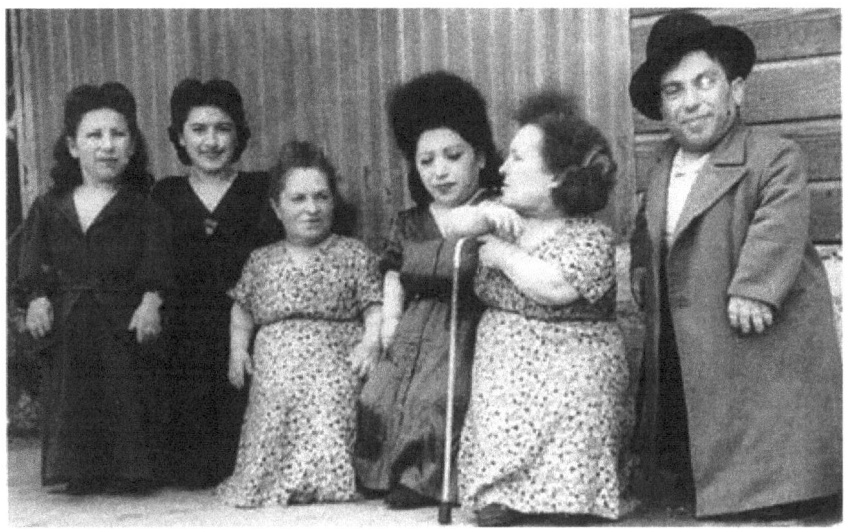

The Ovitz Family.
Courtesy of the Ovitz Family.

Ovitz Family

Many sources claim the Ovitz family to be circus performers.[7] This was absolutely not the case, however, and is simply an assumption based on their short stature. We included them here as a clarification on their behalf. As far as circus goes, in fact, the Ovitz family consciously refused to be a part of it. They were, however, proud musical and theatrical entertainers. Perla Ovitz once said on the matter, "Circus was not for us, as we didn't have the physical strength or inclination. We abhorred the idea of being animals in a human zoo... We never wanted to make a living out of exhibiting our deformity. We always wanted to be taken seriously as professional actors" (Koren and Negev, 31).

Hailing from Transylvania, the Ovitz family was distinguished by being the largest recorded family with dwarfism. This included the father, Rabbi Shimshon Elzik, and seven out of 10 children. Elzik served as the "wandering rabbi of Maramures County." For a week or two at a time he would go to a town to lead prayers and preach (Koren and Negev, 9). When he died young, the family decided to gain financial stability by becoming a traveling music and entertainment group, first going by the name of the Jazz Band of Lilliput, and later The Lilliput Troupe. They sang, played instruments, and put on theater performances.

They managed to travel and perform while hiding their Jewish identity, but in May 1944 they were arrested and sent to Auschwitz. Mengele was, tragically, very intrigued by the Ovitz family and performed horrific experiments on them.

[7] See, e.g. https://www.aish.com/jw/s/Jews-and-the-Circus-7-Fascinating-Facts.html.

After the liberation of the concentration camps, they continued to perform throughout Europe as a singing family ("The Ovitz Family"). In 1949, they moved to Israel, where they continued to perform until they retired in 1955. (Koren and Negev).

Sara Hauptman

Sara Hauptman (1918-2014) was a Belgian who lived in Brussels and joined the resistance during World War II. She helped create false identity papers and delivered messages and packages, saving many people in the process. She worked with Cirque Royal as a cover for her work in the Belgian resistance, first as an usher and later as a lion tamer. As an usher, she felt too

Sara Hauptman.
Courtesy of the Hauptman Family

exposed to the many Nazis who showed interest in her, so she started working as a lion tamer, which felt safer to her. She was eventually outed as a Jew, brought to the Malines transit camp, deported to Auschwitz, and then Dachau. While at Malines, the head of Cirque Royale tried to negotiate her release, telling them that she was the star of the circus and offering to perform for the camp in exchange for her freedom, but he was unsuccessful. Sara survived through liberation and was reunited with her husband and children. Though she was asked to return to the circus as a performer, she ultimately chose not to return to that lifestyle. She later moved to the United States with her family, and lived in El Paso, Texas, and in Colorado Springs, Colorado. (Hauptman and Oliver)

Zirkus Konzentrazani

In concentration camps, the Nazis used music in a variety of ways: as punishment, as a way to make a statement to the outside world, and to entertain themselves. Some camps also had cultural events to entertain the guards. The Börgemoor camp held an event called "Zirkus Konzentrazani," or "Concentration Circus," on August 27, 1933. They set up a type of circus ring and had a number of performances including music, acrobats, wrestling, a parody of boxing, clowning, and a barbershop quartet. Inmate Wolfgang Langhoff,

Wolfgang Langhoff, 1962.

a German actor who was arrested by the Gestapo, accused of being a Communist, was the force behind it. The night before the circus had been particularly brutal at the camp, as SS officers attacked inmates, beating them with wooden boards. The circus was partially intended to lighten the spirits of the inmates.

Eugen Eggerath, who was also at Börgemoor, described the circus as follows:

> On Sunday there was a great circus! Konzentrazani with "oxen", "camels" and other rarities. If it had been the Circus Sarasani, (sic) I would have gladly paid five for it. All joking aside, it was a great show. The director Wolfg. [Wofgang (sic) Langhoff] created a show about three hours long! Nine hundred detainees and 60 members of the SS were in the audience!! Some of the songs had original music and lyrics and were in four-part harmony! A five-person orchestra, direction Dr "Moor Blower", the "Moorsänger" [Moor Singers], "Riesenmoorballett" [The Great Moor Ballet], the "Bergische Nachtigall" [Mountain Nightingale] and others. In short, it was the best day of the last six months! In a very funny announcement, Dr "Moor Blower" said that next Sunday we should bring our wives and children. (Fackler)

The circus was so impactful on the inmates that they took the idea to other camps they were eventually transferred to, and a similar event later took place in Neuengamme. Two former Moor soldiers, Heinrich Pakullis and Ernst Saalwächter, created a circus in Neuengamme saying that there should be "circus in life, circus in dying, and circus in death." (Fackler)

Marcel Marceau

Marcel Marceau (1923-2007) was born as Marcel Mangel in France. During World War II, he and his brother took on the last name of Marceau to avoid being identified as Jews. He joined the French resistance and saved hundreds of Jewish children, helping them escape from France to Switzerland by embarking on treacherous journeys through the Alps. During these journeys he started using mime as a way to entertain and calm the children while also being silent. His first major performance was for the United States Army, entertaining thousands of troops after the libera-

Marcel Marceau as Bip the Clown, 1974.

Ziratron posters.
Courtesy of Hadi Orr, Israel.

tion of France in 1944. He then went on to a brilliant career as an entertainer, becoming one of the most famous mimes of all time.(Goldfarb)

Ziratron

Israel's first permanent circus, Ziratron, opened in 1950 in Tel Aviv. Founded by 36 ex-soldiers as a cooperative enterprise, Ziratron had audience seating for 2,000 and included performances by jugglers, trapeze artists, clowns, acrobats, and other circus acts. Israel in its infancy consisted primarily of immigrants from various countries, and they did not all speak the same language. Ziratron's performances did not rely on language, and thus all could enjoy its entertainment. Many of the performers were circus artists who had significant careers in Europe. Some had survived the horrors of the Holocaust, whether in hiding or in concentration camps, and yet they were still able to perform, even as clowns. (Meishar; JTA)

Frank Avruch: Bozo the Clown

Frank Avruch (1928-2018) was the first Bozo the Clown, whose television program was syndicated across the United States. He was born in Boston to Russian Jewish parents. The character of Bozo was originally created by record producer Alan W. Livingston, who trained many who portrayed Bozo and developed the look of the clown. Avruch, who originally changed his name to Frank Stevens, played Bozo from the 1950s through the 1970s; after his army service he went back to using his family name, Avruch. In addition to his work on TV, he performed around the world as Bozo for UNICEF and received a United Nations award for his work with children. (Bush; *Times of Israel*; *Ha'aretz*)

Big Apple Circus
(Paul Binder and Alan Slifka)

The Big Apple Circus was cofounded by Paul Binder, (b. 1942) a Jewish man from Brooklyn. After a performing career in Europe, he returned to the United States and sought to bring a one-ring circus to the United States. Together with his cofounder,

Frank Avruch as Bozo the Clown. Chicago, 2017.

Michael Christensen, (b. 1947) they created the Big Apple Circus in New York City in 1977. Alongside its performances, the Big Apple Circus at different times had several community service arms, including Beyond the Ring, which brought circus to inner-city youth; Circus of the Senses, which adapted circus for children with sensory issues; and a Clown Care Unit program bringing "clown doctors" to pediatric wards.

Big Apple Circus: "Dream Big," 2022.
Courtesy Ayal Prouser.

The Big Apple Circus was originally the performing arm of the New York School for Circus Arts, a nonprofit institution whose first chairman was Alan B. Slifka, a Jewish philanthropist (1929-2011). Slifka was a great promoter of circus, both in the United States and in Israel. He saw circus as a unifying cultural event. Slifka claimed that "the circus is something you feel with your belly, not with your head. And belly stuff is where humans connect. [At the United Nations Night at the Big Apple Circus] People from completely different backgrounds and cultures sit around the ring and laugh at the same time, worry at the same time, and applaud at the same time. The ambassador of Israel once told me, 'I come to this event every year, and it gives me hope for the world.' It puts us in touch with our shared humanity." (History of the Big Apple Circus)

References

Asso, Annick. "Zoltán Hirsch (1887-1944), a Hungarian Lilliputian Circus Star, murdered in Auschwitz." Diverging Fates, August 9, 2017. http://www.divergingfates.eu/index.php/2017/08/09/zoltan-hirsch-1887-1944-a-hungarian-lilliputian-circus-star-murdered-in-auschwitz/.

Burnam, Kalman A. "The Jewish presence in the London theatre, 1660-1800." *Jewish Historical Studies*, 33 (1992-1994): 65-96. https://www.jstor.org/stable/29779912.

Bush, Lawrence. "Bozo the Clown." *Jewish Currents*, January 2, 2013. https://jewishcurrents.org/january-2-bozo-clown.

CandyGuy. "The Ovitz family - Nazi Experiments." The Human Marvels. 11/12/2008. https://www.thehumanmarvels.com/the-ovitz-family-nazi-experiments/.

DeCastro, J. *The Memoirs Of J. Decastro, Comedian: In The Course Of Them Will Be Given Anecdotes Of Various Eminently Distinguished Characters... Accompanied By An Analysis Of The Life Of The Late Philip Astley*. Palala Press, 2015 (reprint).

Dibdin, Thomas. *The Reminiscences of Thomas Dibdin of the Theatres Royal, Covent-Garden, Drury-lane, Haymarket, Etc*. London: J. Major, 1836.

Fackler, Guido. "Music and the Holocaust: Circus Shows at Borgermoor." https://holocaustmusic.ort.org/places/camps/music-early-camps/borgemoor/zirkus-konzentrazani/.

"First Permanent Circus Organized in Israel; Will Open in Ramat Gan Tonight." *Jewish Telegraphic Agency* 5/16/1950.

Goldfarb, Phil. "Marcel Marceau: The Legendary Mime Who Saved Jewish Children and Fought Nazis." 6/23/2020. https://blog.nli.org.il/en/lbh_marceau/.

Hauptman, Sara, as told to Sue A. Oliver. *The Lioness of Judah: A Jewish Lion Tamer's Memoir of Resistance and Survival*. Colorado: Dancing Queens Press, 2006.

History of the Big Apple Circus. https://web.archive.org/web/20101225044154/http://bac.binary-design.com/About/StudyGuide/pdf/BAC_StudyGuide_Ch4.pdf.

Jando, Dominique. "The Circus on Tsvetnoy Boulevard." *Circopedia*. http://www.circopedia.org/Circus_Nikulin.

"Jewish Performer Who Played Bozo the Clown Dies at 89." *Times of Israel*, March 23, 2018. https://www.timesofisrael.com/jewish-performer-who-played-bozo-the-clown-dies-at-89/.

Koren, Yehuda, and Negev, Eilat *In Our Hearts We Were Giants: The Remarkable Story of the Lilliput Troupe: A Dwarf Family's Survival of the Holocaust*. Da Capo Press, 2005.

"The Little-Known Jewish History of the Late 'Bozo the Clown.'" *Ha'aretz*, 3/22/2018.

Meishar, Stav. "Past: Zishe Breitbart." The Escape Act's Blog: Circus Jews. 9/6/2018. http://www.theescapeactshow.com/blog/past-zishe-breitbart.

———. "Past: Zoltan Hirsch." The Escape Act's Blog: Circus Jews, 9/18/2019. http://www.theescapeactshow.com/blog/past-zoltan-hirsch.

———. "Extra: Israel's First Circus." The Escape Act's Blog: Circus Jews. 4/17/2020. http://www.theescapeactshow.com/blog/extra-israels-first-circus.

Portnoy, Edward. "Freaks, Geeks, and Strongmen: Warsaw Jews and Popular Performance 1912-1930." *The Drama Review* 50 (2006): 117-135.

Rubens, Alfred. "Jews and the English Stage, 1667-1850." *Transactions & Miscellanies.* Jewish Historical Society of England, 24 (1970-1973): 151-170.

Wittman, Matthew. "The Transnational History of the Early American Circus." Bard Graduate Research Forum. https://www.bgc.bard.edu/research-forum/articles/289/the-transnational-history-of-the. Originally published in Weber, Susan, et al. *The American Circus.* New York, New Haven, London: Yale University Press, 2012.

Wolf, Lucien. "Astley's Jews." *Jewish Chronicle,* May 26, 1893.

Young, Susan. "Making a World of Difference: Alan Slifka's Venture Philanthropy." *Harvard Business School Alumni Bulletin.* October 1, 2001. https://www.alumni.hbs.edu/stories/Pages/story-bulletin.aspx?num=2943.

The Circus Performance. Irene Aronson. Lithograph, 1958.
Image: Art Resource, NY © The Metropolitan Museum of Art.

An Embodied Epistemology

Lori Wynters

We all have bodies; thus all knowing is embodied and felt...unless we have been taught differently. In *Poetry is Not a Luxury*, Audre Lorde writes, "The white fathers have told us I think therefore I am, but the Black mother in each of us whispers, I feel therefore, I can be free."[1] When I read this essay over 25 years ago, I remember being curious about transgressing the boundaries we have been given on what thinking, feeling, sensing, knowing, being, and doing are. It occurred to me then, that meaning making and constructing knowing was all of these, in fluid movement, never static and always in a process of unfolding and becoming "*eheyeh asher eheyeh*,"[2] with aliveness to the present moment and our relationship to our social, cultural, historical, political, religious, and ecological context of our day-to-day living. This is how my body/mind/spirit arrives at an understanding and practice of an "embodied epistemology." When I began teaching at Goddard College in 2004, my dear colleague and friend S.B. Sowbel called me a "body scholar." I think we are all body scholars. We either just forgot, or were educated out of that knowing.

When I first read Lorde's writing, I remember my breath and belly softening, my jaw falling open a bit more and my body dropping more deeply into an ease that affirmed my lived experience that was not centered in most of my education as valuable knowledge. In the 1960s, something called "affective education" emerged from humanistic psychology. In affective education, educators tend to the sensory and emotional experience, valuing the beliefs, feelings, personal education, and attitudes of students, honoring all that as part of thinking and meaning making. Plato also spoke to a holistic curriculum about the balance in learning the arts, math, science, character, moral judgment, and physical education, in *The Republic*. The term "social-emotional learning" was coined at Yale in the 1960s by James Comey. Daniel Goleman's book *Emotional Intelligence: Why It Can Matter More than IQ* also speaks to this.

The language of embodiment theory in academia has a short history with (white Christian hetero-patriarchal intellectual) roots dating back to the early 20th century philosophers which include, but are not limited to, Merleau-Ponty,[3] Martin Heidegger, Emanuel Kant, Simone de Beauvoir, and John

---

[1] Audre Lorde. *Sister Outsider: Essays and Speeches*, Berkeley: Crossing Press, 2007.

[2] This is the divine name God shares with Moses at the scene of the burning bush (Exodus 3:14). It is translated by Robert Alter as "I will be who I will be." Robert Alter, *The Hebrew Bible: A Translation with Commentary*, New York: W. W. Norton and Company, 2019.

[3] I had the privilege of studying Merleau-Ponty's work extensively as an undergraduate earning a BA in Existentialism and Phenomenology, longing to learn about our lived experiences as knowledge.

Dewey whose treatise *Experience and Education* informed the roots of "progressive education" in the United States. When we study Torah, we investigate, get curious and inquire to see what we can learn from the texts. Simultaneously, we also ask what voices are absent from this conversation...and in particular, whose body or bodies have not been included.

I refer to scholar Audre Lorde's quote about Descartes because it is the Cartesian motif, "I think therefore I am," that has contributed to the mind-body split in dominant academic culture. In my experience as a philosophy undergraduate in the late 1980s, it is still a place that currently needs investigation, repairing the rupture that has been imposed on our thinking, on our bodies. We know this concept when we are young, but it seems that in dominant K-12 United States education systems, there is a shift from holistic learning and teaching to valuing our thinking over other ways of knowing, our affect and sensing selves. David Abrams notes, "I believe it is possible to experience Merleau-Ponty's radical undoing of the traditional mind-body problem by dropping the conviction that one's mind is anything other than the body itself."[4] It may be useful to ask why we have been taught that there is a "mind-body" problem at all.

In my work as an educator, psychologist, Jewish college chaplain, dancer, and musician, I have repeatedly asked this question: What if our mind/body/spirit is one being and what if we could practice allowing ourselves to live in and inhabit that complexity with each other, honoring our lived experience, our felt experience, as knowing, as epistemology?

A brief overview of embodiment theory & studies

One basic definition of embodiment theory/studies is that we use our bodily experience and processes to construct knowledge and make meaning of our lived and felt experiences. I suggest that this concept can be found in all cultures. The thinking that has informed contemporary language of embodiment theory/studies has been primarily Western white Christian hetero-patriarchal European phenomenology, Buddhist thought, Yogic philosophy and practice, and models of dominant western neuroscience. More recent perspectives include intersectional feminist approaches to race, class and gender, Black feminist thinkers and Indigenous knowledges. The list is vast and some of them may have places of overlap or intersection which is why it is difficult to name a specific definition of "embodiment theory." It depends whose body, stories and lived experiences are being valued, seen, centered and matter. Having our lived experiences, our stories, validated, witnessed, recognized, and honored from our particular

---

[4] David Abram. *The Spell of the Sensuous: Perception and Language in a More Than Human World.* New York: Random House, 1997.

bodies informs our epistemologies. When our lived experiences are not seen or valued, dismissed or centered, we learn to dismiss, devalue, and decenter our own knowing. For those of us who have had this experience, we need to reclaim and learn to listen to and trust our bodies' knowing. This is how I have come to explore embodied epistemology.

An embodied epistemology: It's in our theology
To start, we must understand that learning and creating meaning is a sensory and intellectual experience; these ways of knowing inform our lived experiences, which inform the way we construct knowledge. As an intersectional feminist theologian, I, along with many of us, have had to unlearn and let go of the dominant paradigm, decolonize the rigid definitions and theoretical axioms about what I learned about how we come to know what we know, our bodies' felt sense, and the discourses we use to share our knowledge, understandings, and questions. In community with other educators and the mothers in our homeschooling and public education community, I have had to remind myself that in most K-12 education classrooms in the United States we start out including the body, our senses and emotions, in our meaning making and epistemologies. However, as we move up in grades from kindergarten, we begin to slowly educate and be educated from the neck up...and slightly to one side, without addressing relations of power that have shaped our discourse and our bodies' knowing, especially when we are discussing what is considered "academic." Distinct from Descartes, "I think therefore I am," Audre Lorde reminds us, "I feel therefore I can be free," and that "...freedom is a possibility that is not just mentally generated: it is particular and felt."[5] It is particular to each of our lived experiences and the social/political/cultural/historical context within which we live.

Embodied learning includes our sensations, emotional and cognitive agencies, and intellectual capacities. It also includes our relationship to the sacred. If our bodies are the location of our knowing, then we cannot *not* investigate and explore the social/political/cultural/racial/religious relations of power if we are to center our lived experiences as knowing. If we ignore our bodies' experiences, we will not bring our whole selves to our lives and the ways we construct knowledge and create meaning. As Jews, we know this practice. We live the questions. Body and movement are built into our epistemology, into our liturgy and our theology. Whose bodies have been privileged is a question. The choreography of our liturgy is deeply embodied. We sway when we *daven* (pray, in Yiddish). We take three steps back, bend over, which brings our head below

---

[5] Lorde, 2007.

our heart, valuing the heart's knowing.⁶ We bow in two directions, stand up and take three steps forward in the *Amidah, Ha T'filah*.⁷ In *Tahanun*,⁸ we lay our head on our left arm, at times weeping and talking to God. We sing, praise and wail from our *kishkes*. *Kishke* comes from the Yiddish word for intestine. And *kishke* has entered mainstream culture in the US as another word for guts. You may hear people say, "I had a feeling in my *kishkes*," meaning I have a perhaps irrational or unexplainable knowing, that is still a reliable felt sense knowing. The raft of research on the "enteric brain" speaks to the neuroscience behind this knowing, so perhaps the wisdom of our ancestors who honored our knowing from our *kishkes* has some insight for us in this time now.

It is through our bodies and heartfelt knowing, which is part of our thinking, that we engage with our unique relationship with *Shekhinah, Ruaḥ HaKodesh, Raḥamim, HaShem*⁹ and the many other names for the Divine, and with what is generative and life-giving for us in each moment. On Sukkot, we shake the lulav in six directions, aware of our body and our relationship to the spaces, the four worlds of *asiyah* (action), *yetzirah* (formation), *briyah* (creation), and *atzilut* (emanation) and the four souls of *nefesh*—our bodies, *ruaḥ*—affect, *neshamah*—thinking, and *ḥayah*—spirit. These can be mapped onto the more known web of body, heart, mind, and spirit.¹⁰ We continue to shake the lulav toward the earth/*adamah* and toward the sky/*hashamayim*, the earth and heaven that surround us. On *Kabbalat Shabbat*,¹¹ we open the door during *Lekha dodi*,¹² rise to standing and walk towards the door, or even outside, to greet the *Shabbat haMalkah*,¹³ with our bodies.

Embodiment, connection, and relationality are in our epistemology. On Yom Kippur, some of us fully prostrate on the earth, feel the heartbeat of the land on our heart and again, bring our head below our heart, so that our intellect can sink into our hearts and bellies. In this gesture, our bodies can become the compass for what is generative, what is life-giving, what we know. What if we embrace this pedagogy in our scholarship?

I began learning the *Ma Nishtanah*¹⁴ at the age of three or four. It was an

---

⁶ This understanding of bowing follows understandings in many yogic practices and in Tibetan Buddhism.
⁷ The central prayer, often considered the core, of every Jewish prayer service.
⁸ A prayer of supplication recited in traditional morning and afternoon weekday prayer services.
⁹ Various names for God, used in different contexts and with different connotations.
¹⁰ Zalman Schachter-Shalomi. *Gate to the Heart: A Manual of Contemplative Jewish Practice*. Netaniel Miles-Yepez and Robert Micha'el Esformes, eds. Boulder: Albion-Andalus, 2013.
¹¹ The Friday evening service welcoming the Sabbath.
¹² A liturgical poem recited at the Friday evening service.
¹³ The Sabbath Queen, the traditional metaphor used for the Sabbath.
¹⁴ The Four Questions recited at the Passover ritual called a *"seder."*

early introduction, learning to value and uplift the practice of a critical agency, to privilege questions over answers and to deepen into them. How many of us have sung those questions over and over again? The waves of sound impact the neural pathways in our bodies and call forth ancestral memory, ancestral bodies, stories and knowledge.[15] Singing, chanting... more embodied practices inherent in Jewish wisdom tradition. Being in song is being in the body.

"...the opposite of faith isn't doubt, it's certainty," says beloved teacher, Bobbie Breitman, MSW.[16]

What if we value critical and analytical inquiry as a felt process? This is an embodied epistemology. Why? Because you must find your questions from your lived experience. You must feel them, listen to them, and trust your experience of your experience. If you are marginalized in multiple ways in your identities, and have a steady diet of not being seen, heard, or valued, the dominant culture often tries to tell you what you are feeling, what you know and don't know. One remedy is daily rigor in tending to one's own lived experiences and seeking out places and people who validate, see, witness, hear, and affirm one's knowing... and being in community. In community, we each need to tend to our reflection and story of our experience, and have that reflected back, rather than the narratives that are often imposed on us about our experiences from the dominant culture. The late Chief Rabbi Jonathan Sacks (*z"l*, may his memory be for a blessing and revolution) teaches that we are a people who hear and listen, differentiated from the ancient Greeks, who were primarily visually oriented.[17] Listening is a deeply sensory experience, from our central prayer, the *Shema*, to *niggunim* when we *daven*, to crying out to God in *Taḥanun,* or when chanting *Avinu Malkeinu*.[18] Hannah cries out to God to be heard (1 Samuel 1). At first the priest, Eli, thinks she is inebriated, and she is not heard. This is a familiar story. But God does hear her. Can we hear each other's prayers? The past has taught us if we don't hear each other's prayers, we will eventually hear each other's war cries. We are asked on Shavuot to listen to the unique call intended for each of us from *Har Sinai* (Mount Sinai). Talmud teaches that each blade of grass has an angel over it chanting, "grow, grow, grow." More embodied epistemology. But to hear what is being asked of us, we need to learn to cultivate listening. And we

---

[15] S. Budisavljevic et al. "Heritability of the limbic networks." *Social Cognitive and Affective Neuroscience*, 11 (5) (2016): 746–757. https://doi.org/10.1093/scan/nsv156.

[16] While this quote is generally attributed to Anne Lamott in her book *Plan B: Further Thoughts on Faith*, 2006, here I attribute it to my teacher Bobbie Breitman, an intersectional Jewish scholar, therapist, and a colleague of mine. She shared this insight with me in 1999.

[17] Rabbi Lord Jonathan Sacks. *The Spirituality of Listening*. The Rabbi Sacks Legacy, n.d. https://www.rabbisacks.org/covenant-conversation/eikev/the-spirituality-of-listening/.

[18] Literally, "Our Father, Our King," a prayer recited during the High Holy Day season.

listen with not just our ears. We listen with our bodies, hearts, our bellies, our deep *kishka* knowing. Chinese tradition teaches of the "dantian" from the 3rd century CE as the elixir of life's energetic field where our essential being lives.

The body and mind are not separate ways of meaning making. To think with our whole being is to include our affective knowing, our physical, sensory, and emotional knowing. And to feel includes our critical agency. We can let go of the Cartesian mind-body split as a common reference point.

There has been extensive research on the enteric brain, also known as the belly brain, located in the gut.[19] It is the place where we feel "butterflies" when we feel seen, valued, and loved. It is where we feel nervous when sensing something is not congruent with our safety. In dominant Western educational culture, we have been trained and practiced at privileging and valuing primarily our cognitive capacities, giving lower status to our "affect," our gut feelings, our embodied and our ancestral knowing. This kind of knowing lives in our cells, in our body's individual and collective history and memory.

Our limbs, ligaments and bones guide us in how we navigate the world, which impacts how we think. The world literally shapes our bodies, our epistemologies, how we come to know what we know, and the discourses we choose to engage with each other about what we know… or what we think we know. Humans not only have always moved, danced, and engaged their bodies as a way of connecting to the Divine, but also as a way of making meaning in their worlds and in connection with one another, which in turn invites a reflective capacity to know and understand the self more deeply, learning to know and understand our internal landscapes that impact our critical agencies. One could reflect that this is deeply absent in many of our educational models. And when our internal landscape emerges with strong feelings, some educators feel that is the place for a therapist or counselor. What if understanding our affect and sensations could be part of intellectual discourse? This is a form of embodiment in education.

We are an integrated whole, and an embodied epistemology integrates these places of knowing, thinking, feeling and being. It means that we must listen to, honor and come to know, feel and trust our own experiences and stories, and then to listen to each other's stories. It means that we must pause, and perhaps sit in the discomfort of not knowing, of recognizing the complexity of our multiple identities, of tending to the places where we hold status and the places where we have been marginalized or silenced. All this lives in our BODIES.

---

[19] *The Brain-Gut Connection*. John Hopkins Medicine, n.d. https://www.hopkinsmedicine.org/health/wellness-and-prevention/the-brain-gut-connection.

When we tend to our bodies' knowing and lived experiences, we can more fully know ourselves and each other, nurture the compassion it takes to know, listen, and trust ourselves to work together in solidarity to dismantle systemic oppressions and for collective liberation.

We have this in our pedagogy too. We listen and understand with our bodies. As Jews, we are often referred to as the People of the Book. And what if we add, we are a people of the body? What if, in addition or instead of "we are in service" to God, "we embody" God?

Questions (to use with your classes)
Let's begin with these questions as a way to tend to the larger social, ecological, cultural, historical, racialized, psycho-spiritual and political context of our lived experience.

1. What are the bodies that we each inhabit or that inhabit each of us? And how does this inform what we know?

2. Who am I and how do I experience myself, my body and how/what I know? Who do other people think I am and how might they experience me, my body and how/what I know?

3. What do I understand, experience or know about my geographical, gender, class, ethnic, racial, religious, able-bodied, neuro-divergent and other identities and how this informs my epistemologies?

I am a woman. I am cis and queer. I am part of a tribe of single mothers and aunties and grandmothers. I have white-skin privilege. I have working class income and I have class access with multiple degrees. I am Moroccan and Hungarian, Russian and Romani. I am Jewish. I am over 50. I am a teacher and a student. I am a Jewish Chaplain. I am a social/clinical psychologist and a theologian. I am a dancer and a musician. I am a student/teacher of Feldenkrais and Somatics. I am a North American. I regularly reflect on the being I am, what/who I resonate and identify with, and how that informs my being in the world. Like God's response to Moshe at the burning bush, *Eheyeh asher Eheyeh*, I am becoming that I am becoming. And if we indeed are *b'tzelem Elohim*, made in the image of them/God, we too are always in the process of becoming.

Our bodies as centers of knowing

What does scholarship and discourse look, sound, and feel like when we value our bodies as centers of knowing, as places of meaning making, as locations of constructing knowledge? We need to move and feel to think... and we express our inquiry, investigation, analysis, our documentation of new learning and understanding in many ways. Some of us think in images, some in movement, some in sound, some through relational connection, some through introspective awareness, some of us through relationship to the elements of the natural world, and some through poetics. For some of us, it is an amalgam of all of these in a dynamic and synergistic combination of each of these ways for creating meaning and constructing knowledge.

I am not the first to ask this question, nor will I be the last. "*Lo alekha hamlakha ligmor V'lo ata ben ḥorin l'hibatel mimena.*"[20] And yet we still need to ask it, until our individual asking and our collective discourse and conversation emerge from our embodied knowing. We keep asking it until the epistemologies, knowledges, stories and memories that we have privileged make room and space for the embodied knowing of those of us whose stories and bodies have been marginalized, objectified, assimilated, changed, violated, whitewashed, dismissed, confused, gaslighted, or completely erased.

This writing engages this conversation. I write and speak from my experience, scholarship, reflection, and practice which is located in my body as an Ashkenazi/Sephardi Jewish cis woman, single mama, first generation college educated, second generation American, liberatory theatre practitioner, dancer and musician, dedicated to valuing our individual journey and stories and our collective liberation.

An embodied epistemology

For those of us who have taught and/or learned in a broad range of educational environments from K-12, to community college, undergraduate and graduate programs in the United States, the dominant and/or conventional pedagogical paradigm of schooling and education often begins by teaching the whole child in kindergarten and early elementary school as an embodied learner, naming and valuing their sensory and emotional agencies with their social and intellectual capacities. Then something HAPPENS. We slowly shift from large circles of learning, connection, relatedness and engaged embodied

---

[20] "You are not obliged to finish the task, neither are you free to neglect it," a Rabbinic saying found in Pirkei Avot/Ethics of the Fathers. Translation from Reuven Hammer, *Or Hadash: A Commentary on Siddur Sim Shalem*. NY: The Rabbinical Assembly, 2003.

activities. We often begin close to the floor, using and valuing our entire bodies for learning, meaning making and constructing knowledge. And then in fourth or fifth grade, or sometimes earlier, we shift to placing more value on sequential, organized, and cerebral learning, but less on critical agency. We start to privilege math, science and reading comprehension, with the arts, hands-on learning, and relational skills as secondary (with the exception of sports, which is an entirely other issue). We implement and seem to value more control and order, or what we call organization. We integrate more regimented rows and methods, guided conversations, written exams and tests, valuing the product over the process. We lift up linear and qualitative analysis over the messiness and, at times, discomfort of the complexity of our stories, identities and bodies, places of intersection and power, transgressing and integrating intellect, emotion, relational connection and the sacred. This is a much messier place to be. This way of being invites uncertainty and a state of "not knowing." But it also invites inquiry, exploration, questions, and reflective agency. It invites an attunement to what we know with our bodies, and the possibility of connection with the mystery and the sacred. And if we can be held or hold our students in this place of inquiry and investigation, we can open the possibility of ways of being where we inhabit more of who we each are and who we are meant to be, potentially bringing us all greater generativity in our lives in the movement for collective liberation.

Many of us have learned to cut off important parts of ourselves and our more organic meaning making process to fit into the dominant paradigm and what I call the "commodity culture and time model of learning," overriding and dismissing rather than honoring our lived experiences. How does one listen to their lived experience and embodied knowing if it is not safe to act upon it, whether it is physically unsafe or shame-based, which was part of the origins of schooling in the United States. Paulo Friere called it "banking education." He wrote in *Pedagogy of Indignation*[21] "...how urgent it is that we fight for more fundamental ethical principles such as respect of the life of human beings, the life of other animals, of birds, and for the life of rivers and forests. I do not believe in loving among women and men, among human beings, if we do not become capable of loving the world this must be present in any educational practice of a radical, critical, and liberating nature."[22] Nancy Tarule and Jill Goldberger in *Women's Ways of Knowing* remind us that "constructivist knowing" is knowledge that draws from claiming our lived experiences.[23] V (formerly Eve Ensler) wrote

---

[21] This text was published posthumously, and edited by his wife, Ana Maria Arajo Friere from his unpublished notes.
[22] Paulo Friere. *Pedagogy of Indignation*. New York: Routledge Press, 2004.
[23] Mary Field Bêlenky, Blythe McVicker Clinchy, Nancy Rule Goldberger, Jill Mattuck Tarule.

the *Vagina Monologues* because it was a way she could make it safe for women to name and claim their bodies in a dominant culture that wanted to extract, use or completely make invisible women's bodies and the deep knowing that comes from all of our sensuality. One of my mentors, Elizabeth Minnich, who wrote "Transforming the Academy," invited me in graduate school to consider thinking as a kinesthetic experience that comes from our felt/intellectual knowing, an integrated body/mind. She speaks of thinking as an art by breaking off from the typical ways of thought and maintaining joy in stimulating our minds. Dr. Minnich noted that as we engage in the exploration of thought work, we might wonder if the ways that we embody thinking and emotion are not already interrelating, mutually informing conjoined twins, so connected that if one is harmed, lessened, so is the other.[24] What if thinking and feeling inform each other and we are curious about dissolving or transgressing that binary?

While quantitative practice has value, I am suggesting that our integrated body/mind/spirits have always been our way of knowing and that we must reclaim this. We are trained in valuing an "objective" lens. We ask that our students let go of the "I" in their scholarship. We are suspicious of "opinion" without considering that literature, scientific and psychological theories, theologies (and more) are composed by real people who are informed by their personal, political, cultural, religious, gendered, historical and embodied (or disembodied) experiences. We forget that each of these theorists, thinkers, artists, cultural critics, or theologians has a particular relationship to power, their bodies and an awareness (or lack thereof) of body, power and status. What if our lived experiences, our stories that come from our body's knowing, inform our scholarship? What if our bodies are also the "text" that we are reading, while we simultaneously read text through our body's knowing? What if we begin to discern what has been imposed on us and start to cultivate our felt sense and trust our lived experiences as ways of knowing?

Exercises/Practice

1. Read a piece of text out loud. First read through it seated. Notice how the words feel and land in your body. Notice the sounds of the words in your mouth. Notice what word or phrase holds vitality for you.

Women's Ways of Knowing: The Development of Self, Voice, and Mind, 10th edition. New York: Basic Books, 1997.
[24] Elizabeth Minnich. *Transforming Knowledge (Second Edition)*. Philadelphia: Temple University Press, 2004.

2. What happens if you read this same text walking around the space you are in? What about reading the text while lying on your back? What happens when you do this lying on your belly? How does it feel to read it aloud sitting back-to-back with a partner/ḥevruta?

3. What would it feel like to chant the written text, in English, Hebrew or other languages? What happens when you chant the text in the *Haftorah* trope of your *b'nai mitzvah*? What is it like to chant it to a contemporary melody or a lullaby or another melody that inspires you?

4. What is it like to read the text while in a balance posture of some kind? How is being balanced on the right leg different from the left leg? What is it like to read it in some kind of inversion or upside down? What do you notice about how you relate to the text that might feel different from other ways of being?

5. What is it like to reflect on reading and thinking in this way, with this intention of attuning to our bodies response and knowing?

Identity Questions

- What kind of body is each of us in?
- What are the many layers of body that we inhabit, or that inhabit us?
- Are we in young or old bodies?
- Are we in bodies that have access to resources, to money, to a comfortable home, to education?
- Are we in a body that receives healthy touch?
- Are we in a Christian body? Or a Muslim body? Are we in a Jewish body?
- A female body? A male body?
- A queer body? A cis body? A trans body? A non-binary body?
- A Black and Brown body? A white body?

- An (dis)able body? A small or large body?
- What bodies are valued?
- What are the stories from these locations?
- Are your stories told?
- What are the memories?
- Whose histories and memories are told from these bodies?
- What bodies get to tell the narratives?
- Whose bodies are centered?

Taking it to our teaching: Reflective practice and scholarship
In the spirit of questions as an embodied way of knowing, perhaps I might offer these questions to continue our discourse and dance with one another.

- How does this inform the ways we as learners and teachers make meaning and construct knowledge from our lived experience?
- How do we invite this and honor this as a location of knowing in our learning environments, in our classrooms, in our own and our students' writing, speaking, discourse, reflective practice and scholarship with each other?

References

Abram, David. *The Spell of the Sensuous: Perception and Language in a More Than Human World.* New York: Random House, 1997.

Alter, Robert. *The Hebrew Bible: A Translation with Commentary.* New York: W. W. Norton and Company, 2019.

Bêlenky, Mary Field, Blythe McVicker Clinchy, Nancy Rule Goldberger, Jill Mattuck Tarule. *Women's Ways of Knowing: The Development of Self, Voice, and Mind.* 10th edition. New York: Basic Books, 1997.

The Brain-Gut Connection. John Hopkins Medicine, n.d. https://www.hopkinsmedicine.org/health/wellness-and-prevention/the-brain-gut-connecti on Budisavljevic, S., Kawadler, J. M., Dell'Acqua, F., Rijsdijk, F. V., Kane, F., Picchioni, M., McGuire, P., Toulopoulou, T., Georgiades, A., Kalidindi, S., Kravariti, E., Murray, R. M., Murphy, D. G., Craig, M. C., & Catani, M. (2016), "Heritability of the limbic networks." *Social Cognitive and Affective Neuroscience, 11*(5), 746–757. https://doi.org/10.1093/scan/nsv156.

Friere, Paulo. *Pedagogy of Indignation.* New York: Routledge Press, 2004.

Goleman, Daniel. *Emotional Intelligence: Why It Can Matter More Than IQ.* New York: Bantam Books, 2005.

Hammer, Reuven. *Or Hadash: A Commentary on Siddur Sim Shalom for Shabbat and Festivals.* New York: The Rabbinical Assembly, 2003.

Lorde, Audre. *Sister Outsider: Essays and Speeches.* Berkeley: Crossing Press, 2007.

Minnich, Elizabeth. *Transforming Knowledge (Second Edition).* Philadelphia: Temple University Press, 2004.

Sacks, Rabbi Lord Jonathan. *The Spirituality of Listening.* The Rabbi Sacks Legacy, n.d. https://www.rabbisacks.org/covenant-conversation/eikev/the-spirituality-of-listening/.

Schachter-Shalomi, Zalman. *Gate to the Heart: A Manual of Contemplative Jewish Practice.* Netaniel Miles-Yepez and Robert Micha'el Esformes, eds. Boulder: Albion-Andalus, 2013.

Wynters, Lori. *In Relational Culture at the Goddard Residency in Teaching Transformation: Progressive Education in Action.* Caryn Miriam Goldberg, ed. Plainfield, Vermont: Goddard Graduate Institute, 2017.

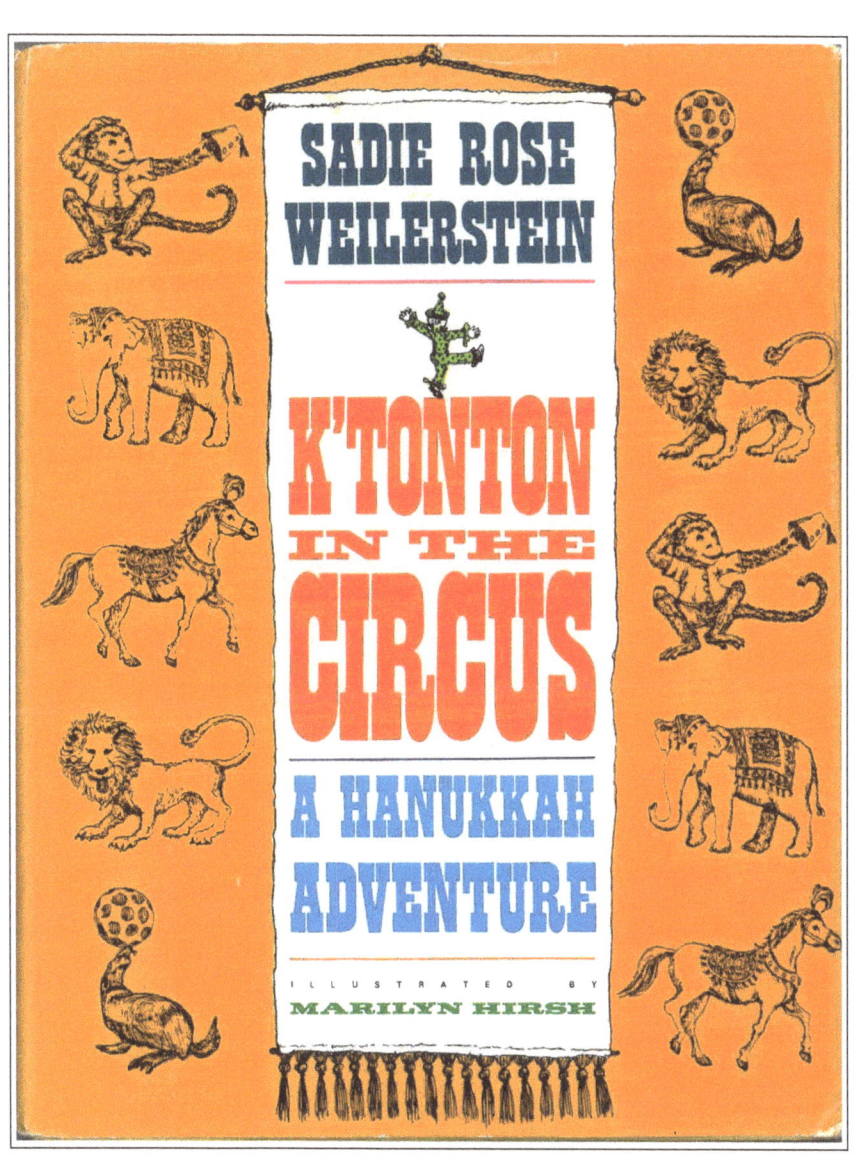

Courtesy University of Nebraska Press.

Early Childhood Hebrew Learning Incorporating Total Physical Response

Shirah Rubin

Juggling. Juggling is not just a simple, fun activity. It is a metaphor for the process of how learning a second language develops. Dr. Patricia Kuhl, internationally recognized expert in early language learning and neuroscience, describes that babies have a critical period for sound development from 0-6 months when the ability to learn more than one language is heightened. Between 6 months and 7 years is a sensitive period in which the brain's development is most flexible for second language learning.[1] Kuhl has been an advocate for second language learning at a young age as a result of her neuroscience research.[2] Jewish preschools should follow this direction.

Dr. Marley Jarvis, Outreach and Education Specialist at the University of Washington's Institute for Learning and Brain Science (I-LABS) and a colleague of Kuhl, describes that young children have the ability to juggle language. These findings demonstrate that introducing a second language to infants, toddlers, or preschoolers will not cause confusion if there's consistency and social interaction with the language. Their research supports early language learning.[3] Studies have shown that social interaction is essential for early language development and that videos and films do not fill the role of human interaction.[4] The field of usage-based approach to second language learning integrates elements of different fields and is based on the assumptions that linguistic inputs are the primary source of second language learning and that learning of any kind contributes to the cognitive mechanisms of second language learning.[5] Social interaction requires a cooperative exchange.[6] Psycholinguist Nick Ellis elaborates that "... the

---

[1] Patricia Kuhl. "Babies' Language Skills," Talk given at *Mind, Brain, and Behavior Annual Distinguished Lecture Series*, Harvard University, April 3, 2012.
[2] Sarah Roehrich. "Kuhl Constructs: How Babies Form Foundations for Language," *E/I Balance* (blog). Cambridge, MA: Conte Center at Harvard University, May 3, 2013. https://eibalance.com/2013/05/03/kuhl-constructs-how-babies-form-foundations-for-language/.
[3] Marley Jarvis as quoted in K.C. Compton.
[4] Patricia Kuhl, F. M. Tsao, and H. M. Liu. "Foreign-language Experience in Infancy: Effects of Short-term Exposure and Social Interaction on Phonetic Learning," *PNAS*, vol. 100, no. 15 (2003): 9096-9101. https://www.pnas.org/doi/10.1073/pnas.1532872100.
[5] M. Bratman (1992) and H. Clark (1996) as cited in Wulff and Ellis.
[6] Stefanie Wulff, & Nick Ellis. "Usage-based Approaches to Second Language Acquisition," In David Miller, et. al. eds. *Bilingual Cognition and Language*. John Benjamins e-Platform, 2018, 37. https://www.researchgate.net/publication/341085352_Usage-based_Approaches_to_Second_Language_Acquisition_Cognitive_and_Social_Aspects.

usage based approach and second language acquisition research emphasize how language is learned from the participatory experience of processing language during embodied interaction in social and cultural contexts where individually desired outcomes are goals to be achieved by communicating intentions, concepts, and meaning with others."[7] "Embodied" is referring to embodied cognition, which is a neuroscientific perspective relating to the mind and body being complex and unified entities that integrate sensorimotor experiences.[8]

Since early childhood education is centered on play, opportunities for early learners to play in a second language can be an invitation for second language development. Play happens through movement, song, and dramatic play.[9]

Studies of individuals learning to juggle show that practicing 30 minutes a day for six weeks resulted in a change in neural development. This was independent of the jugglers' level of competence. The main takeaway from this research is that learning a new skill results in unique brain development.[10]

Dr. Kuhl similarly found that introducing young children to second language learning early enough resulted in cognitive flexibility. Her brain research studies of babies provides us with knowledge about why babies learn language from humans and not screens.[11] This chapter delves into the benefits of using movement and culturally authentic music in teaching Hebrew as a second language, learning through immersion in preschool settings. Movement and music are used together as strategies to advance cognitive development in early childhood teaching with benefits in the areas of second language acquisition, memory retrieval, and listening skills.

Benefits of Hebrew immersion learning

Toddlers in preschool can barely speak English, so why should preschools teach Hebrew to these young children? Hebrew is important to Jewish early childhood learning because it is one of the foundational elements for young children to connect with Judaism and Israel. Judaism is a text-based religion, and the ability to read those texts is a central point of connection. Including Hebrew language in preschools is particularly desirable as it is one way that children may connect

---

[7] Nick Ellis. "Essentials of a Theory of Language Cognition," *The Modern Language Journal*. Vol. 103 No. 1. (2019): 45.
[8] Manuela Macedonia. "Embodied Learning: Why at School the Mind Needs the Body," *Frontiers in Psychology*, (October 2019): 1-4. https://www.ncbi.nlm.nih.gov/pmc/articles/PMC6779792/.
[9] Patrice Baldwin. *With Drama in Mind: Real Learning in Imagined Worlds.* London: Continuum International Publishing Group, 2004. This book provides a detailed discussion on language development through drama.
[10] Ibid.
[11] Peri Klass. "Hearing Bilingual: How Babies Sort Out Language," *The New York Times*, October 10, 2011. https://www.nytimes.com/2011/10/11/health/views/11klass.html.

to Jewish culture and community, both in the diaspora and in Israel.

Jewish educators have developed experiential ways to use movement, music, and play to make Hebrew learning come to life. When, as educators, we plant early seeds of connections to Hebrew, we are setting the stage for future positive Hebrew learning experiences. The preschool becomes the launchpad for lifelong Hebrew learning by young Jewish families just as they are in the midst of forming a Jewish family identity. Hebrew learning initiated early has the potential to launch families down a Jewish learning path that may include the exploration of subsequent Jewish Day School or supplementary school options.

Looking at larger trends in second language learning, studies have demonstrated the beneficial impacts of early second language learning. For example, research has demonstrated that early exposure to a second language supports brain development and increased academic achievement. Second language learning benefits a variety of skill development including higher order and abstract thinking; enriches cognitive development; promotes success in standardized tests; and narrows the achievement gap of students from different socio-economic backgrounds. Early second language learning shapes the architecture of the brain and promotes valuable attitudes regarding achievement.[12]

Language development
Toddlers 18-36 months old begin vocal development including naming people, objects, feelings and actions. Language skills for children between the ages of three to five years become more complex.[13] Linguist Stephen Krashen developed a number of language development theories. His Acquisition-Learning theory distinguishes between first language learning (innate language development informed by the surrounding environment) and second language learning (in which an additional language is learned as the product of formal instruction). Second language learning requires the conscious teaching and acquisition of rules and grammar. He is a proponent of second language acquisition in a fashion modeled by first language learning. As the natural progression of first language learning is speaking before reading, and reading before writing, Krashen believes that children should learn the second language in the same progression, which will make learners less self-conscious.

---

[12] U.S. Department of State: National Security Language Initiative, "The Benefits of Second Language Study." *Regarding World Language Education*, NEA Research (December 2007): 1-6. https://portal.ct.gov/-/media/SDE/World-Languages/BenefitsofSecondLanguage.pdf.
[13] Ricardo Schütz. "Stephen Krashen's Theory of Second Language Acquisition," *English Made in Brazil*, published April 1998; revised October 2019. https://www.sk.com.br/sk-krash.html.

Embodied cognition

Embodied cognition is a relatively new field that describes how cognitive processing is changed by the actions of the rest of the body much like the study of jugglers. Embodied cognition, however, relates to a far larger scope of impact and influence, and aspires to understand how our perceptual, cognitive, and motor skills are informed by the physical body.[14] Cognitive activity is rooted in bodily states and actions.[15] Embodied cognition poses the question, "How do the body and the mind relate to each other to enhance and maximize learning?" One approach to that question is the methodology of Total Physical Response or TPR, which was originated by Professor Emeritus from San Jose State University, John Asher, in 1960. Asher's TPR has received renewed attention of late and the theory has been adapted into a practical tool by second language teachers around the world. The approach that has been developed has become popular because it's playful and can reduce the stress often associated with second language learning. It encourages gestural experiences that increase memory retrieval and creates meaningful communicative frameworks. Words that are learned through movement are internalized in ways that enhance memory.[16]

TPR put into practice is a method of teaching language or vocabulary concepts by using physical movement to react to verbal input. Students follow the teacher's physical directions to complete the command without speaking. Gradually the commands become more complex and new commands are added. Students speak when they are ready, without prompting, in ways that are similar to the way one learns their first language.

TPR is a particularly positive tool for early learners because the focus is on language comprehension and actions. There is a useful vocabulary for beginning TPR that focuses on action verbs like stand up, sit down, lift/raise, lower, point to, lay/place, take, pick up, jump, skip, walk, turn around, clap, open, shut, hold, drink, eat, and wave. Adjectives and adverbs are then added. Finally, nouns denoting body parts, classroom objects, parts of the room, colors, and numbers are added. Using this vocabulary and the commands also invites children to use their imagination once they have demonstrated understanding. As Dr. Vera Savic states, "TPR utilizes body movement (large-motor skills) that can reinforce language learning and potentially strengthen physical

---

[14] Robert A. Wilson, and Lucia Foglia. "Embodied Cognition," In Edward N. Zalta ed. *The Stanford Encyclopedia of Philosophy Archive* (website), 2017. https://plato.stanford.edu/archives/spr2017/entries/embodied-cognition/.

[15] D. Atkinson. "Extended, Embodied Cognition and Second Language Acquisition," *Applied Linguistics*, Vol. 31 No. 5 (2010): 599-622, https://doi.org/10.1093/applin/amq009.

[16] Drora Arussi. "Hebrew through Movement (in Hebrew)," *The New Ulpan Newsletter* #104, Fall 2015, Mofet Institute. https://meyda.education.gov.il/files/AdultEducation/hed_haulpan/hed_104_drora_arussi.pdf.

development of children; enjoyment created in stress-free activities that focus on physical movement can further foster children's engagement, enhance motivation for participating in action games, and make foreign language learning truly effective."[17]

According to Asher, this method contributes to learning a target language in a fashion similar to how native languages are learned. The use of TPR promotes low-stress environments that lead to rapid understanding of the target language regardless of the student's academic aptitude, and has been shown to lead to long-term retention. Asher also supports language immersion for this learning and he does not believe in translation as he believes it does not contribute to long-term understanding, but rather only toward short-term comprehension. Utilizing the TPR technique is an alternative to translation as the relevant classroom experiences create a knowing of facts through experienced gestures.[18] The TPR method has now been used worldwide in over 500 schools. TPR is often adapted by educators, for example, *TPR Storytelling* by Blaine Ray, a high school Spanish teacher in the 1990s. This technique involves story co-creation using high-frequency vocabulary and has become a popular adaptation of TPR.[19]

Another TPR method is called Embodied TPR. Teachers are experimenting with using TPR and integrating multiple types of physical embodiment.[20] Gesturing and physical activity have been demonstrated to enhance children's learning and health. A recent study demonstrated that combining physical activities with task-relevant gestures leads to even better learning performances in terms of cued recall. In addition to these benefits, children preferred a combination of physical activities and gestures to gestures alone.[21] Embodied cognition recognizes that the body not only demonstrates knowledge but also is an impactful tool to additionally store knowledge. Researchers Ullman and Lovelett state that "Second language learning instruction can definitely take advantage of techniques that involve procedural memory in order to enhance memory."[22]

---

[17] Vera Savic. "Total Physical Response Activities for Early English Learners," Conference paper for Физичка култура и модерно друштво. Vol. 17. Jagodina, Serbia: Faculty of Education, January 2014.

[18] John Asher. "TPR: After forty years, still a very good idea," *TPR World*, February 5, 2007. https://tpr-world.com/zexpertsbu/.

[19] Karen Lichtman. "Research on TPR Storytelling." In *Fluency Through TPR Storytelling*. Command Performance Storytelling, 2019, 300.

[20] Marianna Ioannou, and Andri Ioannou. "Technology-Enhanced Embodied Learning." *Educational Technology & Society*, Vol. 23, No. 3 (2020): 81-94.

[21] K. Toumpaniari, S. Loyens, M.F. Mavilidi, et al. "Preschool Children's Foreign Language Vocabulary Learning by Embodying Words Through Physical Activity and Gesturing," *Educational Psychology Review*, 27 (2015): 445-456. https://doi.org/10.1007/s10648-015-9316-4.

[22] Michael T. Ullman, and Jarrett T. Lovelett. "Implications of the Declarative/Procedural Model for Improving Second Language Learning: The Role of Memory Enhancement Techniques,"

I propose that TPR be widely used as a tool in Jewish preschools to build strong and emergent Hebrew programs for children 2-5 years old. Jennie Berger, a Hebrew language and Israeli dance teacher from the Milton Gottesman School in Washington, DC, uses TPR regularly. She breaks down types of TPR into categories such as responsive hand motions, pointing hand motions, and gesture hand motions. One example she describes is teaching the colors and the Genesis creation story to kindergarten children. She introduces new vocabulary by breaking a word into syllables and teaches a gesture for students to produce the word. "When TPR activities are games, it is suitable for kinesthetic learners who especially enjoy learning through physical response or connecting to memory through actions. Besides kinesthetic learners, TPR appeals to visual children who take visual cues from seeing the actions associated with the instructions given. When TPR involves learning songs, learners will particularly benefit from rhythms associated with movement which support language learning. The commands and vocabulary become memorable to the learners."[23]

The importance of immersion for teaching Hebrew

Young children in preschool are capable of learning Hebrew from 20-45 minutes a day immersively.[24] It is suggested that preschool directors consider creatively thinking about staffing, preferably having a Hebrew teacher and a Hebrew speaking volunteer, possibly parents or older adults, who could serve in that role.

The American Council on the Teaching of Foreign Languages (ACTFL) was developed in 1982 by a group of researchers and practitioners to examine best practices.[25] They wrote in their 2012 position paper that the target language needs to be taught for a minimum of 90 minutes each week, which could be broken down to 18 minutes each day. This includes lesson content, managing classroom behavior, giving instructions, and implementation of the activities in the target language.[26]

An immersion model focuses on meaning rather than grammatical rules and the environment promotes a learning community in which students are

---

Second Language Research, Vol 34, No. 1. (2018): 36-65.
[23] Vanessa Reilly and Sheila M. Ward. *Very Young Learners (Resource Book for Teachers)*, Oxford: Oxford University Press, 1997.
[24] "Early Language Learning," *American Council on the Teaching of Foreign Languages* (website), Published July 29, 2012. https://www.actfl.org/news/early-language-learning.
[25] https://www.actfl.org/about-actfl.
[26] Siddens, Stephanie. What Is Language Proficiency? Ohio Department of Education. July 5th, 2021. https://education.ohio.gov/Topics/Learning-in-Ohio/Foreign-Language/Model-Curriculum-for-World-Languages-and-Cultures/Introduction-to-Learning-Standards/Proficiency-and-Research-Based-Proficiency-Targets.

comfortable developing a growth mindset for making mistakes and taking risks. Young children who learned in an immersion model were observed to be more at ease and confident using the language in the future.[27]

ACTFL developed the Proficiency Approach, which is the main immersion tool that enables schools and teachers to articulate standards and learning goals, support language acquisition, and guide students in internalizing language learning.[28] It focuses on the learner and uses constructivism theory, in which educational goals follow the curiosity and interests of the children based on the belief that learning occurs best when children are actively involved in the learning process rather than passively receiving information. Renowned scholar Dr. Bill VanPatten, from the field of second language acquisition, focuses on communication that is based on participation and negotiating meaning. His theory emphasizes the process and development of communication as a priority over grammar and vocabulary.[29] His theory supports an immersion model.[30]

Constructivist teaching is manifest in the Proficiency Approach in that the approach fosters critical thinking and creates motivated and independent learners. Constructivism recognizes that learners are central to the learning process and that students construct understanding and knowledge through curiosity. This process involves teachers and students engaging in developing, inventing, and constructing meaningful learning opportunities and experiments that become integrated into their prior knowledge.[31] The Proficiency Approach is flexible and can be used with diverse teaching methods and curricula. It provides standardized assessment tools to follow progress and performance in the areas of listening, speaking, reading, and writing. Dr. Vardit Ringwald, the founding Director of the School of Hebrew at Middlebury College and current Director of the Consortium for the teaching of Hebrew language and culture at Brandeis University, has contributed, as part of a team, to the development of the Hebrew guidelines for the ACTFL Proficiency Approach. These Hebrew

---

[27] Helena Curtain. "Using the Target Language & Providing Comprehensible Input," From *STARTALK*, a program of the National Foreign Language Center at the University of Maryland, published on *Teachers Effectiveness for Language Learning*. http://www.tellproject.org/wp-content/uploads/2017/02/AdvanceLearning_TargetLanguage_Overview.pdf.

[28] https://www.actfl.org/resources/guiding-principles-language-learning.

[29] Bill VanPatten. "The Principles Of Comprehension-based Communicative Language Teaching" with Angelika Kraemer.and Walter Hopkins, Talkin L2 with BVP, podcast audio, May 22, 2019, Episode 33, 1:01:51. https://www.listennotes.com/podcasts/talkin-l2-with-bvp/s1-episode-33-the-principles-RkgsbC9ImOz/.

[30] More resources from Dr. Bill VanPatten are available at his weekly call-in show that discusses second language learning, teaching, and acquisition, related to research-supported knowledge and practices intended for language teachers and practitioners. http://www.teawithbvp.com/

[31] B.A. Marlowe, and M.L. Page. *Creating and Sustaining the Constructivist Classroom* (Rev. ed.), Thousand Oaks, CA: Corwin, 2005, 7-14.

proficiency curriculum frameworks were developed for secondary and post-secondary education for both the ACTFL and the United States Department of Education. She notes, "The Proficiency Approach has provided a framework within which the institution, the educator and the learner are all partners in a clearly defined journey and, on the way, they are all winners as the school's vision is strengthened, the staff is empowered and the students are guided to use the Hebrew language naturally, the language of our heritage, continues to thrive and be passed to another generation."[32]

Teachers, even in preschool, are encouraged to create learning frameworks, scope and sequence, and learning objectives that relate to children's interests. Professional development can support teachers in mapping out the big picture themes for the year. Building off the Proficiency Approach, the Teacher Effectiveness for Language Learning (TELL) Project is a community of teachers who reflect upon their instruction, define best practices, and measure effectiveness. The network offers a plethora of language learning frameworks which guide instructors in the areas of learning experiences, collaboration, performance, and feedback, among other domains.[33]

Authentic resources are materials developed for real-world situations, most often from the native country, and not created for language learning purposes (e.g., books, newspapers, music, magazines, menus, signs, and such). These are used as supporting materials to enrich and reinforce the target language and culture. Authentic materials are defined as "written by members of a language and culture group for members of the same language and culture group."[34] It is preferred that authentic resources be used whenever possible to reflect the culture of the language. In a Jewish context, this often implies connection to contemporary Israeli culture rather than to an Americanized Hebrew. Exposing Jewish-American children to Israeli songs, books, and materials provides students similar cultural touchstones to similarly aged kids in Israel. The use of authentic materials also legitimizes the language for the learner as it reminds them that there is a broader group of children who use the language as a primary language. Hebrew can further be a cultural bridge for friendships between children in the diaspora and in Israel.

For students ages 3-6, using a large-font Hebrew print to label objects and furniture in classrooms is recommended as a pre-literacy introduction to He-

---

[32] Ringwald, Vardit. 2021. Interview.
[33] Ibid.
[34] Vicki Galloway as cited by Eileen Glisan. "Use Authentic Texts," *ACTFL* (website). https://www.actfl.org/educator-resources/guiding-principles-for-language-learning/use-authentic-texts. [Note: This quotation and citation information is provided online by ACTFL, but it is not entirely possible to follow the citation trail, since Galloway has several 1998 publications.]

brew language in their environment. The use of authentic songs with a school and home library is critical. Creating a preschool library of Hebrew books that can go home with students can enhance the process. Parents can be provided with book lists if they want to enhance their Hebrew book selection at home. A useful resource for newly published Hebrew books is the Institute for the Translation of Hebrew Literature, which disseminates new titles of both Hebrew and English books. *Sifriyat Pijama B'America*/PJ Library Israel sends Hebrew books to kindergartens in Israel in an effort to enhance literacy and those can be useful in secondary language programs in the United States.

Hebrew Play, a program that promotes Hebrew as an integral part of Jewish identity in America by inspiring families to play together in the language, was replicated in seven sites in three states. It was adapted from a family program into a Hebrew immersion preschool curriculum. The goal was to support families in learning Hebrew through immersive methods using Israeli culture and community building. The program used both the classic and contemporary Israeli children's literature, music, movement, and sensory activities to connect both Hebrew speaking families and families interested in learning Hebrew.[35]

Family & preschool collaborative connections
Families of preschool aged children are often more open to partnering in their child's learning than at other stages, so it's particularly important to have strategies for how language learned at school may be reinforced at home. Teachers can share vocabulary, songs, and games with parents that can be played at home with daily or weekly goals and objectives. It is encouraged that content parallel the larger thematic curriculum in the class because it reinforces concepts that are already in the students' learning schema and environment. For example, if students at a preschool are learning about a farmer's market, the Hebrew curriculum could relate to popular Israeli vegetables and shopping at the *shuk* (market).

However, early language researcher Patricia Kuhl has identified a challenge. "Parents worldwide have a common problem: They want their children to speak a second language, but many don't speak that language themselves. We know that zero to 5 is a critical age, a window of opportunity for second language learning, and our newest study shows that when teachers in early education classrooms are trained online to use our method and curriculum, children's learning seems almost magical."[36] Dr. Kuhl conducted studies on how to solve

---
[35] https://www.hebrewplay.net/.
[36] Kim Eckart. "UW Research Expands Bilingual Language Programs for Babies," *UW News*, January 23, 2020. https://www.washington.edu/news/2020/01/23/uw-research-expands-bilingual-language-program-for-babies/.

this problem, and two of them revealed positive findings. In 2017 and 2020 the researchers studied English second language learning and retention based on a 36-week tutor intervention training they were developing at an early childhood center in Madrid. The tutors were native English speakers who met the children for 45 minutes a day. The training was based on six principles:

1. Tutors addressed the children frequently and interactively.

2. Tutors used parentense, which is the high pitched exaggerated intonation and slower use of one's voice.

3. Tutors used highly social interactions.

4. Children were encouraged to "talk" and interact.

5. Children received English language input from multiple native speakers.

6. There were adults modeling play in a way that encouraged high-level language use.

This work was valuable in revealing the potential for learning that was possible in an intensive structure of 45 minutes a day for 36 weeks. The study demonstrated across-the-board increases in English language learning independent of socio-economic backgrounds. These robust results demonstrated to administrators and directors that second language learning is not simply contributing to a child's overall development but proved that children demonstrated language learning at a young age.[37] This study was a boon for revealing the effectiveness of early language learning. Kuhl and her team were creating an online teacher training program called SparkLing that applied the research data and transformed it into early childhood second language educational curricula.[38]

Hebrew classes that take place once per week are unlikely to change a child's brain development. However, an interactive, supplementary, home-reinforced program using library-based materials and experiences can nevertheless re-

---

[37] Naja Ferjan Ramírez, and Patricia K. Kuhl. "Early Second Language Learning through SparkLing: Scaling Up a Language Intervention in Infant Education Centers," *Mind, Brain, Education*, (2020): 98. https://ilabs.uw.edu/sites/default/files/2020_ferjanramirez_kuhl_earlysecondlanguage.pdf.

[38] Reilly and Ward. *Very Young Learners*.

sult in thinking that is more receptive to language learning.[39] Books open the children's minds to play, especially for games that promote turn-taking, which promotes the important skill of self-regulation.

I encourage parents and children to play in Hebrew. TPR is an especially useful tool for learning the body parts in Hebrew. Some favorite activities are teaching songs that relate to body parts. For example, in my own work with families, I have created and shared thematic YouTube-based folders of music for them to listen to at home with their children. Some of my favorite songs regarding learning body parts include "*Yesh Li Shtay Yadayim*" (I have two hands), a song by Mirik Snir, *Af Sheli, Af Shelach*" (my nose and your nose), and "*Afo Agudol*" (Where is Thumbkin?). A tool that I often employ is a chant to repeat when doing routines. Many short songs with repetitive tunes can be adapted to introduce new words. Some English songs in Israel have been adapted to Hebrew, such as "If You're Happy and You Know It Clap Your Hands." Despite not representing the purest of authentic materials, these can be helpful for parents who themselves are not Hebrew speakers.

Curriculum parallelism
As a teacher working with toddlers and preschoolers, I am a firm believer in curriculum design and constructivist education. Developing a curriculum for one's teaching is a process that provides a map. Sometimes children's interests create learning adventures and detours but the advantage of creating this map is that it serves as a learning compass. To develop a curriculum is to consider the variables of scope and sequence not only in relation to Hebrew teaching for a specific grade but the ways in which the content, learning, and teaching becomes more complex in subsequent years.

From my experience of teaching Hebrew to children 6 months to 5 years I have adapted curricula for different classes. In order for a Hebrew curriculum to have resonance and relevance it is beneficial that it be both rooted in the student experience and routines as well as reflect a content parallel to that of the emergent curriculum. Children learn best through play and prompts that spark curiosity and creative problem-solving. Hebrew teachers are encouraged to develop thematic emergent curricular goals shaped by children's interests and the teachers' thematic choices. It is critical that the content selection is in curricular alignment because this provides opportunities for reinforcement of concepts and content. To create a language immersion program that supports

---

[39] Betsy Diamant-Cohen, and Saroj Nadkarni Ghoting. *The Early Literacy Kit: A Handbook and Tip Cards*. Chicago: American Library Association, 2010.

children's curiosity, and allocates time for students to seek out the responses to bigger questions, provides students with opportunities for meaningful learning experiences.[40]

Conclusion
Supporting preschools and kindergartens to build Hebrew immersion for second language learning benefits children's brain development and is achievable by established methods. Essential elements such as encouraging school directors to incorporate immersion, supporting teachers with implementation, building a library of authentic resources, and reinforcing instruction at home with families will result in success. Learning Hebrew as a living language for young people shapes identity and supports different perspectives and cross-cultural awareness. Linguistic juggling is possible for every student, especially with an early start.

---

[40] Paula D. Fortier, and Marielle Hamon. "Teaching 100 Languages in a Second Language," Published by McDowell Foundation as part of the Teaching and Learning Research Exchange, October 2014, 41.

References

Arussi, Drora. "Hebrew through Movement (in Hebrew)." *The New Ulpan Newsletter* #104, Fall 2015, Mofet Institute. https://meyda.education.gov.il/files/AdultEducation/hed_haulpan/hed_104_drora_arussi.pdf.

Asher, John. "TPR: After forty years, still a very good idea." *TPR World*, February 5, 2007. https://tpr-world.com/zexpertsbu/.

Atkinson, D. "Extended, embodied cognition and second language acquisition," *Applied Linguistics*, Vol. 31 No. 5 (2010): 599-622. https://doi.org/10.1093/applin/amq009.

Baldwin, Patrice. *With Drama in Mind: Real Learning in Imagined Worlds*. London: Continuum International Publishing Group, 2004.

Barsalou, L. "Grounded Cognition," *Annual Review of Psychology*, 59 (2008): 617-45.

Compton, K.C . "Zero to 3: Never a Better Time to Learn a Second Language." *Early Learning Nation* (ResearchLab blog), February 9, 2021. https://earlylearningnation.com/2021/02/zero-to-3-never-a-better-time-to-learn-a-second-language/.

Curtain, Helena. "Using the Target Language & Providing Comprehensible Input." From *STARTALK*, a program of the National Foreign Language Center at the University of Maryland, published on *Teachers Effectiveness for Language Learning*. http://www.tell-project.org/wp-content/uploads/2017/02/AdvanceLearning_TargetLanguage_Overview.pdf.

Diamant-Cohen, Betsy and Saroj Nadkarni Ghoting. *The Early Literacy Kit: A Handbook and Tip Cards*. Chicago: American Library Association, 2010.

"Early Language Learning." *American Council on the Teaching of Foreign Languages* (website). Published July 29, 2012. https://www.actfl.org/news/early-language-learning.

Eckart, Kim. "UW Research Expands Bilingual Language Programs for Babies." *UW News*, January 23, 2020. https://www.washington.edu/news/2020/01/23/uw-research-expands-bilingual-language-program-for-babies/.

Ellis, Nick. "Essentials of a Theory of Language Cognition." *The Modern Language Journal*. Vol. 103 No. 1. (2019): 45.

Fortier, Paula D. and Marielle Hamon. "Teaching 100 Languages in a Second Language." Published by McDowell Foundation as part of the Teaching and Learning Research Exchange, October 2014, 41.

Glisan, Eileen. "Use Authentic Texts." *ACTFL*. https://www.actfl.org/educator-resources/guiding-principles-for-language-learning/use-authentic-texts.

Ioannou, Marianna and Andri Ioannou. "Technology-Enhanced Embodied Learning."*Educational Technology & Society*. Vol. 23, No. 3 (2020): 81-94.

Jacobs, Heidi Hayes. *Mapping the Big Picture: Integrating Curriculum & Assessment, K-12*. Alexandria, VA: Association for Supervision and Curriculum Development (1997): 63.

Jarvis, Marley as quoted in K.C. Compton, "Zero to 3: Never a Better Time to Learn a Second Language." *Early Learning Nation* (ResearchLab blog), February 9, 2021. http://earlylearningnation.com/2021/02/zero-to-3-never-a-better-time-to-learn-a-second-language/.

Klass, Peri. "Hearing Bilingual: How Babies Sort Out Language." *The New York Times*, October 10, 2011. https://www.nytimes.com/2011/10/11/health/views/11klass.html.

Kuhl, Patricia. "Babies' Language Skills." Talk given at *Mind, Brain, and Behavior Annual Distinguished Lecture Series*, Harvard University, April 3, 2012.

Kuhl, Patricia K., Barbara T. Conboy, Denise Padden, Tobey Nelson, and Jessica Pruitt. "Early Speech Perception and Later Language Development: Implications for the 'Critical Period.'" *Language Learning and Development*, 1(3&4), 237-264.

Kuhl, Patricia, F. M. Tsao and H. M. Liu. "Foreign-language Experience in Infancy: Effects of Short-term Exposure and Social Interaction on Phonetic Learning." *PNAS*, vol. 100, no. 15 (2003): 9096-9101. https://www.pnas.org/doi/10.1073/pnas.1532872100.

Lichtman, Karen. "Research on TPR Storytelling." In *Fluency Through TPR Storytelling*. Command Performance Storytelling, 2019, 300.

Macedonia, Manuela. "Embodied Learning: Why at School the Mind Needs the Body." *Frontiers in Psychology*. (October 2019): 1-4. https://www.ncbi.nlm.nih.gov/pmc/articles/PMC6779792/.

Marian, Viorica and Anthony Shook, "The Cognitive Benefits of Being Bilingual," *Cerebrum*, (September-October 2012): 13.

Marlowe, B. A. and Page, M. L. *Creating and Sustaining the Constructivist Classroom* (Rev. ed.). Thousand Oaks, CA: Corwin, 2005, 7-14.

Nemeth, Karen. "Dual-Language Learners in the Pre-school Classroom." *Extensions Newsletter*. Vol. 30 No. 1.(2016). https://highscope.org/wp-content/uploads/2018/08/170.pdf.

Ramírez, Naja Ferjan and Patricia K. Kuhl. "Early Second Language Learning through SparkLing: Scaling Up a Language Intervention in Infant Education Centers." *Mind, Brain, Education*, (2020): 98. https://ilabs.uw.edu/sites/default/files/2020_ferjanramirez_kuhl_earlysecondlanguage.pdf.

Reilly, Vanessa and Sheila M. Ward. *Very Young Learners*. Oxford: Oxford University Press, 1997.

Ringwald, Vardit. 2021. Interview.

Roehrich, Sarah. "Kuhl Constructs: How Babies Form Foundations for Language." *E/I Balance* (blog). Cambridge, MA: Conte Center at Harvard University, May 3, 2013.https://eibalance.com/2013/05/03/kuhl-constructs-how-babies-form-foundations-for-language/.

Savic, Vera. "Total Physical Response Activities for Early English Learners." Conference paper for Физичка култура и модерно друштво. Vol. 17. Jagodina, Serbia: Faculty of Education, January 2014.

Schütz, Ricardo. "Stephen Krashen's Theory of Second Language Acquisition." *English Made in Brazil*, published April 1998; revised October 2019. https://www.sk.com.br/sk-krash.html.

Siddens, Stephanie. "What Is Language Proficiency?" Ohio Department of Education. July 5th, 2021. https://education.ohio.gov/Topics/Learning-in-Ohio/Foreign-Language/Model-Curriculum-for-World-Languages-and-Cultures/Introduction-to-Learning-Standards/Proficiency-and-Research-Based-Proficiency-Targets.

Teachers Effectiveness for Language Learning. http://www.tellproject.org/.

Toumpaniari, K., Loyens, S., Mavilidi, MF. et al. "Preschool Children's Foreign Language Vocabulary Learning by Embodying Words Through Physical Activity and Gesturing." *Educational Psychology Review*, 27 (2015): 445-456. https://doi.org/10.1007/s10648-015-9316-4.

Ullman, Michael T. and Jarrett T. Lovelett. "Implications of the Declarative/Procedural Model for Improving Second Language Learning: The Role of Memory Enhancement Techniques." *Second Language Research*. Vol 34, No. 1. (2018): 36-65.

U.S. Department of State: National Security Language Initiative, "The Benefits of Second Language Study." *Regarding World Language Education*, NEA Research (2007): 1-6. https://portal.ct.gov/-/media/SDE/World-Languages/BenefitsofSecondLanguage.pdf.

VanPatten, Bill. "Tenets of Comprehensible-Based Language Teaching with a Focus onCommunicative Ability." May 2019. https://docs.wixstatic.com/ugd/089f69_8dd3d93f826e-4beea19a6b2fc2752556.pdf.

VanPatten, Bill. "The Principles Of Comprehension-based Communicative Language Teaching" with Angelika Kraemer.and Walter Hopkins, Talkin L2 with BVP, podcast audio, May 22, 2019, Episode 33, 1:01:51. https://www.listennotes.com/podcasts/talkin-l2-with-bvp/s1-episode-33-the-principles-RkgsbC9ImOz/.

Wilson, Robert A. and Lucia Foglia. "Embodied Cognition." In Edward N. Zalta ed. *The Stanford Encyclopedia of Philosophy Archive* (website), 2017. https://plato.stanford.edu/archives/spr2017/entries/embodied-cognition/.

Wulff, Stefanie & Ellis, Nick. "Usage-based Approaches to Second Language Acquisition." In David Miller, et. al. eds. *Bilingual Cognition and Language*. John Benjamins e-Platform, 2018, 37. https://www.researchgate.net/publication/341085352_Usage-based_Approaches_to_Second_Language_Acquisition_Cognitive_and_Social_Aspects.

Wimpel (Torah Binder)
Photo: Zev Radovan. © The Center for Jewish Art, Gross Family Collection, Jerusalem.

An Invitation to Dance Toward our Spiritual Identity
Dance as a Medium for Self-Expression, Exploration and Transformation

Daniella Pressner

A spiritual moment

The room was dark and silent. You could hear the sound of 150 children waiting to see their role models, the Jewish sleepaway camp's 7th-9th graders, perform a dance they had been preparing for since their first days at camp as members of an elective entitled "#danceruption." This elective exposed moments of potential presence and absence in the first book of the Torah, *Breishit*. Quiet whispers emerged as the dancers took their spots: eight of them, sitting on chairs in what looked like a large drum circle. Tonight, the young adults would be acting out their understanding of human existence as it unfolded from the Garden of Eden. As the lights came up, each dancer was confidently frozen with an apple (their representation of this "forbidden fruit") gripped firmly in hand. Instead of one apple, the dancers had chosen eight. As the music unfolded with heavy drumbeats enveloping the dancers, they carefully picked up the apples to the beat and, in cascading form, took bites and passed each of their bitten apples to the peers to their left. It quickly became clear that this group of high-schoolers decided to retell the first narrative in the Book of Genesis in a way that would be consequential for them as individuals and as a community. Not only would each of them dare into the unknown; all of humanity would take part.

Though some of the children in this elective had gone to Jewish day school, most of them had not yet had an opportunity, as young adults, to delve deeply into this first narrative in the Torah. They had never considered the question of whether eating the forbidden fruit was a mistake or perhaps a required act to forever propel us into a world of action and consequence. They had never questioned the purpose of this narrative and its place in their history as a people and they had not yet thought about this narrative's relationship with the story of Cain and Abel, or Noah or Abraham—all stories about individuality and community; all stories about purpose and power. In the early days of the elective, the campers spent hours debating what they would have done had they been placed in similar situations and reflected on times in *their lives* when desire and curiosity had the potential to conflict with their concepts or their community's concept of honesty and honor. They generously and vulnerably shared moments in their lives that were raw with jealousy and anger and reflected on why and how they may have acted differently had they had more time and space to process. They also spoke about times when they would not have changed their minds and while they did not feel content with how their experience ended, they felt strongly that they had made the right choice for themselves at that moment.

That summer, our outdoor pergola, known as the "green *sukkah*," became a petri dish and a lab for their experiences and a stage for questions of deep consequence that they had just begun to explore. It was like a rite of passage; every time the students entered the *sukkah*, they knew that thorny, complex, and controversial questions would present themselves—questions that, at times, shook them to the core—*and* they knew that they would be given *the time and the responsibility* to hear each other, feel comforted by each other, and question each other from a place of deep love and wonder. They also knew that at the end, they would be tasked with choreographing a piece of work that would showcase their learning and a message they hoped to share with the camp world.

While they could not all agree on what they would have done in any of the situations presented, they all expressed a deep desire to be *active* agents in their future. Thus began the creation of their first movement, "Apples for All," a statement on their desire for wonder to merge with consequence; the teens specifically did not want the scene to demonstrate truth or falsehood but rather a different possibility for what could have been. What if all of humanity had taken charge and had eaten this first fruit? This was their question of consequence. What if all of humanity came to a space of wonder and acceptance? After much work, conversation, discussion, and practice (which will be explored in the context of this piece), the first act of their choreographed piece on moments of disruption and consequence in the Torah began to unfold.

The beauty and the struggle around the vignette above is that it did not come in the absence of intense toil. The children had spent hours learning about the texts for which they would choreograph. The preparation was hard and messy and at times even heated because they came to care so deeply about the representation and reinterpretation they yearned to share with their audience. The campers disagreed every day and needed to learn how to speak to each other and listen to each other even in their disagreements; eventually they did.

As the dancers ended the piece, it became clear that this was a dance of transformation for many of them. Their faces beamed with pride. This time, the pride was different even for those who had danced before; the type of work they put into this choreography was unlike any dance they had performed until that evening. This dance was born from hours of introspection, intellectual acuity, and careful responsibility for and reflection on how this work would be perceived. The evening was magical. The children were responsible for every piece of the performance, and for so many, it represented a spiritual journey; they recognized that the time spent to uncover who they were was invaluable to who they were becoming.

This chapter explores the role of choreographed dance as a potent pedagogical tool for deep learning, community building, and an opportunity to guide our children through their spiritual journeys. While there are many styles of choreography and dance that one could use as a pedagogical tool, for this chapter, I refer to narrative or representational dance, specifically where the choreographer's intent and the dancer's role is to tell a story or share an idea through the dance. Drawing on over a decade of experience working with children in Jewish day school and various camp settings, I discuss the gains and challenges of this approach and invite you to explore the potential this has to transform the educational journey for more children and young adults in this world.[1]

Creating ethical, spiritual, and flexible minds and souls

Our world needs more flexible, creative, and ethically grounded minds and souls. When approached intentionally and with resolve, dance can serve as a powerful pedagogical tool to help actualize greater commitment to learning, reflection, and purposeful action in our children. When we consider integrating dance into the *Jewish* experience, it is uniquely situated in that the dance experience magnificently reflects many of the same values and commitments so present in Jewish educational thought and learning. First, just as dance requires full sensory engagement, a rich and active Jewish life demands a full sensory experience. Second, just as a choreographed work creates a community of artists and dancers through reflection and idea formation, the *community* is of utmost importance in Jewish life. Communal purpose and communal learning are key to growth and one's participation in one's own spiritual journey. Third, just as dance engenders the possibility for a more in-depth and empathic understanding of this world and of others, so too Judaism calls upon us to feel and hear and see the plight of all those around us. Dance, then, becomes a beautifully powerful medium to engage every child in their spiritual quest as individuals and as part of their larger communities.

---

[1] Akiva School is a K-6 community Jewish day school in Nashville, TN. Students come from diverse religious, socioeconomic and cultural backgrounds. The only requirement for admission is that the child have one Jewish parent. Camp Yavneh in Northwood, NH is a summer camp for students entering into second grade through high school. The camp defines itself as an institution where all counselors, teachers and campers continue to dialogue with each other to understand the other's point of view and, like Akiva School, is committed to a very diverse camper body.

In a world that is often so benchmark-focused and test-centered, educators must communicate that while *mastering* benchmarks is certainly a worthwhile goal, our ultimate goal is to be *masters* of our lives. We need to be able to look honestly at ourselves and feel as though we have given our children the tools, the questions, and the experiences to feel whole, proud, and at peace with who they are and who they are becoming. More importantly, they must feel safe and comfortable with continuous questioning and an uncertainty that is born of a desire to wonder, to grow, to question, and to become. Identity work is hard and requires both time and safe space. The arts, and specifically dance, are uniquely situated to help our children both learn and grow.

Creating ethical, spiritual, and flexible minds and souls:
Dance as a sensory experience

Dance, as a full sensory experience, beautifully epitomizes the full sensory commitment that is so present in an active Jewish life. The Jewish calendar dictates that in almost every month we participate in some sort of sensory experience to commemorate a past event or rededicate ourselves to our Jewish learning or living. For example, many have reflected on how the Passover *Seder* is perfectly orchestrated to be an example of the best educational experience in its ability to capture an individual's full sensory experience.[2] Children hear the sounds of the songs being sung and the Haggadah being read. They reenact the experience of slavery and freedom. They feast their eyes on the symbols of the holiday and carefully taste these symbols as the blessings unfold. Children touch and crumble the crispy *matzah*, the smooth and luminous egg, the sweet, fragrant, *charoset,* the saltwater-dipped herb—and they taste it all with an understanding of what each of these foods symbolizes. This is the type of understanding and experience that we can work to engender for every child through identity work alongside and within the arts. It is these carefully crafted experiences that have the potential to bring about a generation of "text children," individuals who believe deeply in their place as agents for change in this world and who continuously reflect on their Jewish identity as they continue to grow and become.[3]

Young children engage their world with a multitude of sensory experiences. They touch the ground on which they crawl. They are constantly putting items in their mouths. They hear the voices that surround them even from their womb and get to know their surroundings through song, dance, art, action and sto-

---

[2] See Laufer 9-15; Sacks 88; E. Brown 84, 96-97.
[3] Although Abraham Joshua Heschel did not coin the term "text children," he did coin the term "text people," which I will reference further in the body of this chapter. (See Heschel 9-20.) This article is based on an address originally delivered at the Pedagogic Conference of the Jewish Education Committee of N.Y.C. on February 15, 1953.

rytelling. The activities toward which children naturally gravitate engage their senses and wire their brains for cognitive growth. Dewey argues that children have four inclinations: social instinct (the desire to communicate with others); constructive impulse (the desire to make things); instinct for investigation; and the expressive impulse.[4] Children's natural tendencies position them perfectly for learning through the arts, where each of these inclinations is both properly explored and nurtured. Dance is a fully multisensory experience, both in action (when you do it) and performance (when you experience it). We see dancers moving through time and space, we hear their breath, the music, the sound of their feet and hands moving through space and interacting with objects and people around them. There is the smell of the air that wafts toward you or the sweat that reflects their exertion. Performers in the dance are immersed in a sensory explosion whether they are in a solo role or in a corps; the choreography and the dancer determine the experience of sculpting through the space.[5] *Students remember these experiences and this learning because they are listening and seeing and touching and smelling all the time.* Dr. Eliot Eisner, educational arts theorist and a leading ambassador for the integration of the arts in education, argued that *it is the role of the schoolhouse* to provide children with the sensory experiences that are so foundational to a young child's experience.[6]

From a very young age, our capacity for gesture leads to engagement and the ability to express needs. Gesture provides the observer with insight into the child's thoughts, though they may not yet have the ability to express them. University of Chicago professor Dr. Susan Goldin-Meadow suggests that gesture "may be involved in the process of cognitive change itself... through two mechanisms that are not mutually exclusive." Dr. Goldin-Meadow discusses that gesture "communicat[es] unspoken aspects of the learner's cognitive state to potential agents of change." These agents of change might include parents, teachers, siblings and friends. In addition, gesture provides the learner with a more basic manner in which to communicate and explore ideas that are more complicated to think through verbally; this ultimately lessens the cognitive burden.[7] Gesture, then, becomes not just an early form of communication but a dance, in which ideas are expressed in the absence of oral expression. While oral

---

[4] Patricia F. Goldblatt. "How John Dewey's Theories Underpin Art and Art Education." *Education and Culture.* 22:1 (2006): 25.
[5] Neuroscience teaches us that experiences with heightened sensory awareness have the capacity for long-term imprinting.
[6] Elliot W. Eisner. *The Arts and the Creation of Mind*, Connecticut: Yale University Press, 2002, 1-14.
[7] S. Goldin-Meadow. "Beyond words: The Importance of Gesture to Researchers and Learners." *Child Development.* 71:1 (2000): 231.

expression has value, gesture has the unique ability to provide something more.

Beginning in kindergarten, faculty members and children at Akiva use movement and dance, specifically, to engage students in their learning. There are many levels at which movement is used for the pedagogic benefit of the teacher and student. Movement is used to help children remember sounds or letters and pantomime is used to help them learn key vocabulary. Gesture and dance are used to help children comprehend a story and they are used to help children recreate or even retell a story. On the most basic level, children in kindergarten use movements alongside letters to remember the letter names as well as their sounds. For example, a child might put their hand in front of their mouth to make an alligator's snout. They will then move it back and forth and say, "a…a…alligator…a..a… alligator.) There are sounds for the entire alphabet and this pantomime alongside sound recognition helps the children connect the most commonly associated sounds with each letter.

In addition to gesture, it is well researched that regular exercise improves brain performance. In the past 20 years, there have been a number of formal and informal studies demonstrating the connection between movement (specifically dance) and its influence on cognitive ability, rate of learning, and identity formation. These studies focus on the influence of the student dancer or mover's experience on their learning. A number of studies point to greater achievement, greater confidence, and greater depth of learning for students who engage their learning either through dance or alongside dance (where a dance class is added as part of the curriculum).[8]

Two such studies indicate the impact of carefully constructed movement on overall academic achievement. Furthermore, the second study I will reference demonstrates not just the academic gain, which is important, but an impact with regard to identity formation and the growth of a stronger and more deeply understood sense of self. In 2003, *The Basic Reading Through Dance Study* demonstrated that "defined and specific movement activities can impact early reading skills," including consonant sound recognition and vowel recognition, as well as phoneme segmentation."[9] *Students' achievement and rate of achieve-*

---

[8] Karen Bradley, et al., "Evidence: A Report on the Impact of Dance in the K-12 Setting," National Endowment for the Arts (2014), 2-65.

[9] This study was performed with a group of 721 first-grade students in Chicago over a 10-week program. 328 students participated in the treatment group and 393 in the control group. The research demonstrated that those who received dance-integrated reading lessons demonstrated improvement in basic reading skills (including moving letter shapes and sounds, creating name dances, and practicing flow from one shape to the next) and demonstrated significant gains in their basic reading skills as compared to the control group over the 10-week span. https://www.artsedsearch.org/study/basic-reading-through-dance-program-the-impact-on-first-grade-students-basic-reading-skills/.

ment increased due to the integration of specific movements into their reading curriculum. In the second study, dance had a more quantitative vs. qualitative impact. Rather than studying the rate of learning, researchers examined the impact that dance connected to conversation had on written expression. In her initial work with adolescent girls living in inner-city Los Angeles, dancer and choreographer Arianne MacBean worked to demonstrate the relationship between the language of movement and the language of text. Students analyzed each other's movements, reflected on pieces of their identity through writing and created small choreographic works that mirrored their writing. MacBean's work, as well as exercises she has shared with other choreographers, has demonstrated that as students write about their lives, the clarity of their choreography and their sense of self improves. She also argues that the opportunity to view and talk about their work, as well as that of their peers, specifically influences this growth.[10]

Throughout their time at Akiva, children are consistently provided opportunities for public speaking. Beginning in kindergarten, every child speaks in front of the entire school every year. This becomes second nature to them and they begin to see themselves as representatives of the community at large and not just independent individuals. The balance between creation of work and the sharing of that work with the audience (whether it be a poem, a PowerPoint or a dance) provides children with unique spaces to reflect on their learning and their growth; this has continued to profoundly affect them throughout their time at Akiva.

One child, who we'll call Isabelle, joined Akiva with a diagnosis of selective mutism. She had not spoken to her teachers at her other school and her parents were unsure whether she would ever speak at Akiva. That first year, Isabelle wrote her words and would stand next to another child speaking them. The second year, Isabelle recorded a video which was shared with the student body. Before, during the preparation for, and after every performance, there were opportunities for the teacher to reflect alongside Isabelle to help create *the space* for her growth to take place. By the third year, Isabelle was performing in the school plays. This is the type of transformation that can occur when children are provided repeated opportunities to step outside their comfort zones and breathe into their whole selves. While this story does not reflect the impact of dance specifically, it does demonstrate the power of practice, persistence and continuous reflection to engender long-term transformation in children. In addition, it highlights the power of presenting multiple mediums for commu-

---

[10] A. MacBean. "Scripting the Body: The Simultaneous Study of Writing and Movement." *Journal of Dance Education*, 1(2) (2001): 48-54.

nication. These attributes are always being worked on when we help children through the choreographic experience.

More recent studies use neuroscience to demonstrate the brain's response to cognition through experience. Galeet Westreich's work demonstrated that students who initially struggle to process oral or written information are more able to connect to the geometric concepts being presented, and enhance their problem-solving abilities, when presented with kinesthetic opportunities.[11] In line with previous studies, the bodily movement gave rise to short-term impact on both the students' achievement as well as their rate of achievement. Westreich also noted that the same students who initially struggled when presented information orally or in writing (in the absence of movement), "showed an eagerness to understand information presented orally or in writing" when it was later presented, independent of kinesthetic opportunity.[12] This demonstrates that the critical byproduct of movement is an enhanced intellectual/cognitive ability and an enriched enthusiasm for learning.[13] It is, perhaps, the second half of the study that is most interesting; if we can continue to engage children, encouraging them to come back to the learning when in the past they may have disengaged, then *opportunity for continued learning endures.*

Akiva students begin their study of Torah in first grade. Every year, the biblical Hebrew, which includes a new set of structures and root formations,

---

[11] It is important to note that these movements were not all connected to the shapes being discovered, as was the case in the *Basic Reading Through Dance Study*. In Westreich's study, educators provided students with opportunities to remove themselves from class activities to move their limbs.

[12] Westreich, 65. Two studies, focusing on mathematics specifically, demonstrate that students who used dance activities to learn their math concepts demonstrated that increased engagement and student interactions (due to the dance activities) led to a more refined and engaged understanding of the math concepts. According to Moore and Linder, the interactions between the students helped them bring their dance poses to levels that were "accurate and acceptable by the standards of everyone in the group." They highlight that this level and type of interaction cannot exist "when students are involved in more traditional paper-pencil instruction and assessment" (Moore and Linder, 107). Westreich's research focused on the impact of kinesthetic learning on understanding of concepts in geometry. Her research indicated that dance "facilitate[ed] the kinesthetic learners' exploration of abstract geometrical concepts, enhance[d] their problem-solving skills, and enable[d] them to develop a mathematical-thinking process that [could] be verbally communicated" (Westreich, 103).

[13] There are a number of other studies that have demonstrated a similar outcome in various disciplines. The Impact of Dance in the K-12 Setting references two other studies in science that demonstrate "engagement, retention, and comprehension in students who dance the concepts in science" (Bradley, 18). In addition, according to *Evidence, A Report on the Impact of Dance in the K-12 Setting,* the DELLTA study demonstrated that learning through the arts increased "motivation, perseverance/task persistence, focus, ownership of learning, spatial awareness, self-confidence, and cooperative learning and collaboration" (Bradley, 29).

becomes overwhelming for some of the children, which can lead them to quickly shut down. In that same classroom, other children can decode the roots more quickly and have a firm grasp on much of the newer vocabulary and its applications within the first three days. This can lead to even greater stress and anxiety for the children struggling to remember the most important vocabulary. In a methodical way, the teacher introduces pantomime to remember key vocabulary as the story of *Breishit* (Genesis) unfolds. For example, before even opening up the Torah text, a teacher might stand in the middle of a circle and share pictures that represent key words for the learning of *Breishit*. These pictures and words might include: *breishit* (a word that is loosely translated as "from the beginning") light, darkness, water, wind, and *tohu vavohu* (a dark abyss). As the educator shares the pictures, they will pantomime gestures that will be consistently used throughout the unit of study both during the reading of the text as well as in its discussion.

As the students begin internalizing the vocabulary, the reading of the text becomes much more natural and more easily understood; they begin to be able to retell key verses using pantomime as their guide. Perhaps surprisingly, the gesture and pantomime become unusual equalizers; the children who remember the words must work on the movements and often those who quickly pick up on the movements had once been struggling with the words. Even those students who quickly learn the words benefit from the gestures as reminders when the vocabulary continues to grow. Of equal significance is that those children who first became stressed get lost in the games and seem to forget the stress that once paralyzed them—emphasizing both the impact of gesture as well as, perhaps, the act of simply moving. This might be considered a first-tier dance experience.

On a very basic level, these studies demonstrate that dance provides a means to continuously engage children in learning. This affects their academic achievement, their overall approach and, ultimately, their sense of confidence, flexibility, and resilience as learners. Each of these is of critical importance for learning. However, when used thoughtfully and intentionally in character education and identity formation, dance has the capacity for even more.

Creating ethical, spiritual, and flexible minds and souls: Dance as a community builder

At the John Dewey lecture at Stanford University in 2002, educator Eliot W. Eisner insisted that education should be conceived as the "preparation of artists," calling on the work of 20th-century English art historian and poet, Sir Herbert Read. Eisner explained that Read's reference was not a call to cultivate more artists, painters, dancers or playwrights but rather…

> individuals who have developed the ideas, the sensibilities, the skills and the imagination to create work that is well proportioned, skillfully executed, and imaginative, regardless of the domain in which an individual works.[14]

Eisner's ideas are beautifully in line with what so many children and young adults yearn for today. Our children are creating their own connections and communities by developing their own apps, hosting their own YouTube channels and crafting their own images through social media. They crave choice and want a say in what they learn and how they learn it. As Dr. Ray Miller, professor of Dance Studies at Appalachian State University, puts it, "being their own creative agents is often viewed as their right."[15] When harnessing this energy, dance can become an incredibly powerful medium for understanding, self-expression, and deep reflection; it has the capacity to provide children with the guided autonomy and creativity to which they so naturally gravitate. Their natural desires guide them toward communities of shared purpose and responsibility. This community is often created unconsciously, but it can also be carefully crafted by skilled educators to create communities of conscience.

For example, in second grade at Akiva, children study Black American experiences in Social Studies; they might be asked to listen to *Swing Low, Sweet Chariot* and *Go Down Moses* to begin to appreciate the impact of the song within the context of its historical underpinnings. With a teacher's guidance, they might question how this slavery is similar to or different than their ancestors' slavery that they learn about yearly in their study of Passover. While this by no means provides them the context to ever fully comprehend the experience of any nation bound by slavery, the children connected in ways that are unimaginable for much of America because their upbringing is one in which they remember and reenact the experience of slavery through Passover each year. They might watch excerpts of Alvin Ailey's *Revelations* to understand how the slave experience was embodied years later, both reflecting on the deep grief as well as the soulful joy that a people were able to create for themselves. As children watch the dance, they are asked about the movements and the music (the words as well as the sounds). From a very young age, they are asked to consider what

---

[14] Elliot W. Eisner. "What Education Can Learn from the Arts About the Practice of Education." *International Journal of Education & the Arts* 5(4) (2004): 8.

[15] Ray Miller. "The Courage to Teach and the Courage to Lead: Considerations for Theatre and Dance in Higher Education." *Theatre Topics* 26:1 (March 2016, E-1).

these movements and sounds symbolize and what movements they might use if they were trying to express the plight of an enslaved nation. Children debate whether they will relay joy in their choreographic work and whether they hear joy in the spirituals, gospel and jazz that are featured in this piece.

The discussions that *precede* the choreography are critical to providing our children with experiences that are relevant to their world and that will ultimately lead to greater engagement and connection. And then, students are asked to dance to a unique piece of choreography that is created as a response to the movements they have come up with and the discussion they have shared in their study. The dance will include movements that the children have created as well as sections that their teacher has choreographed, enabling them to be creators, consumers, and performers. The children and their guides become a community of learners. As they reflect and create, they form ties and mutual understanding regarding their commitment to themselves and each other in the learning. Miller challenges dance educators to become co-investigators and co-creators so that the "enthusiasm and energy that comes to the studio is there because the student sees herself as an agent in her learning" (Miller, E-4). One could argue that Miller's words are applicable to education in general.

Children continue to crave defined moments to express their feelings and ideas in safe spaces. They need space to disagree with others' conclusions, have others disagree with their conclusions, and friends who will charge them to see their learnings from a multitude of perspectives. This is a moment in history where it is not only our right but our responsibility to encourage children to reflect together on primary texts from key moments in their history or the texts of their tradition. We must then provide productive and meaningful ways for them to dialogue with each other and themselves. As guides, we can provide context but also must work to *help them ground themselves* in *their* tradition, culture and history. As Goldblatt elucidates, "Art in education nurtures thoughtful reflection and a sense of community, which is essential for transformation."[16] When this time has been invested, I have seen incredible transformations take hold.

Creating ethical, spiritual, and flexible minds and souls: Dance as a medium for empathy and ethical courage

In 1953, Rabbi Abraham Joshua Heschel gave a speech in which he called for Jewish educators to be "text people:"

---

[16] Patricia F. Goldblatt. "How John Dewey's Theories Underpin Art and Art Education." *Education and Culture*. 22:1 (2006): 23.

> To guide a pupil into the promised land, [the teacher] must have been there himself. When asking himself: Do I stand for what I teach? Do I believe what I say? He must be able to answer in the affirmative. What we need more than anything else is not text-books but text people. It is the personality of the teacher which is the text that the pupils read, the text that they will never forget.[17]

For years, Jewish educators have used this phrase to push each other to be more mindful of the impact of our actions and the importance of having *mensche*s as teachers and not just those who are brilliant or well-read. For years, this verse has pushed educators to be fervently committed to lifelong learning; after all, how can we expect our children to continue to learn if we do not model that for them? Heschel pushed educators to refuse dogma and to think deeply about every choice and every action so that our outer beings mirrored our inner beliefs; this, of course, is of prime importance for our middle schoolers and our high schoolers who are always searching. There is, however, another element we as educators need to push ourselves to articulate and actualize: our need to develop text children. As important as it is for educators to own and mirror the texts they teach, our children live in a world where their desire to feel rooted and connected is critical to their overall mental and spiritual health, their sense of connection to their learning and, ultimately, their Jewish identity. And while this case specifically applies to Jewish children, one could argue that all children should have opportunities to be "text children," to genuinely engage in questioning and analyzing and creating works of art that center on *their* reflections on the texts and experiences of their tradition. When we provide our students with spaces to become "text children," what we communicate to them is that their thoughts matter, their individuality matters, and that their lives matter; they have something meaningful to contribute to this world and it is our role as educators to help them uncover what *that* is.

The process of guiding a student to become a "text child" is beautifully supported with dance as a medium. One of the most crucial factors for the ability to engage in raw and real questioning and discussion with others is one's ability to empathize and become comfortable positioning and understanding others in their experiences. These opportunities help cultivate empathy. While this cultivation can happen in many ways, dance is uniquely situated to provide this training with a direct, established, and keenly focused approach. Having

---

[17] Abraham Joshua Heschel. "The Spirit of Jewish Education" *Jewish Education* (Fall 1953): 9.

to understand and then embody another choreographer's vision challenges dancers to see a situation or an idea from a different perspective. It requires the learning of a set pattern and remembering the intent behind what is being copied. As senior research scholar in the Department of Dance at the University of Maryland, College Park, Dr. Judith Lynne Hanna points out that dance is "a constructed version of what is imitated."[18] Dancers must harness their empathy to consider whether they have ever been in a similar experience or whether they can imagine the feelings and sensibilities behind the experience. They must consider whether they have felt the emotion the dance is trying to convey, whether the emotion is love, contempt, despair or joy. Then the dancer must live out the choreographer's intent by expressing this emotion through their breath, their movements, and their facial expressions. More so, a dancer must figure out the choreographer's intent, perhaps their take on a controversial moment in history, potentially a commentary on society's malaise about a specific topic. And if the dancer is also a choreographer, then they must figure this out *before and even, at times, during* the transmission of the dance to the dancers.[19] This flexibility and ability to hold judgment as it is figured out in time and space is a powerful lesson for dancers and choreographers and a critical message for today's learners. Not everything is black and white. In fact, most things are gray, and it is our profound commitment to this world to figure out healthy and productive ways to see the bounty of possibilities in the gray.

In *Releasing the Imagination: Essays on Education, the Arts, and Social Change*, Maxine Greene argues that the arts have the capacity to challenge "givens," which are defined as perceptions that become fixed. Whether we are consuming or creating, the arts provide us with an altered lens and a desire to delve more deeply into understanding, and potentially articulating, the issue at hand. "Once we can see our givens as contingencies, then we may have an opportunity to posit alternative ways of living and valuing..."[20] When a student dancer is asked to recreate a moment of history, for example, they must consider what this moment felt like for the person involved. What would their body language communicate if they were stuck in the middle of a war, or a moment of social unrest, or a watershed event? As the work continues to unfold, this questioning uniquely positions the artist in the past, present and future at the same time. As Dr. Patricia F. Goldblatt so eloquently puts it:

---

[18] Judith Lynne Hanna. "A Nonverbal Language for Imagining and Learning: Dance Education in K-12 Curriculum." *Educational Researcher* 37:8 (2008): 496.
[19] See, for example, the film documentary *Make Me Dance*, featuring choreographer Darrell Grand Moultrie. *Make Me Dance*. Tatyana Bronstein, 2017. Film.
[20] Maxine Greene. *Releasing the Imagination: Essays on Education, the Arts, and Social Change*. San Francisco: Wiley, 2000, 23.

> The artist's work initiates a dialogue that calls for inquiry, recalling the past, or dwelling on present experiences... by triggering imaginations to think and behave differently in the present or future, art forms a bridge. As midway points between artists and viewers, art is a vehicle of understanding or reflection.[21]

In the formation of the dance, student choreographers and dancers must wrestle with the audience's vantage point and calculate whether their movements will communicate the intended message. The work to define one's choice in movements (if choreographing) and/or refine them (if dancing), continuously propels the student back to the text of inquiry or moment of history being discovered. This back and forth between the learning and the dance deepens the students' understanding of the material at hand as they are constantly asked to question, analyze, reflect and experiment, while in conversation and collaboration with others. This is not always as simple as it may sound. Students have had heated debates over the use of specific gestures or formations and have walked out on each other. While it is crucial to provide them with space and the language to ultimately come back together to make decisions about how to move forward, it is just as important to honor their passions and convictions as they are such a central part of the children's transformational journeys. At times, this may even mean that a dance that was originally intended to be a dance of one movement becomes one of two movements. In demonstrating this flexibility and the role of choice in every debate, we can teach our children that there is not *one answer* to any given problem, but that more often than not, there are many.

Dr. Eliot Eisner, a champion for preserving the arts in education, proposed 10 ways in which the arts are crucial to developing skills in young students. While each way is significant, and we have already referenced some of them, there is one that stands out in its ability to push children to be positive change-makers in this world. Eisner taught:

> The arts teach children to make good judgements about qualitative relationships. Unlike much of the curriculum in which correct answers and rules prevail, in the arts, it is *judgment rather than rules* that prevail.[22]

---

[21] Patricia F. Goldblatt. "How John Dewey's Theories Underpin Art and Art Education." *Education and Culture*. 22:1 (2006): 30.

[22] *Emphasis mine.* Taken from Eisner's 10-point manifesto for arts education in schools. For the entire list, see E. Eisner, *The Arts and the Creation of Mind,* 70-92.

As an artist creates a work of art, whether it be a poem, a painting or a dance, they must consider, "Is it right?" This question does not have a definitive "yes" or "no;" rather, it comes with a host of other questions, both quantitative and qualitative. Should I add more dancers into the corps? Does this movement need to be tweaked due to the dancer's position on the stage? Does this work communicate the message I hope to share with the world? Is the work *morally responsible*? In a world where we so often chase *tzedek*, (justice), where there is assumed to be a right and a wrong, this approach asks each student to move toward *emet* (truth). In Judaism, truth is a concept that is imbued with *chesed*, lovingkindness. In the spirit of *imitatio dei*, truth requires empathy and a deep and constant pursuit of reflection, inquiry, and wonder. For mortals, it is certainly not black or white or even definitive, and more qualitative than quantitative. It is this uncertainty and process-oriented approach that can be so anxiety-provoking (and, at times, crippling) for our children. It is precisely this uncertainty that we must be committed to helping our children breathe into and walk alongside. Teaching our children to live uncompromisingly fully and wholly in a world of uncertainty is a gift.

Scholars have pointed out that it is precisely this questioning that helps build one's identity as a lifelong learner and seeker.

Dr. Lisa Miller teaches:

> A spiritual life is characterized not by knowing the answers but by asking the questions. Children are born with an innate capacity for spirituality... just as they are born with the capability to learn a language.[23]

Indeed, every child is born with this innate capacity, and it is our world, which is so focused on the notion of one truth, or the value of quantitative vs. qualitative results, or *our need for* certainty, that steals this mature innocence from our children.

As Eisner teaches:

> The arts teach students to act and to judge in the absence of rule, to rely on feelings, to pay attention to nuance, to act and appraise the consequences of one's choices and to revise and then to make other choices. ...as we learn in and through the arts, we become more qualitatively intelligent.[24]

---

[23] Dr. Lisa Miller on Here and Now, "What Does it Mean to Raise a Spiritual Child?" https://www.wbur.org/hereandnow/2015/10/01/spiritual-children-lisa-miller. See also, Miller, *The Spiritual Child*.

[24] Elliot W. Eisner. *The Arts and the Creation of Mind*, Connecticut: Yale University Press, 2002, 208.

Bringing the arts into the classroom in a responsible and thoughtful way allows this uncertainty to take hold and helps our children live more peacefully and confidently in this beautifully unscripted world. Grappling with these realities, students tell their own stories. Dr. Ray Miller argues that the arts lead students to learn "in a framework of immediacy, collaboration, and interactivity," something which he argues is crucial to making learning relevant to students in today's world.[25] Dr. Patricia Goldblatt expands on this, saying that as "students learn they possess the ability to change things," their engagement and learning increases, and students become deeply invested in the message they aspire to share with their art.[26] When this learning occurs with the use of foundational texts or moments in history that are important to that child's tradition, there are cogent implications for identity formation and long-term mental and spiritual health, as each child begins to learn and articulate their spiritual story.

In the 5th and 6th grade years at Akiva, students are expected to lead the *Yom HaZikaron* (Israel's Memorial Day) ceremonies and *Yom Ha'Atzmaut* (Israel's Independence Day) celebrations for the school. Every year, these days call on children to express a piece of their learning through the performing arts. Importantly, children must first spend years learning about their history and the history of their people to come to this space. In addition, in lessons appropriate to their age level, children learn about diversity within Israel's thought and culture. They learn about wars that led to the formation of the State of Israel and the wars that came after. Children learn about the Holocaust and consider whether the Holocaust should be connected to the formation of the State of Israel. Nothing is taken for granted and in every moment, children are encouraged to question and consider: *What does this mean to me?* Children learn about those who immigrate to Israel for safety and those who lose their life in Israel. They learn about the Knesset, the Israeli government, and a democratic society that is very different from the one they are used to in America. This history is fraught with tension and hard for many adults to comprehend, let alone 11- and 12-year-olds, but what our children learn is that joy and happiness and freedom do not come without struggle and responsibility—a message that has the capacity to impact their thinking and their choices forever.

Quickly, our children realize that this history is complicated, wrought with tension and sadness and great joy and that, at times, there are no words to express their understanding of history. Then students engage in particular units of study including *Israel and the Arts* and *Israel's Landscape*. Using what is learned

---

[25] Ray Miller. "The Courage to Teach and the Courage to Lead: Considerations for Theatre and Dance in Higher Education." *Theatre Topics* 26:1 (March 2016, E-4).
[26] Patricia F. Goldblatt. "How John Dewey's Theories Underpin Art and Art Education." *Education and Culture.* 22:1 (2006): 25.

in these classes, the students set out to create a dance that is showcased on *Yom Ha'Atzmaut*. In these performances, children have danced scenes including a mother mourning the loss of her child, the loss of multiple soldiers and friends at war, the controversial proceedings that led to the establishment of the State of Israel, as well as the diverse, cohesive, and divided Israel. None of these ideas is easy for a 5th or a 6th grader to comprehend, but in merging their study of the texts using primary and secondary sources alongside the creative process, children leave with a more in-depth and richly nuanced understanding of the moment of history in the spotlight. Furthermore, they have grappled with their history in a way that has invited them to learn and express something meaningful to them in a cacophony of challenge, despair and hope. While the final product is meaningful for the students, and especially their peers, *it is the process* that most deeply influences their growing sense of self and their spiritual journey.

Creating ethical, spiritual, and flexible minds and souls:
The role of the educator and practical implications in the classroom
Until now, we have focused primarily on the students' experiences, and this is of critical importance. Just as important, however, is the setting in which this takes place and the pedagogues who surround our children in these spaces, including the spaces themselves. The spaces for this learning must be set up so that students can move freely through the room or have opportunities to do so when necessary. In addition, the materials we provide matter. Do we ask them to create a dance with a prop? Do we ask them to create a dance that is performed in a certain room with certain architectural elements that they must work around? What do we provide them with for their costuming and why? These questions matter because each of the materials and spaces allotted allow children to communicate in specific ways, which then may translate into different forms of learning.

None of this is possible without conscious design of an approach and a curriculum that value unique individuals over a uniform collective. We have to ask whether *we* are ready to enter a space not knowing the end result from the very beginning or in many moments throughout the process. For this type of learning to be fully honest and rich, the thinking, questioning and reflection needs to be a part of the overall school culture and not just one unit of exploration. The educator and guide are there to help encourage these conversations and bring out greater questions; the children often bring out their own questions within minutes of this open forum beginning. They begin pushing each other by asking questions that include: What do you think this experience meant to this character? Would you have made this choice and why? Are there moments that seem to be missing from the text and should we come up with what we think happened? Could your view on what happened alienate another's point of view and what might this mean? The processes that are most impactful are those that ask our children to think about how *they* connect to and understand the texts at hand.

Dancer/choreographer Arianne MacBean asks, "How do we construct our art to move the audience the way we want them to be moved, given that the value of our art is always in relation to the reader/observer?"[27] We must make sure there is time for our student artists to think together about what they want their audience to feel and what they, personally, experience as they dance. These conversations help the students more deeply reflect on and connect to the texts, their rich culture and the histories of their tradition.

The curricula must be committed to flexibility and the recognition that not everything can be "measured, mandated or managed" as it would be in a factory.[28] Standards and assessments both have a place and a purpose and *our charge* is to create spaces of inquiry where children inculcate these values with freedom, confidence and agency; compliance has its place in the world but not in place of our children's agency. Unless we provide students with repeated opportunities to take on the delicate responsibility of meaning making and change-making, they will not be prepared to lead with the values of courage, dignity and deep reflection at their core and I wonder whether *their unique spiritual stories* will ever be shared.[29]

Bringing dance and choreography to the center of a pedagogical experience allows both children and their teachers to learn together in a process that is not dictated by hierarchy but by honest investigation of truth—a truth that is admittedly multifaceted and leaves room for multiple possibilities.

At Akiva, as young adults and guides work alongside each other, they must consider emotions they hope to elicit from their audience and to think about the movements that will evoke these emotions. Students are tasked with finding key themes for their movements or creating a series of symbolic movements that will be repeated throughout their piece. They must determine their choice

---

[27] A. MacBean. "Scripting the Body: The Simultaneous Study of Writing and Movement." *Journal of Dance Education*, 1(2) (2001): 49.

[28] Elliot W. Eisner. "What Education Can Learn from the Arts About the Practice of Education." *International Journal of Education & the Arts* 5(4) (2004): 5.

[29] For more, see Ann Kipling Brown, "A Model for Dance Education: Promoting Personal Voice and Communal Learning." *International Journal of Education Through Art* 10.2 (2014): 182. Ann Kipling Brown argues that "[dance] students are socialized to accept authority and the dominance of the authoritative voice. They come to distrust their own voices and devalue their intrinsic abilities to think and contribute to their own learning."

of music (whether it be self-composed or already written) or whether they will perform in silence. Having these conversations requires children and young adults to put themselves in others' shoes: the shoes of their ancestors and the shoes of their peers. They draw upon compassion and understanding as they recognize that sometimes the most difficult choices are made with intellect and heart and still may not turn out as planned. This then guides the students in thinking about their moral responsibility in the message they communicate, as the choreography becomes their mirror and their platform to humbly and vulnerably share their learning and their spiritual journeys with the world.

The way we speak with our students needs to communicate that finality and perfection are not our goals. Rather, students should feel safe and comfortable enough to ask questions and to question themselves, to take risks they have never taken before, and to be able to sit with discontent until reflection, time, and perseverance help them move forward. Finally, our approach throughout the entire process needs to be deeply committed to an arc of learning that may ebb and flow depending on the outcome of the learning along the way. Prediction and control must cede to exploration for the students and their guides[30]. Importantly, this does not mean that we don't meet academic standards; rather, they may be met in a more open, cyclical and dialectical fashion instead of a direct route.

When we ask ourselves whether we are ready for this and the answer is yes, we must then think deeply about what needs to be true in the culture of our classroom, in the makeup of our classroom and in the materials we have available to help students move from vision to reality. Some dances may feel more profound than others. Some may feel dark or scary or even trite; but all, when done in an honest fashion, will reflect something deep within each child's soul. Opportunities to express these soul stories shape our children's ability to connect and stay connected to this world forever. Michael J. Shire teaches:

> As educators begin to [watch] their students' spiritual narratives, some will be philosophically profound, others will be unsettling to the perception of adults. *All of them will be singular probing questions about the nature of life.* This searching is an expression of a child's spirituality and their identity. Educators may encourage children on a philosophical quest *but words* cannot fully express a spiritual experience. We provide our children with gifts when we provide them with artistic

---

[30] Eisner, "What Education Can Learn," 5.

outlets to express their souls.[31]

Students' expressions become a beautiful tapestry of their intellectual and compassionate understanding. They truly become "text children," developing a vision for self-expression and joy in the most complicated and unchartered aspects of their spiritual journey because *you and we* invited them in.

As the eight dancers left the stage, one stopped and turned around. She looked at me, her eyes dark and filled with purpose and humility. After placing both palms together in the traditional dancer's gesture of thanks, she looked deep into my eyes and it was clear to both of us that she had changed. She entered the elective that summer as a dancer, just hoping to dance, with little interest in exploring her identity. That evening, she left the stage a "text child," hungry for continued depth and meaning in her spiritual journey. She had the courage, conviction and humility to enter into a completely foreign experience. And while this new space was complicated and messy—and, at times, even pushed her to the limit—she was able to develop into a more richly nuanced and deeply thought-out version of herself.

As she turned and walked away from the performance area, a tear rolled down my face. *She* had become a "text child," and *I* had the most humbling privilege of simply *inviting her in*. At that moment, "the limits of our cognition [were] not defined by the limits of our language."[32] Both of us knew that while it was dance that first propelled her into this experience, it was her newly formed relationship with this sacred text and this community of learners that would bring her out.

---

[31] Michael J. Shire quoted in Miller, Grant, Thompson, eds. *International Handbook of Jewish Education*, vol. 1. New York: Springer, 2011, 310.
[32] Eisner, "What Education Can Learn from the Arts About the Practice of Education," 10.

References

"ArtsEdSearch | Arts in Education." n.d. Www.artsedsearch.org. Accessed February 26, 2023. https://www.artsedsearch.org/.

Bradley, Karen, et al. "Evidence: A Report on the Impact of Dance in the K-12 Setting," 2014. https://www.arts.gov/sites/default/files/Research-Art-Works-NDEO.pdf.

Brown, Ann Kipling. "A Model for Dance Education: Promoting Personal Voice and Communal Learning." *International Journal of Education Through Art* 10, no. 2 (2014): 179-188.

Brown, Erica. *Seder Talk: The Conversational Haggada*. Jerusalem: Magid, 2015.

Dewey, John. *Human Nature and Conduct: An Introduction to Social Psychology*. New York: Modern Library, 1925.

Eisner, Elliot W. *The Arts and the Creation of Mind*, Connecticut: Yale University Press, 2002.

Eisner, Elliot W. "What Education Can Learn from the Arts About the Practice of Education." *International Journal of Education & the Arts* 5, no. 4 (2004): 1-14.

Goldblatt, Patricia F. "How John Dewey's Theories Underpin Art and Art Education." *Education and Culture*. 22, no. 1 (2006): 17-34.

Goldin-Meadow, S. "Beyond Words: The Importance of Gesture to Researchers and Learners." *Child Development*. 71, no. 1 (2000): 231-39.

Greene, Maxine. *Releasing the Imagination: Essays on Education, the Arts, and Social Change*. San Francisco: Wiley, 2000.

Heschel, Abraham Joshua. "The Spirit of Jewish Education." *Jewish Education* (Fall 1953): 9-20.

Hanna, Judith Lynne. "A Nonverbal Language for Imagining and Learning: Dance Education in K-12 Curriculum." *Educational Researcher* 37, no. 8 (2008): 491-506.

Laufer, Nathan. *Journey: The Seder's Meaning Revealed, and the Haggadah's Story Retold*. Vermont: Jewish Lights Publishing, 2005.

MacBean, A. "Scripting the Body: The Simultaneous Study of Writing and Movement." *Journal of Dance Education*, 1(2) (2001): 48-54.

Miller, Grant, Thompson, eds. *International Handbook of Jewish Education*, vol. 1. New York: Springer, 2011.

Miller, Lisa. *The Spiritual Child: The New Science on Parenting for Health and Lifelong Thriving*. New York: Picador, 2016.

Miller, Ray. "The Courage to Teach and the Courage to Lead: Considerations for Theatre and Dance in Higher Education." *Theatre Topics* 26, no. 1 (2016) E-1-E-7, https://doi.org/10.1353/tt.2016.0001.

Moore, C. and Linder, S. Using Dance to Deepen Student Understanding of Geometry. *Journal of Dance Education* 12, no. 3 (2012): 104-108.

Sacks, Jonathan. *The Jonathan Sacks Haggada*. Jerusalem: Koren, 2013.

WBUR. "What Does It Mean to Raise a Spiritual Child?" WBUR: Here & Now, October 2015. https://www.wbur.org/hereandnow/2015/10/01/spiritual-children-lisa-miller.

Westreich, G. B. An Analysis of Kinesthetic Learners' Responses: Teaching Mathematics through Dance." American University. Washington, DC. Unpublished Manuscript, 2000.

Le Grand Cirque, 1988. Guillaume Azoulay. Serigraph on paper.
Courtesy of the artist.

Dance as a Way of Knowing: Studying Jewish Texts Through Dance

OFRA ARIELI BACKENROTH

> You see, this thing, namely the dancing, in fact it's nothing but a result of the legs, but it raises the body to the level of the soul. A man walking aimlessly doesn't make an impression on us, he is one of those thousands, millions of people, for it is the nature of man to walk, just on the other hand man is wont to stand or sit or lie for all those functions are in the nature of man. And yet, let a man lift his feet and launch into a dance, then his spirit is exalted, and his soul soars so high that we say that all his limbs, all his body are transformed into soul, for thus the body transforms was elated and his whole body became all soul.
> —S. Y. Agnon[1]

This quote from *Only Yesterday* (*T'mol Shilsom*) by S. Y. Agnon underscores my relationship with dance and what I teach my students at the William Davidson Graduate School of Education at the Jewish Theological Seminary of America. Movement is life. It is when we are active, moving, creating, that we feel most alive and thriving. Movement allows us to experience ideas through our bodies, rather than only through our minds. Dance is an embodied art in which we are able to be in touch with all of our being: body and soul become one and are incorporated into a concrete form—our body. It is a holistic form of movement that is creative and affects us not only on the physical and emotional level but also on the spiritual level.

In this chapter, following a short introduction about dance in Jewish life, I plan to explore a few aspects of dance as a way of knowing and learning Jewish texts and of responding to the following questions:

- What is so special about dance?
- What is the place of dance in Jewish tradition?
- What can we teach through dance and why are we looking for alternative ways to teach texts?

---

[1] Agnon, Shmuel. *Only Yesterday* (Translated by Barbara Harshav), Princeton: Princeton University, 1945, 2018. Agnon is the 1966 recipient of the Nobel Prize for Literature.

- How can we teach an audience to observe dance, feel it and learn from it?

Dance has existed since the beginning of humankind. Before verbal or written communication existed, people used movement to communicate. This medium was instrumental in helping ancient peoples comprehend meaning in their world, and in helping to influence our world. Moving rhythmically is innate to human beings and is an intrinsic form of self-expression. Dance communicates in a kinesthetic form. Its vocabulary is steps—movements arranged in patterns—and is suitable for expressing those moments in life that are ineffable and can be expressed solely through the arts: music, and dance. Isadora Duncan, a pioneer of modern dance, once remarked, "If I could tell what it is, I would not have to dance it."[2] Through dance we are able to express these unique moments as well as having the ability to express knowledge. Sharon Mâhealani Rowe, in her research on tribal dances, posits that dance is more than just entertainment. Its steps and motions tell the history, the life stories of people, tribes and nations. It expresses religious beliefs and allows for demonstration of social and political issues. We dance to express that knowledge.[3] Religious Studies scholars, Adams and Apostolos-Cappadona, underscore the tight connection between dance and spiritual and religious engagement; they emphasize how movement can be an excellent mediator in the psychological and spiritual understanding of the Bible and liturgical texts.[4]

Since dance is not a linear process and may include more than one participant at a time, it can present divergent points of view and multiple layers of meaning simultaneously and help educators in showing complexity and nuance. Additionally, since dance has been a form of cultural expression for many years, dance history is an excellent source of learning about multiculturalism and the styles of different ethnicities. Being a group project, it also reflects a cooperative style of learning which has social ramifications. Betty Block, a dancer and a researcher of dance education, posits that dance is an embodied art in which bodies are expressing a tangible and visible form of an idea, quality, or feeling. The dancer's body serves as a vehicle to meanings and ideas presented by the dancer. Exploring dance as a form of embodiment provides a uniquely powerful insight into the body, not only as a subject, but also to the body as a knower of content, and the body as an expresser. Few human experiences express so

---

[2] I. Duncan. *My Life*. New York: Norton & Company, 1927.
[3] S. M. Rowe. "We Dance for Knowledge." *Dance Research Journal*, 40(1) (2008): 31-44.
[4] D. Adams, D. Apostolos-Cappadona, eds. *Dance as Religious Studies*. New York: Crossroad, 1990.

vividly and so totally the meaning of an embodied being-in-the-world as does a human body dancing. Block further posits that "an analysis of movement, and particularly of dance, helps us to see in an extraordinarily effective way the meaning of embodiment."[5] Block adds that it is very valuable to look at experiences of dance through the eyes of dance theorists and philosophers who consider dance and movement as the embodiment of experiences. The study of movement and dance encompasses the fullest meaning of embodiment. Being-in-the-world, being fully active in experiences, and taking part in observing dance, actively looking at each movement and gesture, creates the same sensation of experience. Thus, active looking and informed observation have important ramifications to the dialogue between the dancer and the observer of the dance.[6]

History of dance and Jewish life
Philosopher Susanne Langer says that "what is expressed in a dance is an idea … of the way feelings, emotions, and all other subjective experiences come and go—their rise and growth, their intricate synthesis that gives our inner life unity and personal identity."[7] Dance is an exuberant and compelling form of physical communication and expression. Composed of patterned sequences of nonverbal body movements that are purposeful and intentionally rhythmic, dance has always been part of human culture and rituals that celebrate significant life passages; and dance has been an integral part of Jewish life. In the communal and religious life of the Jewish people, dance has been regarded as an expression of joy and sorrow since biblical times and is today an integral part of religious, national, community, and family celebrations. The Bible introduces us to dance as an expression of feelings: happiness, sadness, disappointment, victory and accomplishment. One of the most famous examples features David and the people of Israel dancing as they are bringing the ark of God to Jerusalem. "David danced before the Lord with all his might" (2 Samuel 6:14).[8] Miriam the prophet is dancing with the women, a timbrel in her hand, following the Exodus: "and all the women went out after her with timbrels and dances" (Exodus 15:20).[9] The Psalmist encourages dance and music in the worship of God: "Let them praise His name in dance, on the timbrel and the lyre let them

---
[5] B. Block, & J. L. Kissel. "The Dance: Essence of Embodiment." *Theoretical Medicine,* 22 (2001): 6.
[6] For more discussion of experience and observation, see Dewey, J. *Art as Experience.* New York: Perigee Books, 1934.
[7] S. K. Langer. *Problems of Art.* New York: Scribner, 1957: 9.
[8] Translation from *The New Oxford Annotated Bible,* 1991.
[9] Translation from Alter, 2004.

hymn to him. For the Lord looks with favor on His people. He adorns the lowly with victory" (Psalms 149:3-4).[10]

Humans have always moved or danced as a way of ritualizing their relationship to the Divine. Movements have been part of the choreographed rituals of prayers during weekdays, Shabbat, holiday and life cycle events. Dance has been a major art form expressing Jewish life, and many milestones connected to Judaism, and to other aspects of Israel and Israeli society. For years dances were choreographed for the stage. Examples might include the staged dances of the Dybbuk[11] or communal folk dances and Israeli dances.[12] Jews were involved in creating dances during the 20th century in Europe, America and Israel. Many dancers of the modern dance movement, shepherded by Ted Shawn and Ruth Dennis at the end of the 19th and beginning of the 20th centuries, were Jews who found their calling in the modern dance movement and later formed the Doris Humphrey and Charles Weidman company, protesting the Jewish quotas imposed by Shawn and Dennis.[13]

This trend continues today as many dancers and choreographers continue to explore Judaism, biblical stories and spirituality. Another trend in dance has been toward Israeli dances and folk dancing in general. Anthropologists who study dance in historical societies, as it reflects other aspects of their culture, claim that folklife thrives in traditional societies and is closely related to religious practice. Dance also functions as a mode of storytelling, communication, and ecstatic celebration.[14] Two of the oldest forms of dance that exist in many cultures are the circle dance and the vertical line dance.[15] Circle and line dances evolved over the centuries, taking on different functions in cultures across the world as they developed. In circle dancing like the *hora*, which means dance in Greek, the dancers hold each others' hands while dancing in a circle. This dance was most widespread in Eastern and Central Europe from 1590 on, and has continued to be prevalent in Jewish life.[16] Line dancing is also a form of dance that takes place with a group of people. Participants line up in rows and execute identical movements in a synchronized manner. These two forms are common today in various forms of folk dancing. Contemporary Israeli dance has developed in two directions: expansion of the folk dance genre which ac-

---

[10] Translation from Alter, 2007.
[11] S. Ansky. *The Dybbuk and other Writing*. New Haven: Yale University, 2002.
[12] Y. Goren. *Fields Dressed in Dance*. Kibbbutz Ramat Yochanan: Hakibbutz Hameuchad, 1983.
[13] P. A. Scolieri. *Ted Shawn: His Life, Writings, and Dances*. Oxford, UK: Oxford University, 2019.
[14] J. Tucker. "Dance midrash: non-narrative Torah text comes alive." *Jewish Education News* (Summer) (1997): 36-37.
[15] J.B. Ingber. *Seeing Israeli and Jewish Dance*. Detroit: Wayne University Press, 2011.
[16] Walter Zev Feldman, "Traditional Dance," The Yivo Encyclopedia of Jews in Eastern Europe, https://yivoencyclopedia.org/article.aspx/Dance/Traditional_Dance.

companied the early settlers in Israel in the rebuilding of their homeland, and the establishment of art dance, leading to stage productions created by professional choreographers and performed by trained dancers.[17]

Israeli dance as an art form was introduced in Israel in the 1920s. Of course Israelis were always dancing in various occasions such as family and life cycle events and holidays, but as more artists found their way to Israel, there was an elevated interest in the arts and in dance as an art form.[18] During this period, the early settlers in Israel (the *Yishuv*) were searching for new forms of culture and that was when the emergence of the dance as a concert form—choreographed dance performed for audiences—emerged. Until then, classical ballet was the only form of concert dance known to the pioneers. With the arrival of Baruch Agadati, Margalit and Yehudit Orenstein, Rina Nikova and Lea Bergstein, a new trend of expressionist dance began to take hold in Palestine.[19] The newly arrived dancer Baruch Koushanski-Agadati, a devotee of dance from the cultural centers of Europe, was interested in expressive and stylized Jewish dance.[20] He is known as the choreographer of the first Israeli folk dance, *Hora Agadati*, which he choreographed for the first Dalia Dance Festival in 1924.[21]

After the establishment of the State of Israel, dance was developed to a high professional level by several ensembles, each founded on, and practicing with, a different orientation and style. One of the first dance companies, the Inbal Dance Company, was founded in 1949 by Sara Levi Tanai and gives voice to the stories of the Bible.

In 1960, Yehudit Arnon, a Holocaust survivor, founded the Gaaton Dance Company that later became the Kibbutz Contemporary Dance Company. This company aimed to nurture and develop the creativity of Israelis living in the north of Israel. Today the company is led by Rami Be'er, who walks in the footsteps of his mentor, Arnon, and continues the legacy of teaching dance to the people of the Galilee, including Arabs, and presenting their dances. Additionally, there are more than a dozen major professional dance companies performing a varied repertoire throughout the country and abroad. The Batsheva Dance Company, the largest in Israel, was established in 1963 by Baroness Bat Sheva De Rothschild and was originally dedicated to training dancers in the

---

[17] N.S. Spiegel. "New Israeli Rituals: Inventing a folk-dance tradition." In S. J. Bronner (Ed.), *Revisioning Ritual Jewish Traditions in Transitions*. Oxford: The Littman Library of Jewish Civilization, 2011.
[18] G. Manor. *Agadati, the Pioneer of Modern Dance in Israel*. Tel-Aviv, Israel: Sifriat Poalim, 1986.
[19] R. Eshel. "Dance in the Yishuv and Israel." In *Shalvi/Hyman Encyclopedia of Jewish Women*. Boston: JWA, 2021.
[20] See Manor (above) for more on the life of Agadati.
[21] "Hora Agadati: One of the Earliest Hebrew Folk Dances." Israelidances.com, www.israelidances.com/horaagadati.htm.

Martha Graham technique and performing Graham dance compositions. In 1990, Ohad Naharin became the artistic director of the Batsheva company as well as its choreographer. He won international acclaim for his dances and his innovative dance language Gaga, which is taught around the world.[22] Gaga is a movement language intended to help practitioners raise physical awareness by focusing on (or in Gaga terms, "listening" to) the rhythm of their bodies which lets them more effectively direct their movement. They then experience the pleasure that movement brings.[23] To help the growing interest in dance, Curtain Up was established in 2005 to assist young choreographers such as Inbal Pinto, Noa Dar, Yasmin Godar and more to create, teach, and offer educational experiences for schools.[24]

In Israel, folk dance was tightly connected to the Zionist goal of producing a new Jewish culture and new traditions to celebrate the emerging society.[25] Because dance embodies a variety of central Zionist goals, folk dance aligned seamlessly with the Zionist ethos of building a new culture based on tradition but each in its own way, creating communities but emphasizing equality and demonstrating a new spirit. Dance became an integral part of the emerging civil religion, representing the secular Zionist aim of connecting to Jewish traditions while breaking away from religious practice. Many folk dances were based on biblical themes and Jewish holidays, but celebrated them in a different way. Thus, song and dance became the new version of public prayer.[26] These trends were evident in Israel as well as in the United States, and folk dance was, and still is, a major attraction for Jewish life and its celebration.[27]

Theories about learning through movement and dance

The contribution of arts education in general and teaching through and with dance are grounded in research. The launching of project Zero[28] in 1967 at Harvard University brought the use of the arts in education to public awareness. Researchers used psychological experimentation and clinical studies of the brain, as well as fieldwork in schools, to research human ability.[29]

Creative dance offers an alternative avenue to the interpretation of material and a new way to exhibit understanding and acquisition of new knowledge for

---

[22] Eshel.
[23] J. Siliezar. "Flowing together." *Harvard Gazette*, 2019.
[24] O. Orfa. "Behind the Move." *The Jerusalem Post*, November 11, 2005.
[25] Spiegel.
[26] C. S. Liebman & E. Don-Yehiya. *Civil Religion in Israel*. California: Berkeley, 1983.
[27] Ingber.
[28] For more information on Project Zero, see http://www.pz.harvard.edu/who-we-are/about).
[29] M. Kornhaber, M. Krechevsky, & H. Gardner. "Engaging Intelligence." *Educational Psychologist*, 25(3&4) (1990): 177-199.

many students, especially those who learn well in a bodily-kinesthetic mode. With the publication of *Frames of Mind* in 1983, Howard Gardner, the father of the theory of multiple intelligences, changed the perception of the arts in educational circles.[30] In addition to the school's regular curriculum, Gardner argued that teachers should provide pathways for students' success and should look for ways to identify and build a curriculum that encourages students' use of their strengths, allowing them to express themselves through their strong and dominant intelligences. Gardner posited that it is not useful to teach students against their own natural grain of intelligence. He argued that learners need to be approached by a symbol system relevant to them and their own inclinations. Looking at learning, he claimed that "a prerequisite for a theory of multiple intelligences, as a whole, is that it captures a reasonably complete gamut of the kinds of abilities valued by human cultures." Therefore, considering the multiple intelligences potential and the value of bodily kinesthetic intelligence[31] justifies and encourages approaching content from different pathways of knowledge. This helps educators target diverse students, each having unique learning capacities.

Gardner argued that there are a number of intelligences that provide a unique profile of each person, and he laid down the criteria for each of the intelligences.[32] He underscored the way each of the intelligences allows for problem solving and knowledge demonstration through the principles that underlie each of them.[33] The following are included in these intelligences: linguistic, musical, logical-mathematical, spatial, bodily kinesthetic, personal-interpersonal, and intrapersonal. Gardner claimed that there is a connection among intelligences, the cognitive skills associated with them, and that people prefer to operate within the intelligence with which they feel most comfortable and successful.[34] The intelligences we explore in this chapter are bodily-kinesthetic intelligence, spatial intelligence and musical intelligence. Dancers need to be in tune with their bodies; they move in space and in rhythm. The audience who watches them needs to be attuned to movement, space, and to the accompanying sounds. Gardner claimed that in general, intelligences are independent of each other, and each has its own strengths and constraints. However, each person can, and most of the time is capable of, operating within more than one domain. As we see, there is an amalgam of a few intelligences that work together to make

---

[30] H. Gardner. *Frames of Mind*. New York: Basic Books, 1983.
[31] Ibid.
[32] Gardner, 73-298.
[33] Gardner, 299.
[34] Gardner, 367.

powerful and meaningful dances.[35]

What is an "intelligence"? For his purposes, Gardner defines intelligence as the ability to solve problems and to create products that are valued and are common knowledge and practice within a cultural setting.[36] Looking at culture and at human inventions, Gardner, in his most influential work about multiple intelligences, where he asserts that teaching and learning can be done through various modalities, posits that in all domains of knowledge, training and practice are necessary components of learning to accomplish a degree of fluency—which opens the ability to express ideas and emotions. It is true that one always needs some form of linguistic intelligence in order to be able to reflect upon the learning process in different domains; however, reaching out to address multiple ways of learning helps students learn and teachers teach. As teachers, we need to help students by providing them with ample opportunity to understand themselves, their actions, and to experience various feelings and emotions. Knowledge and awareness of various intelligences help us give our students these opportunities and experiences. Intelligences are always expressed in the context of specific tasks, domains, and disciplines. The intelligences are linked to content and creativity, which means the ability to solve problems in a certain way within a specific domain, in a field that is being recognized within a given culture. This process lays the groundwork for acquisition of new knowledge that has its own symbol system.[37] Often, these intelligences are being nurtured outside the context of school. In her article about the arts, Jane Remer laments the absence of the arts during the school day.[38] Jason Ohler hopes for the day the arts become the fourth R in the educational system, an idea espoused by educators who realize the importance of the arts.[39] In his essay, "In some important ways, the day only starts at 3," Richard Rothstein underscores the impact of arts classes as extracurricular activity and highlights the notion of many children who are able to shine only after school hours during extracurricular activities when they are allowed to express themselves through the arts and be creative.[40] Learning from Thomas Armstrong and Eric Jensen's respective research on the effect of adhering to knowledge of multiple intelligences and respecting the preferred tendencies of learners, educators realized that working with students by highlighting their own strengths enhances cognitive

---

[35] Gardner, 268.
[36] Gardner, 274.
[37] C. Geertze. *The Interpretation of Cultures*. New York: Basic Books, 1973.
[38] J. Remer. *Changing Schools Through the Arts*. New York: ACA, 1990.
[39] J. Ohler. "Art Becomes the Fourth R." *Educational Leadership*, 58(2) (2000).
[40] R. Rothstein. "In some important ways, the day only starts at 3." Education section. *New York Times*, January 9, 2002.

skills, improves learning and retention, and develops creativity, self-esteem and self-concept.[41] Additionally, utilizing dance and movement tends to reduce stress, increase energy, and make learning fun.

Dance in the classroom
In my work as an educator, I seek to familiarize my students with the possibility of using creative dance as a modality of learning academic content and to introduce the possibility of learning text through dance: by doing dance and by observing dance works. By learning through dance I hope that students achieve mastery of both cognitive and affective layers of the text, of reinforcing knowledge of the content matter in an experiential way, and of establishing a connection to the emotional content of the lesson.[42] As a Jewish educator I found that through dance, learners were able to express moments of spirituality and their reactions to Jewish texts, and reflect on the essence of Jewish learning. Learning through dance can help learners observe and present divergent points of view and multiple layers of meaning simultaneously, an important aspect of all learning which highlights the ability to respect opposing and divergent points of view.

In order to teach dance, we need to consider some of the aspects we explored earlier: the theories of teaching through dance and movement. The creative process of expressing ideas through dance and movement is not a one-time event, but a continuous journey. The actual doing and practicing of improvisations in motions are just as important as the final product. Just like any other skill, dancing in a creative and original way can be learned and needs to be done regularly and practiced. The exploration of the ideas that initiate the movements and the process of putting the movements together into a phrase are the practice of being creative. Students learn that creativity is not an "awakening" to a grand idea, but a result of hard work, thoughtful and purposeful practice, and trial and error.[43] Therefore, creative dance is a process that requires mastery not only of the content, but also knowledge of the elements of dance.

Creativity needs fostering and nurturing. The teacher's belief that everyone

---

[41] T. Armstrong. *Multiple Intelligences in the Classroom*. Alexandria: ASCD, 1994; E. Jensen. *Teaching with the Brain*. Alexandria, VA: ASCD, 1998; E. Jensen. *Art with the Brain in Mind*. Virginia: ASCD, 2001.

[42] O. Backenroth. "Enriching instruction with dance," In A. F. Marcus (Ed.), *The New Jewish Teacher's Handbook*. Denver: A.R. E. Publishing, Inc., 2003.O. A. Backenroth. *The Blossom School: Teaching Judaism in an Arts-Based School* (Ed.D), Unpublished Dissertation, The Jewish Theological Seminary, New York, 2005. O. A. Backenroth. *"Weaving the arts into Jewish education," Journal of Jewish Education*, 70(3) (2005): 50-60.

[43] D. B. Wallace. and H. E. Gruber. *Creative People at Work*. Oxford: Oxford University Press, 1989.

can create new and exciting dances based on innovative and interesting ideas is a crucial aspect of the creative process. Educators need to support students by showing interest in what they create, responding positively, providing reinforcement, and giving them opportunities to discuss their creations. Teachers need to recognize and showcase the individuality and uniqueness of each student. In addition, teachers should help students articulate reasons for their choice of movements and how they combine them in dance sequences. This reinforces the creation of new movements and interpretations by giving ample time for thought and concentration and encouraging students to come up with meaningful expressions.

Teaching through dance may be done in two ways: asking students to move and explore the ways movement enriches their knowledge and understanding of the text, or asking them to observe the dance and explore how the dance they have analyzed sheds new light on the text they have learned. In both cases, teachers need to prepare students so they see the connection between the movement and the text.[44] To help students, most of whom may be new to the world of dance, and to enrich their movement vocabulary and inspire them, I teach the language of dance and give the students plenty of opportunities to experience different types of movements. Toward this end, I explore with students basic dance vocabulary so they can create new independent expressions with the movements and basic concepts of improvisation they have learned and practiced. Exposing students to some of the elements of dance such as space, time, force, levels, and patterns of movement, and explaining that dance takes the body through space in a certain way or shape, using a certain amount of effort or force, and at a certain speed or tempo, helps students feel more comfortable with movement. Gradually introducing new elements into the practice enriches their dance vocabulary and allows students to become more expressive and confident moving and dancing.[45]

The end goal of teaching dance vocabulary is to help students solve textual problems through movement. In this example it is a Bible class and the students read the first chapters of Genesis. They choose to explore Cain's murder of Abel by creating four different tableaux (a group of motionless figures representing a scene from a section of narrative). The students focus on Genesis 4:8-10.

> And Cain said to his brother Abel, "let us go out to the field."

---

[44] S. Bauer. "Dance as performance, fine art in liturgy." In D. Adams & D. Apostoplos-Cappadona (Eds.), *Dance as Religious Studies*. New York: Crossroad, 1990; Warburton, E. C. Of meaning and movements: "Re-languaging embodiment in dance phenomenology and cognition." *Dance Research Journal,* 43(2) (2011): 65-83.

[45] For more information, see also Tucker and Freeman, 1990, 1994, 1997.

And when they were in the field, Cain rose against Abel and killed him. And the LORD said to Cain, "Where is Abel your brother?" And he said, "I do not know. Am I my brother's keeper?" And He said, "What have you done? Listen! your brother's blood cries out to me from the soil!"[46]

The students were asked to study the verses carefully, identify the leading characters in the story (including objects that might be personified), play a role in a tableau (bodies frozen in a movement sequence) and investigate the relationships among them. They also consulted scholars' interpretations of the verses. The students were then to explore the movement of each of the characters. The culmination of the study was creating the four tableaux in which each of them took a turn in creating the roles of Cain, Abel, the blood, and God. Here, students experimented with movements by matching them to an idea. The students, rather than the teacher, were the choreographers, creating their own sequence in response to a stimulus. The impact on the students was powerful; students usually experience narrative only through words. Moving through the text, wearing the characters of the story on their bodies and bringing text to life,[47] allowed the students to encounter feelings of loss, anger, envy and frustration in a new experiential way. The use of dance as a means of studying sacred texts allows students to further develop their understanding of the Bible. While discussing various interpretations of the Bible, as they were formulating the moving *midrash*,[48] students were engaged in traditional forms of Biblical study namely, discussion and *chavruta*.[49] The flow of interpretation of the Bible to dance forms that were not necessarily narrative-focused forced the students to think abstractly and symbolically. The students experienced interpreting the texts in a new way that led them to internalize the meaning of the text. In my classes I have been using dance to help my learners in their study of biblical texts, showing them that just like storytelling, art and music, dance is a way of expressing knowledge and conveying conveying their thoughts and feelings about the sacred texts.

---

[46] Translation from Alter, 2004.
[47] O. Backenroth, S. D. Epstein, & H. Miller. "Bringing the Text to Life and Into Our Lives: Jewish Education and the Arts." *Journal of Religious Education*, 101(4)(2006).
[48] A traditional method of biblical interpretation dating back to the rabbinic period that still continues in traditional and contemporary forms today.
[49] A traditional form of study in pairs or small groups.

Critical observation of dance works

Welcoming audiences to dance performances at Jacob's Pillow, one of the most celebrated dance centers in the world, Executive Director Executive Director Ella Baff called the audience to dance with her. "Let's dance" were her signature opening words as she introduced each presentation of dance on the stages of this magical place in New England.[50] Obviously, the audience was not going to perform on stage. That place is reserved for the professional dancers. Baff believes that only through active personal engagement with the dancers on stage can the audience truly have a genuine experience with dance. This reflects the philosophy of John Dewey, the father of progressive education, who believed in experience as an integral part of the educational process.[51] Dewey called viewers to actively look at a work of art and to try to to emulate the artistic process of creation; similarly Baff is calling for an active observation by each member of the audience, encouraging them to experience the dance as if they are dancing themselves.

In my experience of teaching graduate students to connect forms of art and Jewish education, and to leverage their enormous potential to inspire learners about Judaism and Jewish texts, I often use dance performances to elicit responses that necessitate close observation. I always wonder how and what students learn by investigating big questions introduced by their dance observation. This work is based on the general backdrop of learning through and with the arts,[52] which encourages imaginative, metaphoric, and creative thinking as well as cultural awareness. This framework gives students of all ages the freedom to learn, express, and explore subject matter through various learning styles. Toward this end, learning in the course is scaffolded in a way that offers students an opportunity to investigate dance performances that comment on social, political and religious topics and gives them space to engage in conversation and to articulate their points of view. Unlike a painting, a dance performance is a temporal process, fleeting away as you watch it. Therefore, observation of dance needs to be well structured. There are various elements that an audience is engaged with while observing dance and movement: the visuals on stage, the physicality of the dancers, the use of space, and the relationships among the dancers. We listen to the music and notice the timing, phrasing of sequence, and dynamics of motion. The novice dance observer might be overwhelmed by the countless things to look for in a dance performance.

The process builds on the teaching of arts observation and arts appreciation,

---

[50] J. Parker. "Ella Baff, looking back on a legacy at Jacob's Pillow." *The Boston Globe*, 2017.
[51] Dewey.
[52] See, e.g., Backenroth, 2006; Burton et al., 1999; and Remer, 1990.

as Dewey[53] and Greene[54] have pointed out but begins with the art exhibit itself. In the beginning of the course, students explore a process that helps them learn how to interpret the arts.[55] To encourage original thinking and creative discussion, my starting point is the dance itself with no background information. I use the following questions: *What do I see? What do I think it is? What do I want to know?* My goal is to encourage students to learn how to describe their observations their observations, to come up with hypotheses, and to be open to research. I introduce appropriate materials such as artists' statements and biographical notes only after the students do their own research into the dance. This method allows students to form their own opinions of the dance and eventually to the topic that is being introduced through the dance.

Since we explore dance not only as a form of art but as a commentary on text, we discuss what it adds to our understanding of the text. We also reflect on the challenges of observing dance and analyzing this art form. Before jumping off to discuss the meaning of the dance and in what ways it adds to their own understanding of the text or differs from it, students are asked to respond to a series of questions that address technical aspects of dance: choreography, music, and space. Students are engaged in a method of slow learning which helps them understand that dance is a unique language and offers its own interpretation of the text.[56] For some students, observing, studying, and learning a creation of dance motivates them to try to to create a dance of their own or to try teaching dance to their fellow students. The discussions that accompany such learning allow students to form their own points of view and, at the same time, creates space enabling a deeper ability to listen to others while learning about diverse points of view, all the while increasing a tolerance of difference.

An example of such an activity is an experiential observation of a dance choreographed by Ohad Naharin, the former artistic director of the Batsheva Company. Naharin is famous for his engaging dance style known as Gaga.

The audience, from their seats, observes the stage as the lights come up, revealing a half-circle of dancers seated on folding chairs. Their number varies from 12 to 120 depending on the troupe performing the dance. Singing the traditional song *"Echad Mi Yode'a"* (Who Knows One?) from the Passover *Haggadah*, they accompany the dance along with drumming and percussive

---

[53] Dewey.
[54] M. Greene. *Releasing the Imagination*. San Francisco: Jossey-Bass, 2000; *Variations on a Blue Guitar*. New York: Teachers College Press, 2001.
[55] R. Sandell. "Form+Theme+Context: Balancing Considerations for Meaningful Art Learning." *Art Education*, 59(1) (2006): 23-37.
[56] J. Thom. *Slow Teaching: On Finding Calm, Clarity and Impact in the Classroom*. United Kingdom: John Catt Educational, 2019.

music by Ohad Naharin, and the Israeli group Tractor's Revenge. The dancers begin the dance seated on chairs. They begin to move in unison, their upper bodies bent over but moving at a fast pace, their heads swinging. They rise up for a second, lifting their arms high above their heads, only to crash to the floor and crawl back to the chairs and pull themselves up to a seated position, bent over their knees. One of the dancers is moving slightly differently, he falls down to the floor, lying flat on his belly and then pulls himself up and stands on his chair before joining the others in their sequence. The sequence, following the rhythm of the song, repeats again and again with growing intensity and elongated movement phrases as the singers sing louder and louder. Toward the end of the dance, the dancers begin to shed their clothes in a frenzy—shirts are flying in the air, ties are thrown off, shoes pile up in the center, and soon the dancers remain only in their undergarments. The dance raises many questions and comments about community, tradition, and the place of the individual within the group. Pairing the dance with a traditional song, a very familiar Passover song for every Israeli, and hearing Israeli dancers praising the name of God, adds additional meaning and raises a question about beliefs. The shedding of clothing throughout the dance brings out other questions that might connect the viewers to Jewish identity and past events in Jewish history where piles of clothes meant destruction and terror. All these questions surface as a result of a close viewing of dance and careful analysis of movement, space, sound and choreography.

Watching a video of the dance during the course serves as a powerful and emotional entry point for the students not only to observe and interpret dance but also to move them from the performance to the text and to discussions about current social and political issues. Through this experience students learn not only how to describe and analyze what they see but also to understand that the dance conveys embedded meaning. Using dance in a text-based class also underscores the fact that artists, choreographers and dancers are active participants in society and that they take a stand about real-life events, and that their art expresses a point of view either in agreement with the text, confronting it, or offering a new explanation.

Conclusion
Through skillful facilitation in a text-based class students learn that dance is an activist art form that deals with serious issues such as violence, death and hostility. Learning to observe dance enhances their learning of nonverbal cues and develops their understanding of the human body and its ability to convey messages through all its parts—torso and limbs—in addition to facial expres-

sion. Skilled observers of dance understand that dance can serve as a catalyst for expressing serious thoughts about the world. Through dance, artists and non-artists can express their opinions, criticism, and feelings about serious social, religious, and political issues in a way that allows for empathy, self-reflection, rethinking and reevaluating previously held assumptions. While observing dance might be challenging, it opens the observer to new ideas and to multiple narratives about difficult issues. Dance presents not just a story or an aesthetic experience; it is a form of public demonstration of ideas that engages the audience in an active debate and creates opportunities for witnessing embodiment of emotions, opinions, and points of view expressed through the moving body. Looking to transform my students' lives, to enhance their spirituality and make the study of Jewish texts powerful, relevant, and everlasting, I feel strongly that dance and movement enrich the lives of my learners.

Appendix
For my class, I use the following guidelines I developed during my many years of teaching students about art and education at the William Davidson School of Jewish Education. They are based on observation of visual art guidelines developed by artist and educator Renee Sandell.

Unlike a painting, a dance performance is a temporal process. There are various elements that the audience is engaged with while observing dance and movement. The audience not only sees the dancers, but notices the space, their physicality, their use of space, and the relationships among the dancers. The audience listens to the music, noticing the timing and the phrasing of the music and how it is depicted in the dance. In short, there are many things to look, see, and listen for in a dance performance.

In my unit of study, the class watches a dance on a video. The students explore the movement as an interpretation of the text and eventually characterize it as a *midrash* on the text. They discuss dance and what it adds to their understanding of the biblical story. I also encourage them to comment on the challenges of observing dance, analyzing this art form, and on their ability to create, or allow their students to create, a dance *midrash* in their own classes. I always ask the students to watch the dance twice:

1. Watch the dance for a first impression.

2. Read the guidelines and watch again.

3. Respond to the questions in the guidelines.

Guidelines to dance observation:

- Reflect on your understanding after reading the texts.
- Understanding a dance performance can be both a visual and a musical process. There are many things to look for. In this second observation we will look again at the same dance video and you will try to respond to the questions.
- What is the intent of the dance? Is it purely abstract movement, or does it tell a story? Does it convey images? Are there ideas about human relationships? Is it based on one idea?
- What is the use of space? Where are the dancers on stage? Do they center on one area or move around a lot? Are they placed symmetrically? What size are their movements? Which levels of space do they use the most? Which body parts do the most moving?
- Which kinds of energy are used? (Remember, in dance the word "energy" does not refer to how many calories the dancers are burning! It has to do with the kind or quality of movement.) Is the energy predominantly sustained, suspended, percussive, swinging, vibratory, or fall and recovery?
- What is the tempo of the dance? (This is a separate issue from the tempo of the music.) Do the dancers mostly move quickly or slowly? Are there sudden or gradual changes? Does one body part seem to express the rhythmic pattern or any accents?
- How is the dance constructed? Do you see a lot of repetition? Is there a lot of new movement? What about the group movement? Does it seem to be in unison or at odds?
- How does the dance relate to the music or to the sounds? Does the dance seem to express the music or move with the music (visualization or conversation)? Would the dance be less understandable if the music/sounds were absent? Or does the dance seem to be completely unrelated to the music/sounds (isolation)?
- How do the costumes, props, and lighting seem to relate to or affect the dance? Are they a significant part, or could they be eliminated without changing the effect of the dance?

Do they seem to complement/support or detract from the dance?
- What do you think this dance is about?
- What does the choreographer want to tell us?
- Is there a message beyond the text this dance associated itself with?

Here are some reactions from students in the class:

"For me, the course highlighted that dancers and choreographers are not only art makers but also agents of change who carry out their artistic work with a critical eye in order to stimulate debate and discussion about the public space."

"Each artistic action is a response to the artist's reality and either comes to strengthen it or challenge it."

"The methodology of first identifying what one sees, then elaborating on what one would like to know, and further re-contemplating and re-thinking about the object's symbolism and meaning, allows for structured means of analytical engagement not only with the art in the course, but with life in general."

References

Adams, D. and D. Apostolos-Cappadona, eds. *Dance as Religious Studies*. New York: Crossroad, 1990.
Agnon, Shmuel. *Only Yesterday* (Translated by Barbara Harshav), Princeton: Princeton University, 1945, 2018.
Alter, R. *The Book of Psalms*. New York: W.W. Norton, 2007.
Alter, R. *The Five Books of Moses: A translation with commentary*. New York: W.W. Norton, 2004.
Ansky, S. *The Dybbuk and other Writing*. New Haven: Yale University, 2002.
Armstrong, T. *Multiple Intelligences in the Classroom*. Alexandria: ASCD, 1994.
Backenroth, O. "Enriching instruction with dance." In A. F. Marcus (Ed.), *The New Jewish Teacher's Handbook*. Denver: A.R.E. Publishing, Inc., 2003.
Backenroth, O. A. "Weaving the arts into Jewish education." *Journal of Jewish education, 70*(3), (2005): 50-60.
Backenroth, O. A. *The Blossom School: Teaching Judaism in an Arts-Based School* (Ed.D). Unpublished Dissertation. The Jewish Theological Seminary, New York, 2005.
Backenroth, O., Epstein, S. D., & Miller, H. "Bringing the Text to Life and Into Our Lives: Jewish Education and the Arts." *Journal of Religious Education, 101*(4)(2006).
Bauer, S. "Dance as performance, fine art in liturgy." In D. Adams & D. Apostolos-Cappadona (Eds.), *Dance as Religious Studies*. New York: Crossroad, 1990.
Block, B., & Kissel, J. L. "The Dance: Essence of Embodiment." *Theoretical Medicine,* 22 (2001): 5-15.
Burton, J., Horowitz, R., & Abeles, H. *Learning in and through the arts: The issue of transference*. Paper presented at the AERA national conference, Montreal, Canada, April 1999.
Dewey, J. *Art as Experience*. New York: Perigee Books, 1934, 1980.
Duncan, I. *My Life*. New York: Norton & Company, 1927.
Eshel, R. "Dance in the Yishuv and Israel." In *Shalvi/Hyman Encyclopedia of Jewish Women*. Boston: JWA, 2021.
Feldman, Walter Zev. "Traditional Dance." The Yivo Encyclopedia of Jews in Eastern Europe, https://yivoencyclopedia.org/article.aspx/Dance/Traditional_Dance.
Gardner, H. *Creating Minds*. New York: Basic Books, 1993.
Gardner, H. *Frames of Mind*. New York: Basic Books, 1983.
Gardner, H. *Multiple Intelligences: A Theory in Practice*. New York: Basic Books, 1993.
Geertze, C. *The Interpretation of Cultures*. New York: Basic Books, 1973.
Ghert-Zand, R. "Rare Glimpse into American Dance." *The Forward*, December 14, 2011.
Goren, Y. *Fields Dressed in Dance*. Kibbutz Ramat Yochanan: Hakibbutz Hameuchad, 1983.
Greene, M. *Releasing the Imagination*. San Francisco: Jossey-Bass, 2000.
Greene, M. *Variations on a Blue Guitar*. New York: Teachers College Press, 2001.
"Hora Agadati: One of the Earliest Hebrew Folk Dances." Israelidances.com, www.israelidances.com/horaagadati.htm.
Ingber, J. B. *Seeing Israeli and Jewish Dance*. Detroit: Wayne University Press, 2011.

Jensen, E. *Art with the Brain in Mind*. Virginia: ASCD, 2001.
Jensen, E. *Teaching with the Brain*. Alexandria, VA: ASCD, 1998.
Kornhaber, M., Krechevsky, M., & Gardner, H. "Engaging Intelligence." *Educational Psychologist*, 25(3&4) (1990): 177-199.
Langer, S. K. *Problems of Art*. New York: Charles Scribner's Sons, 1957.
Liebman, C. S., & Don-Yehiya, E. *Civil Religion in Israel*. California: Berkeley, 1983.
Manor, G. *Agadati, the Pioneer of Modern Dance in Israel*. Tel-Aviv, Israel: Sifriat Poalim, 1986.
Metzger, B., & Murphy, R. (Eds.). *The New Oxford Annotated Bible*. New York: Oxford University Press, 1991.
Ohler, J. "Art Becomes the Fourth R." *Educational Leadership*, 58(2) (2000).
Orfa, O. "Behind the Move." *The Jerusalem Post*, November 11, 2005.
Parker, J. "Ella Baff, looking back on a legacy at Jacob's Pillow." *The Boston Globe*, 2017.
Remer, J. *Changing Schools Through the Arts*. New York: ACA, 1990.
Rothstein, R. "In some important ways, the day only starts at 3." Education section. *New York Times*, January 9, 2002.
Rowe, S. M. "We Dance for Knowledge." *Dance Research Journal*, 40(1) (2008): 31-44.
Sandell, R. "Form+Theme+Context: Balancing Considerations for Meaningful Art Learning." *Art Education*, 59(1) (2006): 23-37.
Scolieri, P. A. *Ted Shawn: His Life, Writings, and Dances*. Oxford, UK: Oxford University, 2019.
Siliezar, J. "Flowing together." *Harvard Gazette*, 2019.
Spiegel, N. S. "New Israeli Rituals: Inventing a folk-dance tradition." In S. J. Bronner (Ed.), *Revisioning Ritual Jewish Traditions in Transitions*. Oxford: The Littman Library of Jewish Civilization, 2011.
Thom, J. *Slow Teaching: On Finding Calm, Clarity and Impact in the Classroom*. United Kingdom: John Catt Educational, 2019.
Tucker, J. & Freeman, S. *Torah in Motion*. Denver, Colorado: A.R.E. Publishing, Inc., 1990.
Tucker, J. & Freeman, S. "Creative Movements Activities." In A. F. Marcus (Ed.), *The New Jewish Teacher's Handbook*. Denver: A.R.E. Publishing, Inc., 1994.
Tucker, J. "Dance midrash: non-narrative Torah text comes alive." *Jewish Education News* (Summer) (1997): 36-37.
Wallace, D.B. and H. E. Gruber. *Creative People at Work*. Oxford: Oxford University Press, 1989.
Warburton, E. C. "Of meaning and movements: Re-languaging embodiment in dance phenomenology and cognition." *Dance Research Journal*, 43(2) (2011): 65-83.

Circus. Nahum Gutman. Ceramic Plate.
Courtesy the Nachum Gutman Art Museum

Motor Skills, Creativity, and Cognition in Learning Physics Concepts[1]
Roni Zohar, Esther Bagno, Bat-Sheva Eylon, and Dor Abrahamson

Introduction

How can one support students in establishing relationships between their naturally developed spontaneous conceptions and the scientific conceptions learnt in school? In other words, what is the connection between naïve knowledge and disciplinary knowledge such as mechanics concepts in physics? Many studies on students' learning of mechanics, at all levels of schooling, show that students experience difficulties in comprehending concepts in this domain, often forming alternative conceptions that are based on intuitive knowledge and are incongruent with normative conceptions of physics.[2]

Physics educators have advocated active learning, beyond mere lecturing, as a method for connecting naïve and disciplinary knowledge.[3][4] Hake et al. for example, examined pre- and post-test data for more than 6,000 students in introductory physics courses and found significantly improved performance for students in classes with substantial use of interactive engagement methods involving active learning. Test scores measuring conceptual understanding were roughly twice as high in classes promoting engagement than in traditional courses.

One approach for connecting experience with conceptual knowledge is "embodiment," a cognitive science paradigm that rejects philosophical dissociations of brain and body. According to this approach, the mind is an activity distributed over the body, the environment, society, and culture.[5] Yet whereas theorists of embodied cognition seek to position sensorimotor activity as formative of all reasoning, "there is limited agreement on what the term 'embodied cognition' exactly means and to what extent 'embodiment' includes sensori-

---

[1] Reprinted with permission from *Functional Neurology, Rehabilitation, and Ergonomics*, Vol. 7, no. 3, pp. 67-76.
[2] McDermott, L. C., Redish, E.F. Resource letter: "PER-1: Physics education research." *American Journal of Physics*. 67(9) (1999): 755-767.
[3] Meltzer, D. E., Thornton, R.K. Resource letter: "ALIP–1: active-learning instruction in physics." *American Journal of Physics*. 80(3) (2012): 478-496.
[4] Hake R. R. "Interactive-engagement versus traditional methods: A six thousand-student survey of mechanics test data for introductory physics courses." *American Journal of Physics*. 66(1) (1998): 64-74.
[5] Abrahamson, D. "Embodiment and mathematics learning." In K. Peppler (Ed.), *The SAGE Encyclopedia of Out-of-School Learning*. Thousand Oaks, CA: SAGE, 247-252.

motor versus higher level cognitive function."[6] Almost a century ago, though, the Soviet cultural-historical psychologist Lev Vygotsky had already made strides in articulating the inherent sensorimotor quality of reasoning:

> Every thought associated with movement induces on its own a certain preliminary straining of a corresponding muscular system that tends to be expressed in movement. If it remains only a thought, then since this movement is not brought to fruition and is not disclosed, it remains concealed in an entirely tangible and effectual form.[7]

Educational researchers informed by embodiment theory have been building and evaluating learning environments that create opportunities for students to engage in sensorimotor problem solving as a pedagogical means of supporting conceptual development.[8] For example, Abrahamson and Trninic[9] report on a study in which embodiment theory inspired an educational design for the mathematical concept of proportional equivalence. Similarly, Scherr and collaborators have been researching a design for the physics concept of energy.[10,11] In these and other studies the role of multimodality, such as manual gesturing, has been theorized as important in mediating action, reasoning, and discourse.[12,13,14]

Educational research on embodiment, and in particular the more encompassing view of the mind, has interfaced with critical-pedagogy literature looking to expand our conceptualization of where and how learning transpires.

---

[6] Koziol, L. F., Budding, D.E., Chidekel, D. "From movement to thought: executive function, embodied cognition, and the cerebellum." *The Cerebellum*. 11(2) (2012): 505-525.

[7] Vygotsky, L.S. *Educational Psychology* (R. H. Silverman, Trans.). Boca Raton, FL: CRC Press LLC., 1997; Original work published 1926, 161.

[8] Abrahamson D., Lindgren, R. *Embodiment and Embodied Design*, 2014.

[9] Abrahamson, D., Trninic, D., Eds. "Toward an embodied-interaction design framework for mathematical concepts." *Proceedings of the 10th International Conference on Interaction Design and Children*. ACM, 2011.

[10] Scherr, R. E., Close, H. G., Close, E. W., Flood, V. J., et al. "Negotiating energy dynamics through embodied action in a materially structured environment." *Physical Review Special Topics-Physics Education Research*. 9(2) (2013): 020105.

[11] Scherr, R. E., Close, H. G., McKagan, S. B., Close, E.W., Singh, C., Sabella, M., et al. "Energy Theater: Using The Body Symbolically To Understand Energy." Aip Conference Proceedings, 2010.

[12] Hall, R., Nemirovsky, R. "Introduction to the special issue: Modalities of body engagement in mathematical activity and learning." *Journal of the Learning Sciences*. 21(2) (2012): 207-215.

[13] Scherr, R. E. "Gesture analysis for physics education researchers." *Physical Review Special Topics-Physics Education Research*. 4(1) (2008): 010101.

[14] Stephens, A.L., Clement, J. J. "Depictive gestures as evidence for dynamic mental imagery in four types of student reasoning." 2006 Physics Education Research Conference.

For example, some researchers have looked to characterize *hybrid learning environments* that bridge home and community practices, identities, and experiences with school practices.[15] In designing a productive hybridity one needs "to ensure that ongoing emergent hybrid practices are guided in ways that promote disciplinary learning goals."[16] In the present study, a dance studio was used as a hybrid environment for embodied learning.

Embodied pedagogy in this study
In this article we describe two case studies of 10th-grade high school students learning the complicated physics concepts of balance and angular velocity. The students participated in a physics course based on the embodied pedagogy described below. The case studies track the students' experiences throughout the course, culminating with their summative projects. The summative projects were delivered in a variety of modalities, such as video art, music, and dance. As we will report, the projects manifested deep conceptual and affective relations with the learnt material.

The learning activities in this study were based on the embodied design heuristic **"Experience first, signify later."**[7,17] That is, the rationale for the proposed design was that students might experience important opportunities to make sense of physics concepts by means of: (A) participating in activities in which they themselves enact these concepts; and then (B) reflecting on the experiences and signifying them within the semiotic register of the physics disciplinary field. In this study, students worked either individually, in pairs, or collectively on a choreographic task that gave rise to problems of coordinating movements. Solving and expressing these solutions, we argue, created significant learning opportunities.

Zohar et al.[18.] articulated the following components of an embodied pedagogy for science concepts:

A. **Directed bodily experiences** that act as a resource enabling the learner to relate complex (often abstract) ideas in physics to the learner's everyday experiences. These Informed

---

[15] Gutiérrez, K. D., Baquedano-López, P., Tejeda, C. "Rethinking diversity: Hybridity and hybrid language practices in the third space." *Mind, culture, and activity.* 6(4) (1999): 286-303.
[16] Ma, J. Y. "Designing Disruptions for Productive Hybridity: The Case of Walking Scale Geometry." *Journal of the Learning Sciences.* 1-37. (2016): 338.
[17] Abrahamson, D. "Embodied design: constructing means for constructing meaning." *Educational Studies in Mathematics.* 70(1) (2009): 27-47.
[18] Zohar R., Bagno, E., & Eylon, B. "Dance and movement as means to promote physics learning." In *Proceedings of the 7th International Conference on Education and New Learning Technologies.* Barcelona: EDULEARN15, 2015, 6881-6885.

Figure 1. An example of improvisation in movement, a component of the embodied pedagogy.

Figure 2. An example of relaxation, a component of the embodied pedagogy.

(All photos courtesy of Dr. Roni Zohar.)

Movements[19] are designed to enhance students' visualization of a new idea as well as its analysis, expression, and actualization. One example is the "collective circular activity" described in the case study of learning angular velocity (see below).

B. **Improvisation in movement** mediates between imaginative reasoning, body actions, and feelings (fig. 1). How this mediation is carried out is described in the case studies below.

C. **Techniques combining walking with talking.**[20] For example, following an improvisation involving circular movements with different parts of the body, students are asked to walk in the studio and think to themselves about circular movements in real life and nature. Then, the students talk with each other about their answers and share ideas with the plenum.

D. **Selected aspects of the Feldenkrais method**[21] intended to increase body awareness and emphasize its connection with physical phenomena. For example in the balance case study we used Feldenkrais exercises related to the issue of stability.

---

[19] Shoval, E. "Using mindful movement in cooperative learning while learning about angles." *Instructional Science.* 39(4) (2011): 453-466.
[20] Science choreography project. Available from: http://sciencechoreography.wesleyan.edu/.
[21] Feldenkrais, M., Eshkol, N. *50 Lessons by Dr. Moshe Feldenkrais.* Israel: Movement Notation Society, 1980.

E. **Relaxation**, for example lying on the floor and using belly breathing (Fig 2.).

The first author acted as the instructor for the lessons described in this paper. Videography of the activities in the case studies was analyzed to track for the emergence and establishment of multimodal actions and utterance that, we conjecture, serves to ground the curricular content in physical movement. We argue that our narratives document individual contributions to, and evolutions through, a classroom sociogenesis of new semiotic bundles, where conceptual meanings are collectively grounded in consensual multimodal referents from shared experiences.

The balance case study
The purpose of this study was to investigate how dance students learn about the physical concept of balance within the framework of dance. We were inspired by Laws' work with dancers[22] to teach students to distinguish between steady and unsteady balance positions. Towards this goal, students became acquainted with conditions for maintaining balance in relation to the constructs of "area of support" and "center of mass."

The students learnt that "Area of Support is the space confined within the perimeter around all the body's contact points with the floor. For example, fig. 3 illustrates the area of support for a standing position with both feet on the floor.

The first author acted as the instructor for the lessons described in this paper. Videography of the activities in the case studies was analyzed to track for the emergence and establishment of multimodal actions and utterance that, we conjecture, serves to ground the curricular content in physical movement. We argue that our narratives document individual contributions to, and evolutions through, a classroom sociogenesis of new semiotic bundles, where conceptual meanings are collectively grounded in consensual multimodal referents from shared experiences.

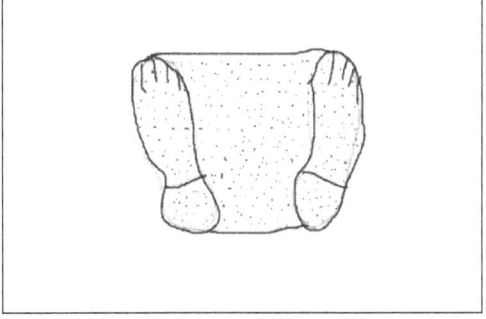

Figure 3. The 'Area of Support' is the dotted area.

---

[22] Laws, K. *Physics and the Art of the Dance.* Second edition. Oxford University Press, 2008.

Regarding the "center of mass," within the context of this case study it was impossible to provide a formal definition involving calculations. The students experienced an intuitive notion of the center of mass as the point in which the downward force of gravity appears to act on the body as a whole. In the dance world, this point is referred to simply as *the center*.

As to the conditions of balance, a person is balanced if the center of mass lies directly above a point anywhere within the area of support. In the context of dancing, the students experienced two possibilities of balance: a steady balance in which applying a force on the person does not lead to a fall, and an unsteady balance in which applying even the slightest force could lead to a fall.

The learning process

In the present research, a group of twelve 10th-grade high school female dance students participated in four consecutive lessons of 90 minutes each. The lessons were conducted in the school dance studio by the instructor using embodied pedagogy, which included a physical experience of each of the concepts prior to their academic learning in class. In the fourth and final lesson, the students were required to present a movement sequence including three balance positions and transitions between them.

The following is a short description of the lessons.

The first lesson. It began with improvisation of feeling balanced and unbalanced. The students realized the contribution of each of the touch points with the floor to their balance. Following the first experience, the instructor explained the meaning of "area of support" and pairs of students marked their partner's area of support for a given position that they formed as shown in fig. 4. In addition, the students were instructed to slightly push their partners and check whether their partners lose balance. At the end of this activity the instructor named each position as steady- or unsteady-balanced positions.

The second lesson. It began with Feldenkrais exercises (see fig. 5) dealing with stability.[20] Following the Feldenkrais exercises some students claimed that

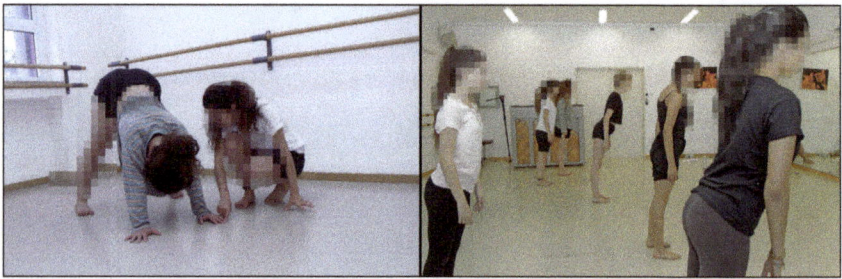

Figure 4. Practice of marking the area of support, in the balance case study.

Figure 5. Feldenkrais exercises, in the balance case study.

"when the area of support is greater, the position is more stable and therefore, it is difficult to fall". The discussion at the end of the lesson involved also cultural and emotional aspects of stability, such as stability in life, financial stability, and stability in relationships.

The third lesson. It began with improvisation. The instructor asked the students to walk around the room when the music was playing and feel the floor. She asked them to imagine that each part of their body, which she named, is like a motor that incites the rest of the body. Following this exercise, the instructor asked them to imagine the body as a small ball and to try and condense their body's weight into the ball as if the ball were the motor that incites the movement. The rationale of this activity was to encourage the students to imagine the ball as a center of mass. At the end of the movement improvisation the instructor asked students where they imagined the central ball to be in their body. Most students believed that their central abdominal area was that point, which is indeed the center of mass when standing up.

The students were surprised to realize that the center of mass is not always in their abdominal area (fig. 6), as experienced previously and depends on their position.

For example, when raising their arms over their head, the center of mass is higher than the abdomen; when moving their arms to the right, the center of mass shifts to the right. The students' greatest surprise was that the center of mass could even be exterior to their body in certain positions such as when leaning forward as shown in fig. 6. Interestingly, this fact is surprising even to professional dancers.

Following the three lessons, the instructor explained the conditions for maintaining body balance. First, she outlined with her finger a perpendicular from the center of mass to the area of support and showed that the smaller the support base, the more limited is the possibility of maintaining balance. This is the case, for example, when standing on tiptoes. Following some demonstrations with one of the students, the students practiced in pairs maintaining a

Figure 6. A - The center of mass is external to the body.
B - Practice of finding the center of mass.

Figure 7. A - Condition for balance: Practice of marking the area of support.
B - Condition for balance: Practice of finding the center of mass.

stable structure with one, two, three or four contact points. One of the students in the pair had to mark the center of mass projected directly above the area of support in the position performed by her partner as shown in fig. 7. Afterwards, the instructor asked one pair to observe another pair of students, to examine the explanation provided by the performing pair and to conduct a discussion.

The fourth lesson. The instructor asked the students to solve some movement problems related to the concept of balance. For example, the students were asked to stand with their legs adjacent to the wall and try to squat as shown in fig. 8. The students realized it was not possible and provided an explanation.

The balance summative project

At the end of the final lesson, the instructor asked the students to divide into groups and create a movement sequence of three balanced positions. After presenting the movement sequence, the students had to determine whether each position was steady or unsteady balanced. The sequential movement task comprising the three balance positions demanded creativity and reflection. The positions chosen by each student were unique for each pair of students, who

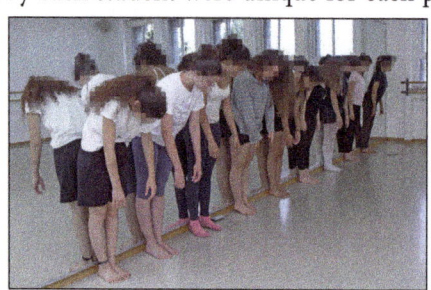

Figure 8.
An example of a movement problem.

Motor Skills, Creativity, and Cognition in Learning Physics Concepts · 191

Figure 9. From the movement sequence: Two pairs of students (A, B) show a position, judge it as steady balanced or unsteady balanced.

presented their movement sequence, including transitions from each position to the next.

In fig. 9a a student explains how the position demonstrates a balance condition. She explained that the area of support is only the foot and showed how the imaginary perpendicular line projects directly from the center of mass point to the area of support. The students showed how swaying forward and backward would not affect the dancer's balance, since the center of mass is still directly above the foot's area of support. Although a movement forward or backward would not cause the dancer to lose balance, the students still defined the position as an unsteady-balance position due to its volatile nature.

In fig. 9b the students explained that although the area of support is relatively wide and includes both feet, the student turned her waist in such a position, which shifted the center of mass to the peripheral area of support in the outer edge of her left foot. Any slight movement of the dancer to the left would have thrown her off balance and therefore this position was categorized as unsteady-balance position.

Movements sequence (figs. 10a-f) of a pair of students and their explanations. The pictures were extracted from the video of the students' presentation. The students chose to elaborate three balance positions (figs. 10a, 10d, & 10f). The students used physical terminology, motor skills, and gestures in their summative projects. They used the terms steady balance and unsteady balance correctly in their work and used body gestures to explain these terms, such as pointing to the center of mass point, to the area of support, and to the imaginary perpendicular line connecting them. An interesting finding was the students' differentiation of a *highly/totally unsteady balance position* as shown in fig. 10f and *relative unsteady balance positions*, which were less unsteady as shown in fig. 10a and fig. 10c.

Frame	Judgment	Explanation of the student
 A	Unsteady balance	Despite the wide area of support, which includes both hands and a foot, the center of mass is situated in the outer rim of the area of support and a slight movement would result in the dancer's loss of balance. Although the position is relatively stable, any movement toward her arms would still maintain the center of mass above the area of support; however, any movement to other directions would result in a loss of balance.
 B	Unsteady balance	Transitional position. This position was not part of the three dance sequence positions required in the project but was a transitional position mandatory when shifting to the next position as shown in fig. 10d. The dancer lost balance when setting her leg down while shifting to the next position.
 C	Unsteady balance	Transitional position when shifting to the next position as shown in fig. 10d.
 D	Steady balance	The area of support surrounds both feet when standing in a straddle stance, and the center of mass still remains above the rim of the area of support even in case of slight movements. It is only if the dancer is pushed vigorously forward that she may lose her balance.
 E	Highly unsteady balance	The center of mass is at the very rim of the area of support.
 F	Highly unsteady balance	In order to remain in this position, she is required to move her arms from behind her back to the front, thus shifted slightly the center of mass. This action assisted in maintaining the center of mass above the area of support.

Figure 10. Movements sequence (Figure 10a-f) of a pair of students and their explanations.

The angular velocity case study

The pedagogical goal in this case study was to teach physics students the difference between linear velocity and angular velocity. Angular velocity was taught within the topic of circular motion. Attached is an example depicting the difference between the two concepts.

In fig. 11, Points A & B are advancing along a circular path in a clockwise direction from time Point 1 to time Point 2. Point A is advancing from A1 to A2, and Point B from B1 to B2. Point B must travel a greater distance (the length of the long arch in fig. 11) compared to the distance that point A travels (the length of the short arch in fig. 11) during the same time. The distance that the two points must travel per time is called linear velocity. Linear velocity is defined as the linear displacement over time. The linear velocity of Point B is greater than the linear velocity of Point A.

Angular velocity is defined as the angular displacement over time of a body in a circular path. The angular velocity of Points A and B moving from their respective Point 1 to Point 2 are the same, because the segments connecting each of the points to the center of the circle advance at the same time in the same angle (in fig. 11, the angle is 60°).

The learning process

The concept of linear velocity was studied during a regular physics class in a standard classroom setting. The concept of angular velocity was taught as part of embodied-pedagogy classes in a dance studio by the instructor of this research. These students were all female art students in various disciplines (art, video art, music, or dance). The research study lasted four months. During this period, each student met with the instructor for a total of seven hours. Some of these meetings were done in groups and some individually. At the end of the process, the students were required to submit a final project in groups, each in her own creative modality, on the topic of angular velocity. They had a month

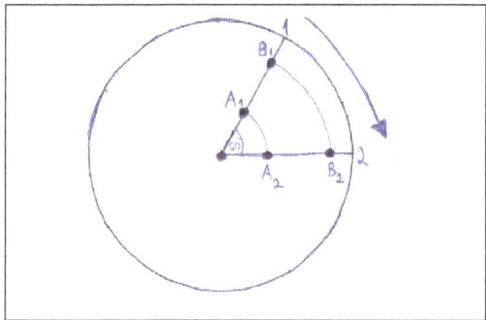

Figure 11. A model manifesting the difference between linear velocity and angular velocity.

Figure 12. Enacting angular velocity by walking around a fixed-point, in the collective circular activity.

to prepare the final project, which will be described and analyzed in depth. The following is a short description of the learning process.

Working in a dance studio, the learning process begins with improvisation in circular movements on different body parts, where the instructions were: "Move your hands in circular way, move your head in circular way; your feet; your hip," and so on. Students may move their limbs as they wish, such as varying movement size and rate. After the improvisation, the students were asked to stand alongside each other in row formation, and a bottle was positioned to the left of the left-most person (see fig. 12).

The students were asked to walk around the bottle, keeping the row intact, which the students interpreted as a straight line. After some trial and error, the students negotiated a collective method to circle the bottle together, with those farther away from the bottle walking faster.

During a discussion of the collective circular activity, described above, the instructor lodged her elbow in the floor as a pivot and rotated her forearm. Specifically, the instructor marked the collective motion of individual dancers along a shared radius as shown in fig. 12. She thus juxtaposed the students' common angular velocity vs. their unique linear velocities. The instructor, herself a dancer, thus used "marking" (a miniaturized version of the full-body movement) as shown in fig. 13. Marking, typically serves dancers "as an anchor and vehicle for thought,"[23] for individual and collective reflection, instruction, and planning of action.

Next, the instructor and students sat on the floor to reflect on the activity. Finally, the instructor asked the students to use paper and pencil to create a representation of the movement in the collective circular activity.

One month after the lessons, the students participated in 20-50 min. clinical interview, which included: (a) a request to draw the collective circular activity and explain the drawings; and (b) a paper-and-pencil physics question, which the students were asked to answer orally. The question concerned the difference between linear and angular velocity. Of the 11 students, 9 succeeded in an-

---

[23] Kirsh, D. *Thinking with the Body.* 2010, 2864.

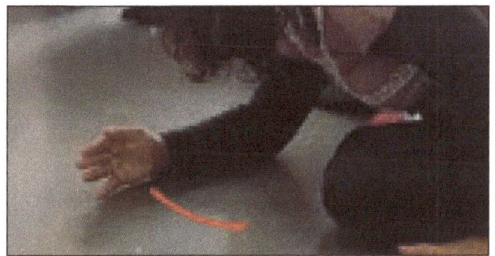

Figure 13. The use of marking referring to the collective circular activity by the instructor.

swering the paper-and-pencil question during the clinical interviews. Of these 9 students, 5 gestured with their forearm, similar to the instructor's marking during the intervention (see fig. 14).

An extended description of the role of the marking in the angular velocity case study in the context of the embodied pedagogy is described elsewhere.[24]

One month after the interviews, the students participated in a concluding lesson, and then each student was asked to explain the concept of angular velocity to three science students from a lower grade, in any way they chose. Of the 8 students who were asked to explain the angular velocity concept to younger students, 7 chose to ask them to stand up and experience the concept of angular velocity in a manner similar to the collective circular activity. All the learning process was videotaped as preparation for micro ethnographic analyses of the multimodal interactions.[25]

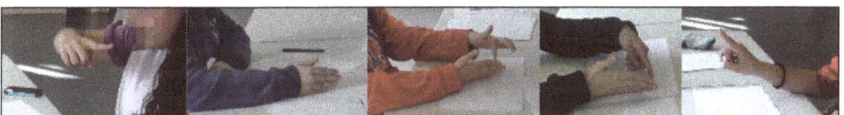

Figure 14. The use of gestures analogous to the instructor's marking.

The angular velocity summative project

At the end of the entire learning process the instructor asked the students to prepare summative projects: "Prepare with one or two partners a creative project associated with the concept of angular velocity." The students had a month to work on the project and were told that they would discuss their project with the class.

We now describe four summative projects. We will provide a detailed description of a video art project of two students.

---

[24] Zohar, R., Bagno, E., Eylon, B., Abrahamson, D. "From collective choreography to angular velocity by leveraging marking and discourse." Paper presented at JURE, Finland. 2016.
[25] Goodwin, C. "Action and embodiment within situated human interaction." *Journal of Pragmatics.* 32(10) (2000):1489-1522.

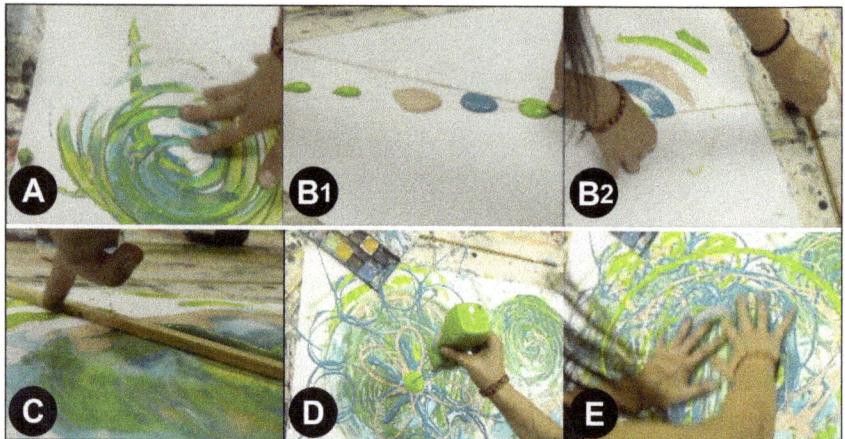

Figure 15. Frames extracted from the original video created by two students. They used water colors, paper, a thread, a stick, their hands, and music lyrics suited for the topic of circular motion.

Project 1.

Two physics students, one of them an Art major and one a Film major, prepared a video clip for the project. fig. 15 presents some frames from the video clip. The video clip can be accessed at http://goo.gl/rFVEmk. The students chose the video clip of "Total Eclipse of the Heart" by Bonnie Tyler. When the words "turn around" in the chorus are played, one of the student trickles drops of paint from a bottle to a paper surface and paints with her finger circles on the paper.

The music then shifts to the Beach Boys song, "I Get Around", and while the music is played the student sprinkles circles on another paper from paint bottles at fixed distances from each other. She then takes a thread (as seen in fig. 15b1) and moves it in circular motion, as seen in fig. 15b2. She then repeats the action with a stick in place of the thread (fig. 15c). The student pours water colors and draws flowers (fig. 15d), and finally she mixes the colors using her hands on the paper in circular motions, as seen in fig. 15e.

The activity done by the students with paint, thread and stick was analogous to the collective circular activity in the dance studio, in which the colors correspond to the students in each circle marked by a different color. Like the collective circular activity, each color used in the project marked a different circle and a different linear velocity. The thread and stick enabled demonstration of the angular velocity, which remains the same for all the differently colored circles. Unlike the elbow-pivot marking, in which the forearm stands in for an undifferentiated student collective, the hand's motion also enables to articulate individual students with individual fingers, thus accentuating the conceptual tension between linear and angular velocity.

Figure 16. Frames extracted from the "circle of life" dance created by two students. They moved on a circle drawn on the studio floor with background music related to circles.

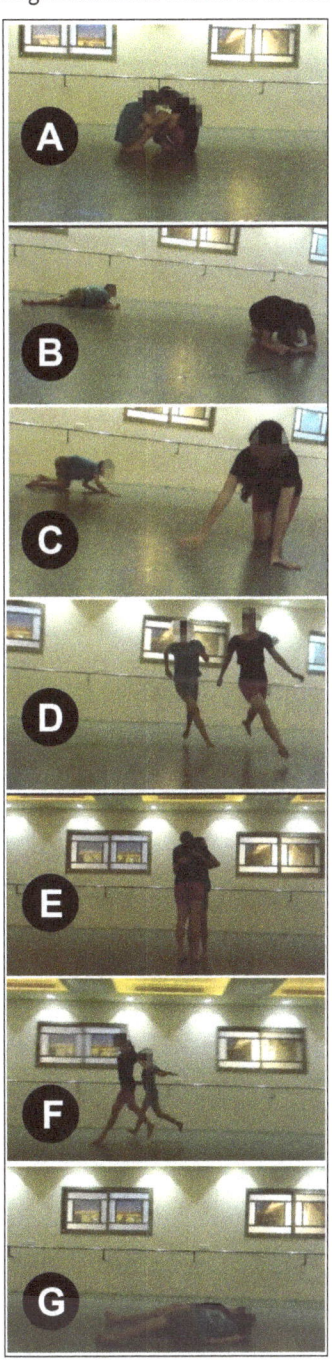

When presenting the video clip, the students explained that they used the same amount of colors for all circles. They claimed that "the color of the outer circle, which is set farthest from rotation axis to which the thread and stick were affixed[by the student]is used up faster, since it is the largest circle and therefore creates the greatest arch." They further explained that "the color which is farthest from the rotation axis has a greater linear velocity compared to the other colors which are closer to the circle's rotation axis. In fact, all colors as well as the paint drops on the thread or on the stick have the same angular velocity." The activity and the students' oral explanation correspond to the difference between linear and angular velocity as seen in fig. 11.

The students clearly incorporated their personal viewpoint and interests in their project. The art students chose to use paint, whereas the video and photography student in the group chose to use her art skill in filming and editing to document the work. The students had the freedom to choose how to present their project and they chose paint, thread, stick, and music. All students reported that they enjoyed working on the project.

Project 2.

Two physics students, one a Music major and one a Dance major, presented for their final project a dance they named "The Circle of Life." Selected photographs from the dance are presented in fig. 16. The dance was choreographed to the song "Circles" by the Israeli composer and singer Idan Raichel. The girls first presented the dance, followed by an explanation. The students explained that the opening position (fig. 16a) portrays an embryo and the final laying position portrays death (fig. 16G). Following the first position, the girls crawled and walked on a circle drawn on the studio floor (fig. 16b) then they stood up and began running (fig. 16d). At first, each student ran separately and later they embraced (fig. 16e) and ran while holding hands (fig. 16f). The students explained that running separately represents the period when each person is single before finding a spouse with whom they continue their life. The coupled run was along two concentric circles representing the individuality of each person within the couple, whereas holding hands represented their unity. The girl dancing in the outer circle explained that she has to run faster and in larger steps in order to keep up with her partner and claimed that "This represents the co-existence of living with your spouse."

At the end of the dance the circles are cut short and the students lay on the floor in the final position symbolizing death.

In this project, we see the students' explicit understanding of the concepts of angular velocity in the coupled run with their hands spread out. In this run, the students claimed that "each one has their own linear velocity and together they share the same angular velocity."

In addition to the understanding of the two concepts the students linked the concepts to real life by analogizing angular velocity to real life as a couple, and linear velocity to life as an individual within a couple. The girls linked the physical concepts regarding circular motion to the notion of the circle of life from birth until death through family life. The dance position chosen for the dance, the music accompanying the dance, and the story revolving around the dance are tightly linked to the embodied pedagogy and the taught concepts. One can recognize in the dance the influence of the collective circular activity in which these students had participated during the embodied pedagogy lessons.

The students ran side by side similar to the circular walk done in the collective circular activity. The students exhibited creativity and a profound understanding of the concepts taught and linked it to their personal world and interest.

Projects 2 & 3.

Fig. 17 depicts artifacts from two more physics projects presented by an Art major and Music major. Unlike the other projects, these students chose to present a model.

The students who made a painted log as shown in fig. 17a, explained: "We selected a log because one can see the age of the tree. You can only see it after the tree is cut and its life ended. The circles created while the tree grows tell us its life story. We decided to add color which adds beauty to the tree life story and this is the way we chose to "thank" the tree for its contribution to humanity.

On the small tree trunk we painted a color mandala created by several circles, while on the larger trunk we created a spiral made of numerous colorful small dots, which represent the growth of the tree." The students who made the olive harvest as shown in fig. 17b, explained: "We imagine people around the paper roll who squeeze the olives."

All the summative projects manifest a clear learning process by the students. The students drew from the physical concepts as well as from cultural and emotional perspectives. All students created interesting projects that incorporated their personal skills, interests, and abstract understanding of life, while linking them to the conceptual knowledge targeted by the science curriculum. We argue that our narratives document individual contributions to, and evolutions through, a classroom sociogenesis of new semiotic bundles, where conceptual meanings are collectively grounded in consensual multimodal referents from shared experiences. We believe the embodied pedagogy enabled the composition of these highly complex projects presented by the students.

Conclusion and discussion

What are best practices for leveraging full-body activity as a means of supporting physics learning? The case studies presented in this article illustrate how this can be achieved through the interplay between the student's naïve sensorimotor knowledge and disciplinary knowledge promoted by an embodied pedagogy. This constructivist pedagogy involves physical-dynamical engagements: directed bodily experiences ("informed movements"); improvisation in movement mediating between imagining and reasoning, body actions, and feelings; techniques combining walking and talking; selected aspects of the Feldenkrais method; and relaxation. The movement activities were carried

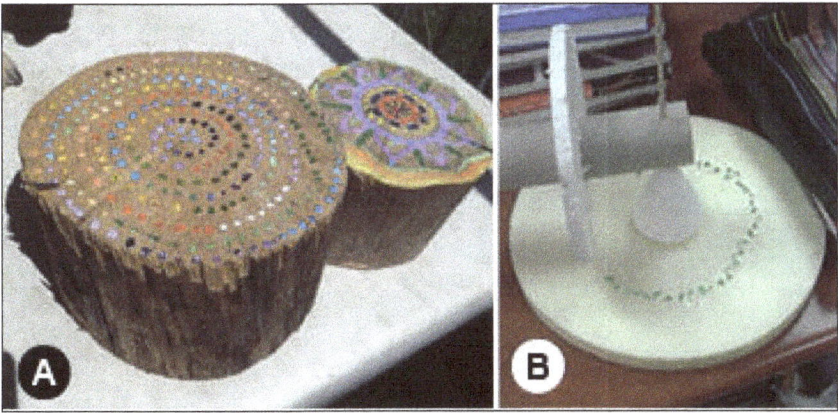

Figure 17. A - A painted log by two students.
B - An olive harvest by two students.

out in a dance studio, which acted as a hybrid learning environment enabling students to connect their artistic interests and talents to school learning. The realization of these connections is a desirable feature of hybrid environments. In the present study, the embodied pedagogy was fitted to a dance studio, but it can be appropriate to sport halls or even an empty classroom.

The case studies analyzed and interpreted summative projects that students carried out after completing the learning modules. Students' summative projects were delivered in a variety of modalities, such as video, art, music, and dance, and included inscriptions and enactment of selected elements from the movement activities. For example, the final projects in the angular velocity case study were influenced directly from the collective circular activity enacted in the embodied-pedagogy lesson, which they had experienced.

In both case studies the students exhibited creativity and a profound understanding of the abstract concepts taught. They linked the ideas to concrete representations, to their personal world and to their private interests. The complexity of the balance and angular velocity concepts is apparent from the learning process described in the case studies. The depth and insight of physics understanding that the students manifested in the summative projects are much beyond what can be achieved in regular instruction. Some of the notions that the students discovered are surprising even to experts. In addition, the students also demonstrated affective life-philosophy relations with the subject matter (e.g., cycle of life and death). Corroborating principles of embodied design, this study has supported the plausibility of STEM (science, technology, engineering, and mathematics) curricula in which: (a) abstract concepts are designed as grounded in sensorimotor problem solving; and (b) multimodal reflective expression plays a key role in raising experiences to collective consciousness and couching insights in disciplinary forms.

Acknowledgement
The first author would like to thank the Israeli students who participated in the study.

References

Abrahamson, D. "Embodied design: constructing means for constructing meaning." *Educational Studies in Mathematics.* 70(1) (2009): 27-47.
Abrahamson, D. "Embodiment and mathematics learning." In K. Peppler (Ed.), *The SAGE Encyclopedia of Out-of-School Learning.* Thousand Oaks, CA: SAGE, 247-252.
Abrahamson D., Lindgren, R. *Embodiment and Embodied Design*, 2014.
Abrahamson, D., Trninic, D., eds. "Toward an embodied-interaction design framework for mathematical concepts." *Proceedings of the 10th International Conference on Interaction Design and Children.* ACM, 2011.
Feldenkrais, M., Eshkol, N. *50 Lessons by Dr. Moshe Feldenkrais.* Israel: Movement Notation Society, 1980.
Goodwin, C. "Action and embodiment within situated human interaction." *Journal of Pragmatics.* 32(10) (2000):1489-1522.
Gutiérrez, K. D., Baquedano-López, P., Tejeda, C. "Rethinking diversity: Hybridity and hybrid language practices in the third space." *Mind, culture, and activity.* 6(4) (1999): 286-303.
Hake, R. R. "Interactive-engagement versus traditional methods: A six thousand-student survey of mechanics test data for introductory physics courses." *American Journal of Physics.* 66(1) (1998): 64-74.
Hall, R., Nemirovsky, R. "Introduction to the special issue: Modalities of body engagement in mathematical activity and learning." *Journal of the Learning Sciences.* 21(2) (2012): 207-215.
Kirsh, D. *Thinking with the Body.* 2010.
Koziol, L. F., Budding, D.E., Chidekel, D. "From movement to thought: executive function, embodied cognition, and the cerebellum." *The Cerebellum.* 11(2) (2012): 505-525.
Laws, K. *Physics and the Art of the Dance.* Second edition. Oxford University Press, 2008.
Ma, J. Y. "Designing Disruptions for Productive Hybridity: The Case of Walking Scale Geometry." *Journal of the Learning Sciences.* 1-37. (2016).
McDermott, L. C., Redish, E.F. Resource letter: "PER-1: Physics education research." *American Journal of Physics.* 67(9) (1999): 755-767.
Meltzer, D. E., Thornton, R.K. Resource letter: "ALIP–1: active-learning instruction in physics." *American Journal of Physics.* 80(6) (2012): 478-496.
Scherr, R. E. "Gesture analysis for physics education researchers." *Physical Review Special Topics-Physics Education Research.* 4(1) (2008): 010101.
Scherr, R. E., Close, H. G., Close, E. W., Flood, V. J., et al. "Negotiating energy dynamics through embodied action in a materially structured environment." *Physical Review Special Topics-Physics Education Research.* 9(2) (2013): 020105.
Scherr, R. E., Close, H. G., McKagan, S. B., Close, E.W., Singh, C., Sabella, M., et al. "Energy Theater: Using The Body Symbolically To Understand Energy." Aip Conference Proceedings, 2010.
Science choreography project. Available from: http://sciencechoreography.wesleyan.edu/.

Shoval, E. "Using mindful movement in cooperative learning while learning about angles." *Instructional Science*. 39(4) (2011): 453-466.

Stephens, A.L., Clement, J. J. "Depictive gestures as evidence for dynamic mental imagery in four types of student reasoning." 2006 Physics Education Research Conference.

Vygotsky, L.S. *Educational Psychology* (R. H. Silverman, Trans.). Boca Raton, FL: CRC Press LLC., 1997; Original work published 1926.

Zohar R., Bagno, E., & Eylon, B. "Dance and movement as means to promote physics learning." In *Proceedings of the 7th International Conference on Education and New Learning Technologies*. Barcelona: EDULEARN15, 2015, 6881-6885.

Zohar, R., Bagno, E., Eylon, B., Abrahamson, D. "From collective choreography to angular velocity by leveraging marking and discourse." Paper presented at JURE, Finland. 2016.

Circus Parade, ca. 1930-1940. Abel Pann (Pfeffermann). Ink on paper.
Photo: The Bezalel Karkiss Index of Jewish Art, Center for Jewish Art, The Hebrew University of Jerusalem.

On Movement and Learning

Roni Zohar[1]

"Movement is the door to learning" (Denison, 2011); but to me, movement is learning. In the wake of the Corona virus pandemic, there has developed an awakening, both in and outside the State of Israel, seeking the incorporation of movement-based exercises in learning and instruction. The proliferation of videoconferencing technology coupled with increased confinement at home has contributed to the lack of movement—adding to the burdens of social isolation, distancing, and anxiety. These difficulties affect learners of all levels as well as the community at large, and there is a sense that the community and the educational system are now more open than they once were to embracing new ideas. Movement, whether or not we feel or acknowledge that it has been lacking, has been recognized as an important and basic need for us all, and most certainly to the community of learners. Movement influences both body and soul and is indispensable—these days, more than ever.

In this article, we will explore movement-based exercises suitable for every learner of every age and every walk of life. I recommend that such exercises be incorporated into any lecture/lesson lasting more than 45 minutes, into everyday life, and into online meetings in general. These exercises will be helpful in providing breaks and enhancing concentration, motivation, stress reduction, regeneration, relaxation, and fun. Some of the exercises are familiar from research literature, particularly in the behavioral sciences; some are drawn from experts in a variety of disciplines such as brain research and sports; others are inspired by a variety of philosophers and Jewish thinkers. What these exercises all have in common is my personal experience with them, with my own body and mind, and the reactions of students, teachers, and the women with whom I work.

About me and my research
The idea of a connection between movement and learning has been in my thoughts and my body for years. My experience with teaching physics in university settings and while preparing for matriculation, the guidance of groups of women with movement improvisation, and my personal experience integrating science and dance, led me to research and think about the potential integration of physical experiences into learning. In the doctoral program in the Department of Science Teaching in the Weizmann Institute in collaboration with the

---
[1] Translated by Joseph Prouser and Ora Horn Prouser.

Education Department at the University of California-Berkeley, we created and researched embodied pedagogy for learning physics (Zohar, 2015). We showed that physical movement, beyond the personal/communal experience, can advance the understanding of scientific concepts and can even influence creativity (Zohar et al., 2017). The findings of my doctoral work were also presented in the video clip of my dance that won in the category of "Dance Your Doctorate" that the journal *Science* organizes each year.[2]

In the last three years, from the time I finished my doctorate, I formulated and conducted academic courses on the topic of movement, science, and learning, and I conducted teacher training with the goal of assimilating the educational approach, embodied pedagogy, in Israel: in schools, institutions of higher learning, and in informal settings. The desire was to facilitate a significant change in educational methods in the sciences and in general. In the context of my postdoctoral work in the Neurobiology Department at the Weizmann Institute, under the direction of Ehud Ahissar and Atan Gross, I used tools to track student eye movements during the delivery of embodied pedagogy. I tried to reveal interesting patterns from the area of vision that constitute insight into the human brain with the goal of establishing a correlation between findings about the behavior of those who learn in this way and scientific findings about the brain and vision.

On the importance and necessity of movement for learners
In his article, Katz (2020) addresses the restriction of movement while sitting in classes during lengths of time, and about students bolting to the door with thunderous clamor when the recess bell rings. And that, as mentioned, was before the time of COVID-19:

> We all need movement, but children need movement more than adults, and among them are children who need movement a great deal more still. But the movement that is recommended during classes doesn't serve merely to satisfy that need, also causing enjoyment and happiness, and eliminating discomfort and distraction. It accomplishes all those goals while impacting on additional functioning essential to the occurrence of absorption and learning on the part of students: the necessary functions of alertness, focus, and attention.

Katz is addressing himself to two senses through which we experience move-

---
[2] https://www.youtube.com/watch?v=oLCTJQ-GCLQ

ment: the vestibular sense (which supplies information about our bodies in space and is related to the regulation of balance) and the proprioceptive sense (which supplies information and body awareness regarding the location of our limbs relative to muscles, joints, and tendons). These two senses are directly connected to the ocular system and their activation in class through movement exercises can assist with educational challenges—from the proper holding of a pencil, through body stability and the ability to pay attention. Various kinds of stress can hinder the process of learning—tension and internal stress or frequent ear infections that relate to the vestibular system. Simple movement exercises can bring about "micro-interventions" (Coulter, 1993) that can bring significant change and improvement.

Embodiment
Embodiment is a cognitive paradigm that sees the body and the mind as one entity. "We think with the body, and it is part and parcel of the processes of creativity, learning, and thinking. In Hebrew we translate the noun *embodied* as *"me'ugan guf"* (Zohar, 2015). Anyone who holds that view understands how important movement is in daily life, and especially in learning. Think about a lecture that you're listening to; have you found yourself taking notes, even if you won't even try to read them later? Movement can anchor thoughts; in this case, fingers do that. Think about people who shake their foot with quick taps while they are trying to listen. Often people think that this movement is a sign of stress and anxiety but there are people who need to move in order to pay attention. Similarly with speech, our explanation to someone else helps us to understand better, as the process of speaking is movement that uses mouth and jaw muscles. There are many for whom any amount of body activity improves understanding or creating thinking, so why not add movement to classes, offices, and anywhere that requires thinking? Even babies move before they speak, so from a developmental perspective, movement precedes everything. Our senses are based on it and connected to it, so why wouldn't we take advantage of this earliest mechanism for processing information that is deep-rooted in our bodies, and stop hiding it and limiting it?

Movement and Vision
Our senses, like our sense of sight, are based on movement. If our eyes weren't always moving we would not be able to see and gather sensory information. The more our eyes move, the more their muscles work together, and effective eye coordination allows for focus—for example, while reading. Therefore it is recommended to consciously blink—for example, when we are in front of a

computer screen. It has been shown that children who are struggling to learn will also have difficulty following a teacher's finger tracking text, for example. Usually this stems from the defective development of eye muscles because of lack of movement (Hanford, 2000). When the head and body are moving, the sense of equilibrium is activated and the eye muscles are strengthened as they respond to the movement. Children come from nursery or daycare environments, which allow space and movement, to school classrooms where they sit at desks where their body is hidden, and their eyes are usually focused in one direction: the front of the classroom and the blackboard. These limitations ignore the fact that the development of vision is connected to movement. The integration of full-body and eye exercises in class from an early age can prevent problems with vision and education and can affect students for the rest of their lives.

Movement exercises recommended for everyday life, and especially for learning

These exercises are recommended for every age and every setting (outside, in the classroom, or on a video call).

Brain exercises

Paul Denison began to develop brain games/exercises in 1970 in the context of his attempts to solve personality problems related to visual difficulties and dyslexia. He helped children and adults for 19 years in the Remedial Group Learning Center in California. The brain exercises (around 46 of them) are simple and delicate and were intended to broaden and establish the neural network that connects the right and left hemispheres of the brain. In his exercises he joined pioneering researchers in the field of sensorimotor training. In 1987 the Educational Kinesiology Foundation was established and throughout the world many behavioral studies were conducted based on brain exercises with impressive results in the improvement of reading, writing, alertness, and math skills, and the ability to concentrate among students in mainstream and special education. The brain exercises also had great influence in the fields of sports, music, dance, and every kind of art, and they contributed to improvements in achievement (Hanford, 2000). The beauty of the brain exercises is in the ease of their implementation: you can do them any time, anywhere, and they're easy to do.

Figure 1. *Figure 2.*

Exercise crossing elbow to knee

Each elbow touches the opposite knee in turn. If it is too difficult, you can touch the opposite knee with the hand. It is recommended to do the exercise at a medium to slow rate a number of times for one-and-a-half to two minutes (fig. 1).

Exercise crossing behind the back, hand to foot

A variation of the original crossing exercise, but it is done behind the back, with the palm of each hand touching the sole of the opposite foot in turn. It is recommended to do this exercise a number of times for one-and-a-half to two minutes (fig. 2).

Another variation to the crossing exercises is touching the hands to the opposite shoulders or feet. Every touch by the right side to the left side of the body or by the left side to the right side of the body is positive; these exercises are also effective while sitting or lying down.

Figure 3.   Figure 4.   Figure 5.

Yoga crossing exercise

With arms and legs crossed, intertwine your fingers, (fig. 3) turning your hands in the direction of your chest and placing your hands upon your chest (fig. 4). If it is hard to stand, bend your knees a bit, and of course take deep breaths throughout. It is recommended to switch the sides of your hands and feet (the palm of the hand that was above will now be below. The sole of the foot that was above will now be below.) You can also do this exercise sitting or lying down. It is good to stay in the final position for one-and-a-half to two minutes (figs. 5 and 6).

Figure 6.

The infinity exercise

My favorite exercise is drawing the infinity symbol (the figure eight horizontally) with my hands. This exercise also works on the concept of crossing the midline of the body, the two hemispheres of the brain. In the fundamental exercise, you draw the infinity symbol with your hand, following the hands with your eyes. You should "draw" the infinity symbol in the air. The movement should be as large as you can make it, and the middle of the symbol, the point where the two circles touch, should be at the center of the body. You can do the movement with one arm, and then with the other arm, and then with both arms together. I like to do the movement without following with my eyes, and actually to dance the pleasant, meditative movement accompanied by music (fig. 7). An addition that can enhance this exercise is to add some sort of silent positive mantra while you do the infinity movement in a large continuous motion. If there is a repetitive movement that we enjoy, accompanying that movement with a positive thought or mantra can affect us in a positive way. It is not appropriate for everyone or for all times, but it can help. It is recommended to repeat this exercise a number of times for one-and-a-half to two minutes each time.

You can scribble the infinity symbol in a notebook when you are bored or even in an unsettled state (with a repetitive movement). There is a story from one of the teachers who followed this suggestion. A girl in a physics class sat for a test and started to cry, saying she didn't know how to start the test. The teacher suggested that the student draw the infinity symbol over and over and to follow the shape with her pen, and it worked! The girl returned to focus and to the test. I will not forget that teacher's description: she said that she herself became stressed by the girl's crying and suddenly remembered my suggestions. She had been very skeptical about them, but when she suggested this exercise to the girl and it worked, the teacher was pleasantly surprised.

Figure 7.

Exercise pulling the ears

A simple brain exercise: Grab your ears with both of your hands and pull them in all directions. Touching an area that we are not accustomed to touching frequently stimulates parts of the brain and can add new neural pathways in the brain. The exercise reminds us of photos from the past where teachers pulled the ears of misbehaving students so that they would pay better attention, as if to open their ears. I don't think they knew that it could help with attention; but when we do it to ourselves, it seems to help. You can do this exercise in a meeting, at a lecture, and certainly during videoconferencing where now and then we can turn off the camera and move by ourselves. It is recommended to do this several times for one-and-a-half to two minutes each time (fig. 8).

Exercises for the improvement of one's mood immediately and lessening of tension and anxiety

Victory exercise

A wonderful feature of our brain is that it's elastic and can change all the time. If we decide to learn to play the piano as adults, or to join our children in a game on PlayStation, and we use our fingers in ways that we are not used to, our brains will also change. Similarly, if we were to look at the brain from the inside, we would see that the part of the brain that controls our fingers will be physically bigger than it was before we practiced the new skill. It will have more neural connections. Sometimes we want to "deceive" our brain for a short time and to confuse it about reality and imagination. If we assume a specific body position like the victory stance (fig. 9), and if we want to add a "Got it!" "Thanks!" or any word, phrase, or freeing yell or sound that relates to the movement verbally or mentally, then our brain/body will feel and act as if it really won. The brain will secrete the same chemicals (endorphins and adrenaline, for

Figure 8. *Figure 9.*

example) as it would on the occasion of an actual victory. This movement can help immediately in situations of stress, sorrow, and even anxiety. From personal experience, it helps! Many practitioners and coaches recommend doing this stance before job interviews, tests, or times of anxiety. It is an important tool for all of us to keep handy.

Clapping hands 7x7

The exercise of clapping hands is an exercise for which the inspiration came from Rabbi Nachman of Bratslav who wrote that "melodies and clapping hands sweeten laws" (*Likutei Moharan* part 1 Torah). In this exercise I try to clap my hands seven times in a row, wait a second, and then to continue to clap seven times. The exercise is freeing and fun, and as in the crossing-the-midline exercises, connects between the right side and the left side of the body. In this exercise there is a connection among touch, movement, and sound.[3]

Soft taps with fingertips on head, face, and chest

In this exercise we use our fingertips to lightly tap the head, forehead, under the eyes, under the nose, on the chin and chest, and, optionally, the armpits (from experience, many teachers, especially of adolescent students, prefer to skip the armpits because of issues of embarrassment, but it's a personal decision). The full exercise was taken from Emotional Freedom Technique (EFT), a technique to release emotion based on channels of energy known in Chinese medicine as the meridian system. According to Chinese medicine, the body has 12 main channels of energy (meridians) that feed the life energy of the different organs both physically and emotionally. In this technique we tap on those areas, as in acupuncture; but instead of needles, we use fingertips. In this technique itself we also use positive and empowering sentences, as you can add a positive thought or an empowering sentence in all these exercises. But I think that even without that the movement itself frees up and helps individuals, and that can be enough. Many practitioners use it to help both physical and emotional issues that, according to this method, stem from an obstruction in the energy

---

[3] In another context, there is a quote from Rabbi Menachem Froman when he sat in Jerusalem with Yasser Arafat's representative from the editorial staff of the weekly Palestinian culture and arts magazine *Al Fajr* (*The Dawn*): "This is a place of applause, bringing together right and left, to be on the border is dangerous but something happens there, is created there." In this exercise the right connects with the left physically, just like the other brain exercises based on crossing the midline of the body. But maybe because of the inspiration from a Jewish source on clapping it is possible to also think about the spiritual connection between an individual's Sefirotic right column and left column and the balance we all seek (Hassidic texts).

Figures 10a-f

that needs to be opened through light tapping. The tapping is done in sequence and then in reverse order (figs. 10a-f). Unrelated to the technique itself, one can choose to focus tapping on an area that is the most pleasant and calming.

Conclusion

The stumbling block before those who use simple movement exercises in order to improve focus and learn is the long-held idea that the brain and the body are separate from each other. The more we adopt the embodiment approach and try to relate to our bodies and minds as one entity, the more we can improve our cognitive abilities and self-confidence, self-worth, and the ability to relieve tension. Just because an exercise is simple doesn't mean it's not effective.

Movement is necessary for healthier and happier lives and it is worth incorporating it in class time and breaks in school, and during the day for all ages. I truly hope that more students, teachers, and lecturers will practice embodied pedagogy and integrate movement in learning, and that we, as a community, will understand how much movement is necessary for all of us.[4]

---

[4] See my demonstration video at https://www.youtube.com/watch?v=XWehK3LMqR8. See all the exercises in sequence at the suggested pace at https://www.youtube.com/watch?v=A394EW1n5_E&t=4s.

References

Coulter, D.J. "Movement, Meaning and the Mind. Keynote Address. Seventh Annual Education Kinesiology Foundation Gathering, Greeley, CO, 1993.

דניסון, ד. פ. (2010) תרגילי מוח התענוג שבלמידה. הוצאת אדוואנס.

הנפורד, ק. (2000) חוכמה ותנועה. הוצאת נמרוד.

זהר, ר. (2015)"שילוב תנועה וידע מחול בהוראת הפיזיקה". מחול עכשיו, 28, 17-23.

זהר, ר., בגנו, א., אלון, ב. ואברהמסון ד, 2017. "יצירתיות וקוגניציה בלמידה מעוגנת גוף של מושגים בפיזיקה", מחול עכשיו, גיליון 32, עמ' 24-30.

כץ, ר. (2020) "החושים שבאמצעותם חווים את התנועה – בשירות העוררות המוחית, הקשב והריכוז – בהוראה ובלמידה". חינוך הטרוגני בלימודי מדע וט־כנולוגיה, גיליון 43.

Clown. Irene Aronson.
Photo: Zohar Shemesh. © The Israel Museum, Jerusalem.

Bringing Physics to the Circus

Alexander Volfson and Yuval Ben-Abu[1]

Circus art "excites, amazes and delights."[2] It captures the imagination of children as well as adults. It presents to audiences human exceptionalism, beauty, courage, passion, glitter and glamor. Circus makes the audience intermittently laugh, worry, and think. Most circus acts[3] (in the basic genres such as acrobatics, equilibristics, juggling etc.) are based on the principles of Newtonian mechanics. Fire shows can be explained in the terms of classical heat theory; illusions usually apply the principles of classical optics and psychology.

The idea to use certain circus numbers and/or single tricks to illustrate physics principles is not new. For instance, the classic *Entertaining Tasks and Experiments*[4] as well as *Fundamentals of Physics*[5] present the example of a bicycle rider performing a dead loop—riding in a vertical circular track—to illustrate the laws of circular motion. Another book, *Fundamentals of Physics*, also illustrates tension and Newton's second law with an aerial gymnast performing on a rope (cord-de-parel); and the law of conservation of energy with a performer sliding on a pole. Science Circus Visindi went even further and built a complete show which brings the basic concepts of Newtonian mechanics to the general public in ways that are relatively easy to understand even for those without a physics background.[6] Why not use circus arts to teach physics?

At the circus, audiences learn a lot about physics without realizing it; they're caught up in the wonder and entertainment of the performances. Therefore actively teaching physics through circus has many advantages over formal frontal lectures. Numerous studies report serious misconceptions regarding physics concepts even after a thorough teaching process.[7] Our previous studies conducted on university engineering students and graduates showed that even after completing learning, participants have difficulty in applying theoretical

---

[1] We dedicate this work to the memory of our teachers and friends in the worlds of science, teaching, research, and circus arts, Prof. Haim Eshach and Mart Bruk.
[2] Z. Gurevich, *About the Genres of Soviet Circus*. Moscow: Art, 1977.
[3] Classical circus shows are composed of relatively short parts. Each part usually presents a different art (acrobatics, juggling, equilibristics, etc.) and is called a number or an act. An individual exercise in a number is called a trick.
[4] Y.I. Perelman, *Entertaining Tasks and Experiments*. Moscow: VAP, 1994.
[5] D. Halliday, et al., *Fundamentals of Physics 10th Edition*. USA: Wiley, 2014.
[6] Schlender, 2013, video reporting about the show: https://www.voanews.com/a/scientist-circus-performers-make-physics-fun/1632653.html; https://www.facebook.com/pg/Visindi/posts/.
[7] See, for instance, Hestenes, Wells & Swackhamer, 1992; Roche 2001; Demirci 2005; Eshach & Schwartz, 2006; Chi, Roscoe, Slotta, Roy & Chase, 2012; Vyas 2012; Ding, Chabay & Sherwood, 2013.

knowledge to explain physical phenomena in real life, for instance, how simple devices work.[8] The sad truth is that many students, ranging from junior high[9] up to undergraduate university level,[10] have an aversion to physics. It is our hypothesis that formal as well as informal physics teaching employing circus can meet these challenges. The present study provides a research foundation for experiential physics teaching through circus shows. Acknowledging the above mentioned ideas, we take it a step further, introducing the idea of group dialogic discussions to physics teaching anchored in circus art.

Dialogic discussions are a way to identify conceptual barriers (misconceptions) and facilitate their further revision thus, producing the desired conceptual change.[11] Indeed, instruction that includes the dialogic aspect is argued to engage students in meaningful learning processes;[12] students' views are sought and valued as a part of the construction of scientific knowledge.[13] Physics educator Michael Ponnambalam argues that "the facts/laws of physics may be cold to many; but the presentation of these laws can be very warm, lively, passionate—and even dramatic and poetic."[14] Introducing physics concepts through *dialogic discussions about circus tricks* (DDCT) may definitely be such a "warm, lively, and passionate" method. Moreover, we, believe that a strong motivation to understand circus tricks, engaged by circus performers (as it takes place in the present study) or by physics instructors, has the power to draw people into a serious study of physics and contribute to changing its negative public image.

Our study originates in 2014 at a Dead Sea hotel. One of the authors (Volfson), being both a physics educator and a circus artist, performed in the hotel during the summer season. One of his numbers included this trick: the artist spins two open bowls connected by a rope and filled with water round and round, combining vertical and horizontal planes of rotation (figs. 1 & 2). The water does not spill out. Once, at the end of this number, the artist asked the audience: *What do you think—why didn't the water spill out of the bowls?* Imagine his surprise when 15-20 children and adults out of about 50 spectators stayed after the show for a serious 15-minute discussion of the physics behind the number—despite the attraction of other entertainment in and around the hotel. After this experience, we developed the idea into an educational circus activity called "Between Circus and Science." This included a full-length circus

---

[8] Volfson, 2018; Volfson, Eshach & Ben-Abu, 2019.
[9] Baram-Tsabari & Yarden, 2005.
[10] Ornek, Robinson & Haugan, 2008.
[11] Eshach, 2009.
[12] Scott & Ametller, 2007.
[13] Lehesvuori, 2013.
[14] M. Ponnambalam, "Popularization of Physics – the Jamaican Experience," *Latin America Journal of Physics Education* 6 (2012), 393.

Bringing Physics to the Circus · 221

Figure 1. Alexander Volfson spins bowls in a horizontal plane.
Courtesy: Alex Vainberg

Figure 2. Alexander Volfson conducts a dialogic discussion.
Courtesy: Omer Armoni, Bazoola Productions.

show and a juggling master class, both based on DDCT dealing with ballistic motion, Newtonian laws, circular motion, rigid body mechanics, heat theory, and more. as can be seen in the following promotion video clip:

https://youtu.be/ZfdrPwePliI

Following our preliminary study which examined the public understanding of the physics of circular motion in DDCT conducted during or after circus shows, we had two goals:

1. Introducing *dialogic discussions about circus tricks* (DDCT) as a diagnostic tool to identify participants' conceptual understanding of Newtonian mechanics, rigid body mechanics and heat issues, as well as examine how participants apply what they have learned in physics classes to explain the physics principles behind circus numbers and tricks.

2. Examining the conceptual changes of participants within a series of DDCT activities circus shows and master classes which include (and sometimes are based on) dialogic discussions between an artist and an audience about the underlying physics principles of the tricks in the performance. This might help us to: examine whether DDCT have the potential to engage people from different age groups and backgrounds in physics; increase our understanding of what particular aspects in DDCT are useful in engaging people with physics ideas; and provide examples of DDCT for future use.

It should be emphasized that bringing circus to physics classes does not require, of course, that every physics teacher should be a professional circus artist. Physics teachers can expose their students to the world of circus by bringing some simple circus equipment to their classes, taking students to circus shows, or analyzing video of circus tricks.

Literature review
Understanding new physics concepts and correcting misconceptions requires conceptual change. According to the seminal work of Posner, Strike, Hewson and William, conceptual change occurs when a learner's central commitments require modification. Here the learner is faced with a challenge to his basic assumptions. In this case, a student

> ...sometimes uses existing concepts to deal with new phenomena.... Often, however, the student's current concepts are inadequate[15] to allow him to grasp some new phenomenon successfully. Then the student must replace or reorganize his central concepts. This more radical form of conceptual change we call *accommodation*.[16]

---

[15] Similarly to other contemporary works in the field of conceptual change, we call these "inadequate" concepts misconceptions.
[16] G.J. Posner, et al., "Accommodation of a Scientific Conception: Toward a Theory of Conceptual

Physics teaching is known to frequently be an arena for educators' dealing with robust misconceptions.[17] Thus, looking for new ways to identify misconceptions as well as facilitate conceptual change is of both theoretical and practical interest in the teaching of physics. In what follows we first summarize the literature on dialogic discussions, we then go on to discuss the possible contribution of circus environment to physics education and finally, we show the potential of DDCT to facilitate conceptual change about physics concepts.

Dialogic discussions

Science education has been mainly limited to the study of *solo cognitive*, rather than *sociocognitive*, processes.[18] This means that the focus of the studies was on the individual's conceptual change process rather than on conceptual construction occurring within groups of learners. The study presented here joins the line of research that focuses on understanding how knowledge is constructed in teacher-led discussions, which has not yet been sufficiently addressed.[19] The "class" in this research is actually the audience of a circus show, and the teacher is the artist.

Scott, Mortimer and Aguiar distinguish between authoritative and dialogic discourse. While in "authoritative discourse the teacher's purpose is to focus the students' full attention on just one meaning... in dialogic discourse the teacher recognizes and attempts to take into account a range of students', and others' ideas."[20] Whole class dialogic discussion (WCDD) is rooted in the premise of social constructivism.[21] Going back to the seminal work of Vygotsky, gives substantial weight to the role of social interaction in learning and sees knowledge as primarily a cultural product. Indeed, the learning of the individual, according to Vygotsky, is preceded and accompanied by inter-individual functioning:

Change," *Science Education, 66*(2) (1982), 212.

[17] See, for instance, Hestenes, Wells & Swackhamer, 1992; Roche 2001; Demirci 2005; Eshach & Schwartz, 2006; Chi, Roscoe, Slotta, Roy & Chase, 2012; Vyas 2012; Ding, Chabay & Sherwood, 2013; Vosniadou, 2013; Volfson, Eshach & Ben-Abu, 2018; Volfson, Eshach & Ben-Abu, 2019.

[18] K. Hogan, Sociocognitive roles in science group discourse. *International Journal of Science Education, 21 (1999),* 855-882.

[19] H. Eshach, "Analysis of Conceptual Flow Patterns and Structures in the Physics Classroom," *International Journal of Science Education* 32(4) (2009), 451-77; S. Lehesvuori, *Towards Dialogic Teaching in Science Challenging Classroom Realities through Teacher Education*, University of Jyvaskyla, 2013; H. Eshach, H. et al., "Misconception of Sound and Conceptual Change: A Cross Sectional Study on Students' Materialistic Thinking of Sound," *Journal of Research in Science Teaching*, 2017. Doi:10.1002/tea.21435.

[20] P.H. Scott, et al., "The Tension Between Authoritative and Dialogic Discourse: A Fundamental Characteristic of Meaning Making Interactions in High School Science Lessons," *Science Education*, 90 (2006), 605-31.

[21] P. Cobb, "Where is the Mind? Constructivist and Sociocultural Perspectives on Mathematical Development," *Educational Researcher, 23*(7) (1994): 13–20; P. Ernest, "Mathematical Activity and Rhetoric: Towards a Social Constructivist Account." In *Proceedings of PME-17*, edited by N. Nohda. Tsukuba: University of Tsukuba, 1993.

higher psychic functions appear in interpersonal interaction before becoming intrapsychic. Dialogic discussions enable students, with the help of instructors' prompts, to reveal their own ideas, compare those ideas with other ideas, adopt or reject ideas, create hybrid ideas, and sharpen their ideas.[22] This is crucially important for detection and identification of misconceptions[23] and may lead the learner to the desired conceptual change.[24]

Dialogic discussions are characterized by an **IRPE** structure.[25] In this structure, *I* stands for initiation—usually a question from a teacher or an artist. *R* is a participant's response to that initiation. *P* is a prompt, which refers to feedback from the teacher (artist) to the participants' responses, in order to prompt further elaboration of their points of view. Finally, *E* stands either for the evaluation of the answers; or in other situations it may function to "extend the student's answer, to draw out its significance, or to make connections with other parts of the students' total experience during the unit."[26] All these are also relevant to *dialogic discussions about circus tricks* (DDCT).

Structures of conceptual flow patterns

Teacher's (artist's) interventions influence student (audience) discourse while, on the other hand, especially in dialogic discourse, the various student (spectator) responses affect the teacher's (artist's) interventions. All these coalesce as *conceptual flow patterns* (CFP). CFP treat the growth, transitions, and sometimes elimination of concepts as they arise during classroom discussions on a certain topic. Science and technology educator Haim Eshach analyzed the CFP of dialogic discussions using diagrams, which he called *conceptual flow discourse maps* (CFDM). He identified the following three patterns (fig. 3):

> A. **Accumulation around budding foci concepts:** a student introduces a new idea into the classroom discussion and this idea becomes the focus of the whole-class discussion. The idea is discussed for a while until another idea buds and the discussion changes its focus to the new idea.

---

[22] Eshach, 2009; Lehesvuori, 2013.
[23] S. Vosniadou, S., et al., "Designing Learning Environments to Promote Conceptual Change in Science." *Learning and Instruction 11* (2001), 381-419; G. Wells, and R.M. Arauz, "Dialogue in the Classroom." *Journal of the Learning Sciences,* 15(3) (2006), 379-428; A. Volfson, "Physics Behind Acoustical Devices: Development of a Diagnostic Instrument for Examining the Understanding of the Underlying Physics Principles Explaining how Simple Acoustic Apparatuses Work." Ph.D. *Dissertation,* Ben-Gurion University, Israel, 2018.
[24] Eshach, 2009.
[25] Ibid.
[26] Wells, G. "Putting a tool to different uses: A reevaluation of the IRF sequence." Chapter 5. In G. Wells (Ed.), *Dialogic Inquiry: Towards a Sociocultural Practice and Theory of Education.* Cambridge: Cambridge University Press, 1999.

B. **Zigzag between foci concepts:** some main ideas are adopted by different student groups. The discussion zigzags between those groups.

C. **Concept tower:** previous concepts and learning experiences are synthesized into the construction of more complex scientific ideas.

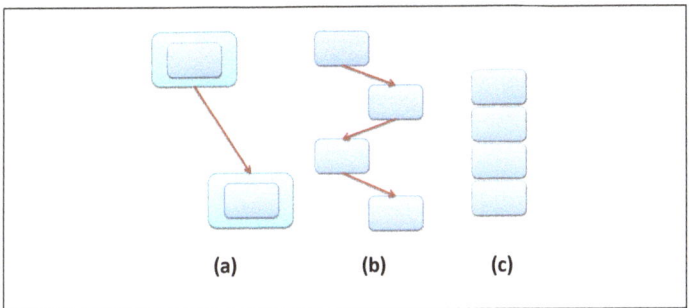

Figure 3. The three CFDM structures (Eshach, 2009):
1. Accumulation around budding foci concepts;
2. Zigzag between foci concepts;
3. Concept tower.

The potential of DCCT in physics education

Circus is full of tricks, props and devices which are all based on simple physics principles. In the present study we shall relate circus to ballistics, Newtonian mechanics (inertia, force, energy, circular motion, etc.), rigid-body mechanics and classic heat theory. By using the term '*simple*' we mean that the background knowledge needed for explaining these tricks, props and devices is only knowledge on the above-mentioned issues and no further knowledge in areas such as electricity, electronics, optics, or quantum mechanics etc. is needed. All the tricks and numbers are demonstrated in real time to the audience/class. Most of them can further be re-demonstrated and/or modified serving the aims of the artist (teacher) providing DDCT. Circus master classes (acrobatics, juggling, fire spinning) relate in addition the embodied knowledge of the participants thus providing another facility for learning the physics principles. Indeed, embodied knowledge (embodied cognition) is not simply knowledge of the body, but knowledge dwelling in the body and enacted through the body.[27] The cognitive

---

[27] C. Craig, C., et al. "The Embodied Nature of Narrative Knowledge: A Cross-study Analysis of Embodied Knowledge in Teaching, Learning, and Life." *Teaching and Teacher Education* 71 (2018): 329-40.

226 · Under One Tent: Circus, Judaism and Bible

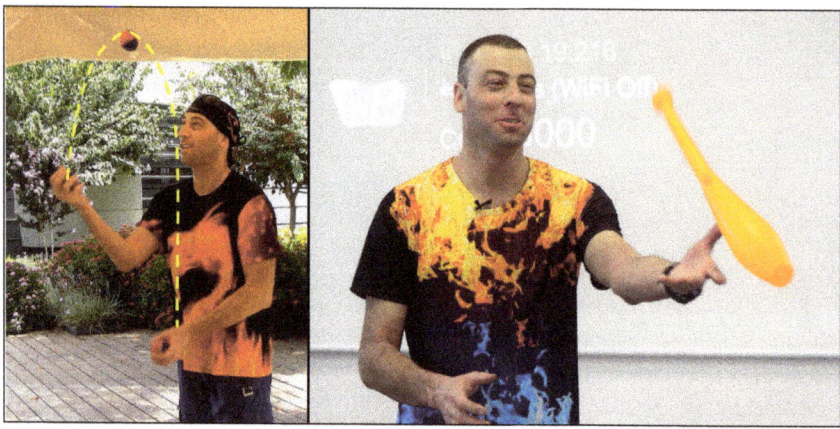

Figure 4. Balls fly in parabolic trajectories.
Courtesy: Marina Aletko

Figure 5. The club performs a parabolic trajectory in the air and spins around its center of mass found near its head. Courtesy: Omer Armoni, Bazoola Productions

systems of learners are affected, even constrained, by action and perception.[28] Let us now demonstrate these in the following examples:

Ballistic motion and center of mass in Juggling

Once thrown, all the props (balls, rings and clubs) fly in parabolic trajectories thus performing the so called ballistic motion (fig. 4). Due to the force of gravity they are found most of the time at the top part of their trajectory. These two facts enable the juggler to predict the motion of the prop, looking at the upper part of the trajectory in preparation to catch the prop when it comes down. Another phenomenon jugglers experience is that the time of the prop on its way up is equal to its time on the way down. Further development of juggling skills with less symmetrical props, such as clubs, shows how every flying object, once rotated, spins around its center of mass (fig. 5). While every club performs a parabolic trajectory in the air, the juggler has to rotate the club in a certain angular velocity so they can catch it properly. The club always spins around its center of mass found near its "head," which enables the juggler to catch it by the handle.

---

[28] S. Weisberg, and N. Newcombe, "Embodied Cognition and STEM Learning: Overview of a Topical Collection in CR:PI." *Cognitive Research: Principles and Implications, 2*(38) (2017), 1-6.

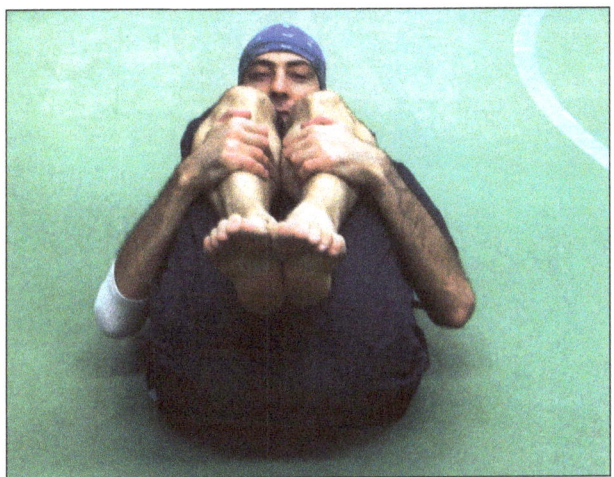

Figure 6. A tight grouping in a somersault.
Courtesy: Marina Aletko

Moment of inertia in acrobatics and spinning props

One of the central movements in a somersault[29] and a salto[30] is the grouping—bending the knees and keeping them bent by holding the shins with the hands; this turns the acrobat into a "ball" (fig. 6). The moment of inertia of a ball is $I_{ball} = \frac{2}{5}mR^2$ where m is the mass of the ball and R is the radius. Therefore the angular velocity of a rolling ball is $\omega = \sqrt{\frac{5E}{m}} \cdot \frac{1}{R}$ when E is the rotational kinetic energy which the acrobat got at the start of the somersault (we look at the acrobat as a spherical body in the first approximation and neglect friction). This teaches us that the tighter the grouping, the smaller the radius of the "ball" and thus, the greater the angular velocity; That is, the acrobat rotates faster[31]. This point can be well observed in different acrobatic jumps involving tight grouping or, on the contrary, salto with a straight body.

Moment of inertia can be considered as the body's resistance to changes of the angular velocity vector,[32] which you can see in various spinning props. Let us look, for instance at a staff—a wooden rod about 1.2m long with rubber bobs (flowers) at its ends (fig. 7 & 8). When spinning the staff around its center of mass, its moment of inertia is $I_{staff} = \frac{1}{12}mL^2 + M\left(\frac{1}{2}L\right)^2 + M\left(\frac{1}{2}L\right)^2 = \frac{m+6M}{12}L^2$.

---

[29] Also called *culbit*—A dynamic or individual element with rotation with hands support to the back and legs.
[30] An acrobatic element in which a person's body rotates 360 or more around a horizontal axis with no hand support during the rotation.
[31] A. Volfson, "Safe and Correct Grouping." Wingate Institute. 2013. https://www.wingate.org.il/Index.asp?ArticleID=6288&CategoryID=267.
[32] I. V. Savel'ev, *Course of General Physics. Volume 1. Mechanics.* Moscow: Nauka, 1998.

Figure 7. Center of mass and moment of inertia of a staff.
Courtesy: Marina Aletko
Figure 8. Flower stick is much shorter and lighter than a staff,
and thus has much smaller moment of inertia.
Courtesy: Omer Armoni, Bazoola Productions

Here, $\frac{1}{12}mL^2$ is moment of inertia of the rod, $M\left(\frac{1}{2}L\right)^2$ are moments of inertia of the left and right weights respectively.

That is, the longer the rod, and the bigger the mass; the whole moment of inertia is higher. This is the reason a staff resists immediate changes of its rotational plane and spinning velocity; the change needs to be made gradually. A flower stick is much shorter (about two feet long) and lighter than a staff and has a much smaller moment of inertia; it is easier to change its rotational plane and spinning velocity.

Bringing Physics to the Circus · 229

Figures 9 and 10. The artist jumps through flaming rings.
Courtesy: Omer Armoni, Bazoola Productions

Fire, heat capacity and heat transfer

Fire shows (fig. 9 & 10) provide the stage to demonstrate and discuss the principles of classical heat theory. Indeed, questions like: What is heat? How does heat propagate in the air, from the flame to our body? Why is heat more intense above a flame than in it? What keeps a fire artist from being burned while performing? These questions deal with the nature of heat, heat transfer, convection and heat capacity, and can be helpful not only in explaining these concepts, but also for addressing people's misconceptions of heat.[33]

---
[33] M.T.H. Chi, et al., "Misconceived Causal Explanations for Emergent Processes." *Cognitive Science* 36 (2012), 1-61; A. Volfson, et al., "Development of a Diagnostic Tool Aimed at Pin-

DDCT and conceptual change

Constructivist educators, who attempt to move students toward a conceptual and qualitative understanding of physics principles need first to understand how students see the physical world, and take their points of view into consideration when designing instruction.[34] One way to identify students' knowledge about scientific concepts is the use of focus group interviews[35] or non-authoritative whole-class dialogic discussions oriented at investigating of students' thinking.[36] These processes, in a sense, are similar. Group members in such discussions should feel relaxed and comfortable, and enjoy sharing their ideas and perceptions.[37] The fact that a large portion of those who came just to watch a circus show in the hotel, remained and actively participated in the after-show DDCT demonstrates that circus indeed offers a unique informal environment for providing comfortable and interesting discussions as the literature requires[38]—thus promising a better cooperation of participants.

At the second stage, the educator must produce the conceptual change toward the correct understanding. According to the classical model of Posner et al., conceptual change can occur by the creation of cognitive conflict through the presentation of anomalies.[39] That is, the educator has to engage dissatisfaction with existing conceptions among the learners as unable to explain the demonstrated/discussed phenomena. Once learners have collected a store of unsolved puzzles or anomalies and lost faith in the capacity of their current concepts to solve these problems, the educator has to come up with the scientifically correct conception. This novel conception needs to be intelligible, plausible and able to predict and explain further alike phenomena. According to Rowlands, Graham, Berry and McWilliam (2007) such an attempt has to

---

pointing Undergraduate Students' Knowledge About Sound and its Implementation in Simple Acoustic Apparatuses' Analysis." *Phys. Rev. Phys. Educ. Res.* 14 (2018).

[34] D. Hestenes, et al., "Force Concept Inventory." *Physics Teacher, 30* (1992), 141-58; Galili & Hazan, 2000; S. Vosniadou, et al., "Designing Learning Environments to Promote Conceptual Change in Science." *Learning and instruction 11* (2001). 381-419; Treagust, 2006; Hrepic, Zollman & Rebello, 2010; Eshach, 2014.

[35] R.M. Dilshad, and M.I. Latif, "Focus Group Interview as a Tool for Qualitative Research: Analysis." *Pakistan Journal of Social Sciences* 33(1) (2013), 191-8.

[36] H. Eshach, "Analysis of Conceptual Flow Patterns and Structures in the Physics Classroom." *International Journal of Science Education* 32(4) (2009), 451-77.

[37] R.A. Krueger, *Focus Groups: a Practical Guide for Applied Research*. Newbury Park, CA: Sage Publications, 1988; R.M. Dilshad, and M.I. Latif, "Focus Group Interview as a Tool for Qualitative Research: An Analysis." *Pakistan Journal of Social Sciences* 33(1) (2013), 191-8.

[38] R.A. Krueger, and M.A. Casey, Focus Groups. *A Practical Guide for Applied Research (3rd Edition)*. Thousand Oaks, CA: Sage Publications, 2000; F. Rabee, "Focus Group Interview and Data Analysis," *Proceedings of the Nutrition Society*, 63 (2004): 655-60.

[39] G. J. Posner, et al., "Accommodation of a Scientific Conception: Toward a Theory of Conceptual Change," *Science Education*, 66(2) (1982), 211-27.

"...involve a meta discourse component that encourages students to reflect on their misconceptions and the coherence of their physics knowledge systems."[40] All these come to fruition in whole class dialogic discussions as outlined by Eshach.[41] DDCT, we suggest in the present study, are in a sense a direct extension of Eshach's discussions conducted in the informal circus environment.

Research Aims and Questions
The present study aims at examining the potential of DDCT as a diagnostic tool for identifying participants' conceptual understanding of Newtonian mechanics, rigid body mechanics and heat issues as well as, examining how participants utilize what they have learned in physics classes to explain the physics principles of circus numbers and tricks; and examining whether and how theoretical concepts in these fields can be learned through DDCT provided in circus shows and master-classes. Thus, the following research questions will guide our study:

- Whether and how DDCT can be used to reveal and identify physics misconceptions?

- Whether and how DDCT can facilitate conceptual change regarding physics concepts?

Methodology

Study population
When our research began in 2014, seven shows incorporating DDCT about circular motion[42] were performed by the KESHET circus artists in a hotel on the Dead Sea in Israel. After each show, the performing artist led a dialogic discussion about the underlying physics explaining the circular motion embedded in the circus tricks. About 50 spectators of various ages watched each show. Of these, 10 to 20 people remained after each show and participated in a discussion (about 105 people in total). Since the 2014 preliminary research (Volfson, Eshach & Ben-Abu, 2020) we have developed the DDCT repertoire

---

[40] S. Rowlands, and T. Graham, "What is Conceptual Change in Mechanics?" In *Proceedings of the Sixth British Congress of Mathematics Education*, edited by D. Hewitt and A. Noyes, 36; held at the University of Warwick, 2005. Available from www.bsrlm.org.uk.
[41] H. Eshach, "Analysis of Conceptual Flow Patterns and Structures in the Physics Classroom," *International Journal of Science Education* 32(4) (2009). 451-77.
[42] A. Volfson, et al., "Development of a Diagnostic Tool Aimed at Pinpointing Undergraduate Students' Knowledge About Sound and its Implementation in Simple Acoustic Apparatuses' Analysis," *Phys. Rev. Phys. Educ. Res.* 14 (2018).

to other fields of physics as well as appropriate shows and master classes. About 30 such shows and master classes have been presented since then. In total, about 5,500 people watched the shows, from which, about 400 spectators actively participated in the DDCT. Most of these discussions were video recorded and transcribed verbatim; others were written down during or immediately after the shows.

The circus act and DCCT
In our approach, every circus act/number/trick provides an opportunity for a DDCT. Following the number, the artist first asks the audience to explain the physics of the trick and further challenges the participants' views with some modifications of the trick, other tricks, or other props. For instance, in the preliminary research, the artist asked the audience: a) Why did the water not spill out of the bowl? b) Can you predict what would happen to the bowls if the rope broke at specific points, e.g. in the horizontal plane, when one of the bowls is in front of the artist, and in the vertical plane when the bowl is at the top of its rotation.

At the beginning of the discussion, the artist asked participants to express their views regarding the presented phenomenon, to refer to each other's explanations, and to consider challenging questions. The artist provided not only verbal prompts, but also used demonstrations to further challenge participants' views. Once the participants expressed their ideas, the artist summarized the discussion and explained, in a qualitative manner, the underlying physics of the circus number. He began with an explanation of Newton's first law and then explained that at every point of the path, each bowl "strives" to continue moving in a straight line in a tangent to the path direction but since the rope holds it, it is forced to move in a circular path, due to the action of centripetal force—in this case, the tension of the rope. The water in the bowl also strives to continue moving in the tangent direction, however, it is blocked by the bowl, which exerts a force on the water. This makes the water stay in the bowl. The artist also emphasized that there is no centrifugal force; on the contrary, there is a force which pulls the bowls to the center of the circular motion path—the centripetal force, in this case, tension. The artist explained all this in laymen's terms, without using any formulas.

What if you offer a prize? In our preliminary research, the artist announced at some shows that there would be a prize for those with correct answers. At half of the shows, the artist gave prizes for all scientifically reasonable answers—that is, not necessarily the correct answer, but every answer with a solid theory explaining the physics principles behind the act. The reward turned the discussions into a kind of game, facilitated the cooperation of participants, and contributed to the atmosphere of entertainment. At the other half of the shows, the artist did not offer any reward at all. In both cases, there was lively discussion of theories, and no measurable difference in the theories participants suggested. Both groups exhibited the same misconceptions, which showed us that these misconceptions are deep-seated ideas, and people weren't suggesting theories just to win a prize.

Common misconceptions
Three misconceptions about circular motion surfaced in post-show discussions of the Bowls Show:
Centrifugal force (40%): According to this view, when we spin an object, an actual centrifugal force appears and pushes the object outside of the path, in a radial direction.[43] This centrifugal force pushes the water to the bottom of the bowls and so it does not spill out. It should be noted that those who expressed the centrifugal force theory: (a) considered it as a real force; and (b) could not go much beyond using the term "centrifugal" to explain why the water doesn't spill out. Also, many of those who expressed this view believed that centrifugal force depends on the rotation speed, i.e., the faster one spins an object the stronger is the centrifugal force acting on it. This argument was expressed especially to address why the water does not spill out in a vertical plane rotation.

Speed of spin (27%): Those who expressed this view referred primarily to the case of spinning the bowls in a vertical plane, although in the show the artist rotated the bowls both vertically and horizontally. According to this view, the artist spins the bowls so fast that the water actually does not have enough time to spill out when the bowls are upside-down at the top of their path. This view should not be confused with the view connecting the speed of spin with the centrifugal force described in the previous section. According to the previous view, rotation speed influences the magnitude of centrifugal force, whereas according to the view presented in this section, the speed of rotation cuts down the time the water needs to spill out. Another variation of this idea is that the water does spill out, but the artist spins the bowl so quickly that he manages to catch the water back at the bottom part of bowl's trajectory. This variation was mostly expressed by the young children in the audience.

---

[43] D. Hestenes, et al., "Force Concept Inventory," *Physics Teacher 30* (1992), 141-58; N. Demirci, "A Study About Students' Misconceptions in Force and Motion Concepts by Incorporating a Web Assisted Physics Program," *The Turkish Online Journal of Educational Technology – TOJET* 4(3) (2005). ISSN: 1303-6521.P. Vyas, Misconception in Circular Motion, *International Journal of Scientific & Engineering Research 3* (2012). 12. ISSN 2229-5518.

Air pressure (15%): According to this view, when we spin the bowls quickly enough, the air exerts an increased pressure on the water. This pressure keeps the water inside the bowls. Some participants explained that there is a friction between the water surface and the air. This friction also pushes the water into the bowls. This view was expressed by adult and adolescent participants.

Course correction

How can DDCT facilitate the process of conceptual change toward the correct concepts? Multiple researchers[44] do not express optimism for revising misconceptions by simply telling the students which concepts are the correct ones, as we usually do in frontal teaching, but rather suggest to "...compare and contrast their existing conception and new ideas, recognize, integrate and evaluate existing and new conceptions and associated commitments, everyday experiences and contextual factors."[45] The artist, who was familiar with these studies, constructed his pedagogic approach to DDCT in the same way. The following scheme (fig. 11) maps the three main misconceptions and the appropriate pedagogic techniques of the artist to confront them. We hope that physics educators will find it helpful.

---

[44] See, e.g., A. A. diSessa,. "Toward an Epistemology of Physics." *Cognition and Instruction* 10(2/3) (1993):105 - 225.M.T.H. Chi,. "Three Types of Conceptual Change: Belief Revision, Mental Model Transformation, and Categorical Shift," In *Handbook of Research on Conceptual Change*, edited by S. Vosniadou, 61-82. (Hillsdale, NJ: Erlbaum, 2008).

[45] Yürük, N. "A case study of one student's metaconceptual processes and the changes in her alternative conceptions of force and motion." *Eurasia Journal of Mathematics, Science & Technology Education*, 3(4) (2007): 306.

Bringing Physics to the Circus · 235

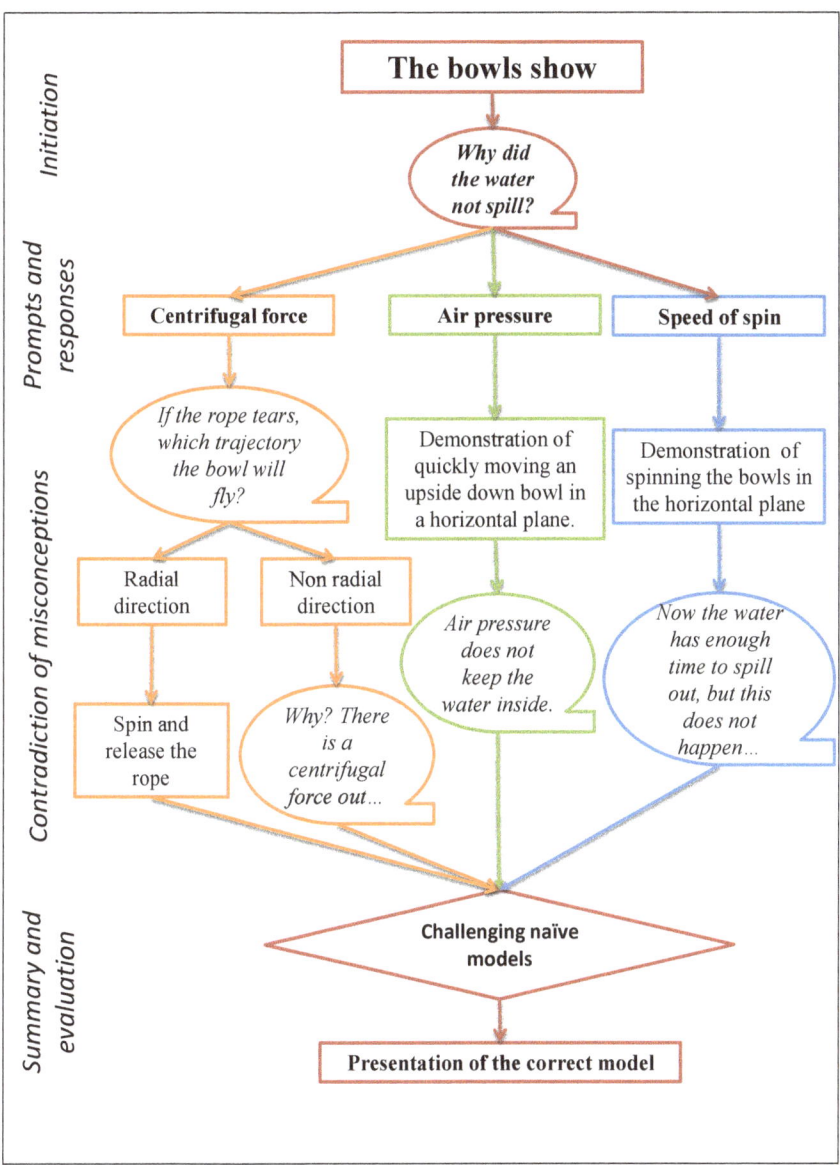

Figure 11. Suggested pedagogic algorithm for preparing students for qualitative understanding of circular motion.

References

Baram-Tsabari, A., & Yarden, A. Characterizing children's spontaneous interests in science and technology. *International Journal of Science Education, 27(7)* (2005): *803-826*.

Beichner, R. Testing student interpretation of kinematics graphs. *American Journal of Physics,* 62 (1994): 750-762.

Chi, M. T. H. "Three types of conceptual change: belief revision, mental model transformation, and categorical shift." In *Handbook of research on conceptual change*, edited by S. Vosniadou, 61-82. Hillsdale, NJ: Erlbaum, 2008.

Chi, M. T. H., Roscoe, R. D., Slotta, J. D., Roy, M. and Chase, C. C. "Misconceived Causal Explanations for Emergent Processes." *Cognitive Science 36* (2012): 1-61.

Cobb, P. "Where is the mind? Constructivist and sociocultural perspectives on mathematical development." *Educational Researcher, 23(7)* (1994): 13-20.

Craig, C., You, J., Zou, Y., Verma, R., Stokes, D., Evans, P. and Curtis, G. "The embodied nature of narrative knowledge: A cross-study analysis of embodied knowledge in teaching, learning, and life." *Teaching and Teacher Education* 71 (2018): 329-340.

Demirci, N. "A study about students' misconceptions in force and motion concepts by incorporating a web assisted physics program." *The Turkish Online Journal of Educational Technology – TOJET 4*(3) (2005). ISSN: 1303-6521.

Ding, L., Chabay, R., Sherwood, B. "How do students in an innovative principle-based mechanics course understand energy concepts?" *Journal of research in science teaching* 50, (6) (2013): 722-747.

Dilshad, R. M. and Latif, M. I. "Focus group interview as a tool for qualitative research: An analysis." *Pakistan Journal of Social Sciences 33*(1) (2013): 191-198.

diSessa, A. A. "Toward an epistemology of physics." *Cognition and Instruction* 10(2/3) (1993):105-225.

Donskoy, D. and Shoyhet, K. "Biomechanical justification of acrobatic exercises technique." In *Sportive acrobatics*, edited by V. Korkin. Moscow: Fizkultura i Sport, 1981.

Ernest, P. "Mathematical activity and rhetoric: Towards a social constructivist account." In *Proceedings of PME-17*, edited by N. Nohda. Tsukuba: University of Tsukuba, 1993.

Eshach, H. and Schwartz, J. L. "Sound Staff? Naive materialism in middle-school students' conceptions of sound." *International Journal of Science Education, 28(7)* (2006): 733-764.

Eshach, H. "Analysis of conceptual flow patterns and structures in the physics classroom." *International Journal of Science Education 32*(4) (2009): 451-477.

Eshach, H., Lin, T. and Tsai, C. Misconception of sound and conceptual change: A cross sectional study on students' materialistic thinking of sound. *Journal of Research in Science Teaching.* 2017. Doi:10.1002/tea.21435.

Galili, I. and Hazan, A. (2000). "Learners' knowledge in optics: Interpretation, structure and analysis." *International Journal of Science Education.* 22 (2000): 57-88.

Gurevich, Z. *About the genres of Soviet circus.* Moscow: Art, 1977.

Halliday, D., Resnick, R. and Walker, J. *Fundamentals of Physics 10th Edition.* USA: Wiley, 2014.

Hestenes, D., Wells, M. and Swackhamer, M. "Force concept inventory." *Physics Teacher, 30* (1992):141-158.
Hogan, K. "Sociocognitive roles in science group discourse." *International Journal of Science Education, 21 (1999):* 855-882.
Hrepic, Z., D. A. Zollman, N.S. Rebello. "Identifying students' mental models of sound propagation: The role of conceptual blending in understanding conceptual change." *Physical Review Special Topics - Physics Education Research,* 6, (2010) 020114-1-020114-18.
Kapon, S. "Bridging the knowledge gap: An analysis of Albert Einstein's popularized presentation of the equivalence of mass and energy." *Public Understanding of Science, 23*(8) (2013): 1013-1024.
Krueger, R. A. *Focus groups: a practical guide for applied research.* Newbury Park, CA: Sage Publications, 1988.
Krueger, R. A. and Casey, M. A. Focus Groups. *A Practical Guide for Applied Research (3rd Edition).* Thousand Oaks, CA: Sage Publications, 2000.
Lehesvuori, S. *Towards Dialogic Teaching in Science Challenging Classroom Realities through Teacher Education.* University of Jyvaskyla, 2013.
Ornek, F., Robinson, W. R. and Haugan, M. P. "What makes physics difficult?" *International Journal of Environmental & Science Education,* 3(1) (2008): 30-34.
Patton, M.Q. *Qualitative evaluation and research methods, 2nd ed.* Newbury Park, CA: Sage, 1990.
Perelman, Y. I. *Entertaining tasks and experiments.* Moscow: VAP, 1994.
Ponnambalam, M. "Popularization of Physics – the Jamaican experience." *Latin America Journal of Physics Education* 6 (2012): 390-393.
Posner, G. J., Strike, K. A., Hewson, P. W., & Gertzog, W. A. "Accommodation of a scientific conception: Toward a theory of conceptual change." *Science Education,* 66(2) (1982): 211-227.
Rabee, F. Focus group interview and data analysis. *Proceedings of the Nutrition Society,* 63 (2004): 655-660.
Roche, J. "Introducing motion in a circle." *Physics Education* 36 (2001): 399.
Roth, W. M. "Affordances of computers in teacher–student interactions: The case of Interactive Physics™." *Journal of Research in Science Teaching,* 32 (1995): 329-347.
Rowlands, S. and Graham, T. "What is conceptual change in mechanics?" In *Proceedings of the sixth British Congress of Mathematics Education,* edited by D. Hewitt and A. Noyes, 144-151; held at the University of Warwick, 2005. Available from www.bsrlm.org.uk.
Rowlands, S., Graham, T., Berry, J. and McWilliam, P. "Conceptual change through the lens of Newtonian mechanics." *Science & Education* 16 (2007): 21-42.
Savel'ev, I. V. *Course of general physics. Volume 1. Mechanics.* Moscow: Nauka, 1998.
Samovarski Sh. *Physics thought coming into being.* Jerusalem: Bialik Institute, 1987.
Schlender, S. "Scientist Circus Performers Make Physics Fun." 2013. https://www.voanews.com/a/scientist-circus-performers-make-physics-fun/1632653.html.

Scott, P. H., Mortimer, E. F. and Aguiar, O. J. "The tension between authoritative and dialogic discourse: A fundamental characteristic of meaning making interactions in high school science lessons." *Science Education,* 90 (2006): 605-631.

Scott, P. and Ametller, J. "Teaching science in a meaningful way: Striking a balance between 'opening up' and 'closing down' classroom talk." *School Science Review.* 88 (2007): 77-83.

Singh, C. & Rosengrant, D. "Multiple-choice test of energy and momentum concepts." *American Journal of Physics,* 71(6) (2003): 607-617.

Thornton, R. K., & Sokoloff, D. R. "Assessing Student Learning of Newton's Laws: The Force and Motion Conceptual Evaluation of Active Learning Laboratory and Lecture Curricula." *American Journal of Physics,* 66 (1998): 338-352.

Treagust, D. F. "Conceptual change as a viable approach to understanding student learning in science." In Kenneth Tobin (Ed.), *Teaching and Learning Science: A Handbook,* 25-32. Lanham, Maryland: Rowman & Littlefield, 2006.

Volfson, A. "Safe and correct grouping." Wingate Institute. 2013.

Volfson, A. "Physics behind acoustical devices: Development of a diagnostic instrument for examining the understanding of the underlying physics principles explaining how simple acoustic apparatuses work." *Dissertation submitted in partial fulfillment of the requirements for the degree of Ph. D.* Ben-Gurion University, Israel, 2018.

Volfson, A., Eshach, H., Ben-Abu, Y. "Development of a diagnostic tool aimed at pinpointing undergraduate students' knowledge about sound and its implementation in simple acoustic apparatuses' analysis." *Phys. Rev. Phys. Educ. Res. 14* (2018).

Volfson, Alexander, Haim Eshach, and Yuval Ben-Abu. "Identifying physics misconceptions at the circus: The case of circular motion." *Physical Review Physics Education Research* 16 (2020).

Vosniadou, S., Ioannides, C., Dimitrakopoulou, A., Papademetriou, F. "Designing Learning environments to promote conceptual change in science." *Learning and instruction 11* (2001): 381-419.

Vosniadou, S. Conceptual change in learning and instruction: The framework theory approach. In *International handbook of research on conceptual change,* 2nd *edition,* edited by S. Vousniadou, 11-30. New York and London: Routledge, 2013.

Vyas, P. Misconception in circular motion. *International Journal of Scientific & Engineering Research 3* (2012): 12. ISSN 2229-5518.

Vygotsky, L.S. *Mind in society: The development of higher psychological processes.* Cambridge, MA: Harvard University Press, 1978.

Weisberg, S. and Newcombe, N. "Embodied cognition and STEM learning: overview of a topical collection in CR:PI." *Cognitive Research: Principles and Implications, 2*(38) (2017): 1-6.

Wells, G., Arauz, R. M., "Dialogue in the Classroom." *Journal of the Learning Sciences,* 15(3) (2006): 379-428.

Wells, G. "Putting a tool to different uses: A reevaluation of the IRF sequence." Chapter 5. In G. Wells (Ed.), *Dialogic Inquiry: Towards a Sociocultural Practice and Theory of Education.* Cambridge: Cambridge University Press, 1999.

Yürük, N. "A case study of one student's metaconceptual processes and the changes in her alternative conceptions of force and motion." *Eurasia Journal of Mathematics, Science & Technology Education*, 3(4) (2007): 305-325.

Zharskih, M. *Study the effectiveness of various instructional methods for teaching children 7-12 years acrobatic exercises.* Thesis submitted in partial fulfillment of the requirements for the degree of Ph. D. The State Pedagogical Institute in Voronezh, 1965.

Zinkovsky, A., Ivanov, A., Sholukha, V. "Computer based synthesis of human motions based on anthropomorphic model with non-stationary constraints." *Russian Journal of Biomechanics*, 4 (2000): 50-60.

Circus Horse and Rider, 1964. Marc Chagall. Lithograph.
© Artists Rights Society (ARS), New York / ADAGP, Paris.

Movement is in the Jewish DNA

MICHAEL KASPER, AYAL PROUSER, ORA HORN PROUSER

Jewish study is traditionally a sedentary activity: one where students sit around a table and study together. Engaging in Jewish study through movement, circus, and dance may seem to be an unexpected approach to sacred literature, but in reality movement is deeply embedded in Jewish thought, life, and history. You could say it's in our DNA.

Every culture has narratives, symbols, or images at the heart of communal identity.[1] To be clear, these are not "Jewish symbols" such as wearing a kippah (head covering) or a Star of David necklace. Rather, they are cultural habits that are typical of a given people. These narratives and images emphasize what is central to the ethos of the culture and help to promote the identity of the people. There are a number of elements we could point to as being part of Jewish culture, peoplehood, and grounding for communal identity. For instance, the idea of "sacred time" is a very Jewish idea going back to the biblical creation story. Genesis 1 is structured by time[2] and has a special focus on Shabbat creating the structure of the full week of Jewish life[3] which continues to this day. Another important concept in Jewish culture is movement. This theme permeates traditional and modern literature and liturgy.

It is in Our DNA

> "Running away with the circus sounds both heroic and liberating. The actual nomadic condition is more ambiguous and challenging than the poetic themes it has spawned as it is rooted in ethnic discrimination."
> —Paul Bouissac, circus scholar[4]

Throughout history, even when Jews have found relative peace and acceptance for decades or centuries at a time, the collective unconscious expresses a sense of impermanence, a sense that the national order of things is to keep a bag packed for the inevitable wandering to come. Science offers a possible explanation for

---

[1] Some have called this "national imagination."
[2] Conversely, many ancient Near Eastern creation stories involve battles among gods. See, e.g., Enuma Elish. See the translation in Pritchard, pp. 60ff.
[3] A good example of this is seen in the psalms for the days of the week recited in the traditional morning service in which the word Shabbat is used to refer to the week.
[4] Bouissac, Paul. *Semiotics at the Circus*, Berlin: De Gruyter, 2010, 11.

this type of cultural phenomenon. The relatively new field of epigenetics[5] posits that "...trauma can leave a chemical mark on a person's genes, which then is passed down to subsequent generations."[6]

Epigenetic changes are usually triggered by the environment. In simple terms, an event in the external environment theoretically can cause a change in the inner environment of the person being affected. Once this happens, the gene connected to this change begins to behave differently. It is thus possible to understand the Jewish impetus to wander as being in some way part of this bio-trauma-cultural phenomenon.

These themes of movement, wandering, and travel appear everywhere from the earliest sacred literature to modern Israeli poetry, with many stops along the way proving that they are central to the Jewish experience. Throughout this chapter we will analyze different manifestations of this genetic coding being turned on its head, from painful origins to sources of strength, growth, and culture. Tracing examples through Jewish text and thought will shine a light on movement's ubiquity in Jewish life.

Movement in Sacred Literature

The Bible

Travel, movement, and walking are major themes that appear throughout the Hebrew Bible, our earliest sacred literature. These themes can first be analyzed through language, especially language surrounding the concept of dance.[7] For example, the root *raqad*—dance—occurs nine times in the Bible. Interestingly, it is more frequently used in the context of nature or chariots rather than people; goats dance about (Isaiah 13:21) and mountains dance like goats (Psalm 29:6; 114:4,6).[8] The synonym *maḥol*, in both noun and verb forms, is used to refer

---

[5] Epigenetics is a theory deemed science by some and pseudo-science by others. As a new field of inquiry there is real conversation regarding its legitimacy as a branch of science and its potential for misuse. We find it interesting as an idea and are struck by its ability to capture the multiplicity of feelings we observe. For further reading: https://developingchild.harvard.edu/resources/what-is-epigenetics-and-how-does-it-relate-to-child-development/; https://www.ncbi.nlm.nih.gov/pmc/articles/PMC6127768/.

[6] Samuels, David. "Do Jews Carry Trauma in Our Genes? A Conversation with Rachel Yehuda." *Tablet,* December 11, 2014. Also see: Lehrner Amy, Yehuda Rachel. "Cultural Trauma and Epigenetic Inheritance," *Development and Psychopathology* 30 issue 5 (2018), 1763-1777. doi: 10.1017/S0954579418001153.

[7] For a full analysis of the language of dance in the Hebrew Bible see Mayer I. Gruber, "Ten Dance-derived Expressions in the Hebrew Bible." in *Dance as Religious Studies*, edited by Doug Adams and Diane Apostolos-Cappadona, 48-66 (Oregon: Wipf and Stock Publishers, 2001).

[8] Note that the word is also used to refer to the movement of chariots in Nahum 3:2 and to the sound of chariots in Joel 2:5.

to dances of joy, celebration, and thanksgiving.[9]

These verses make it clear to us that dancing, especially by women, was an act of celebration and joy. It was a way to rejoice as a community and honor an individual. Significantly, it is not just young women who are involved in this dancing, as is often depicted in modern art. For example, Miriam is over 80 years old when she leads the women in dance after the crossing of the sea.[10] Nearly all individuals described as dancing are women, which makes it all the more interesting to see David dancing so obviously and with such abandon (2 Samuel 6).[11] Clearly, dance was a part of communal life and had important ritual and societal roles.

Early rituals in Israelite cultic life were also movement-based, including priestly anointing, shaking, and sprinkling blood.[12] Israelite cultic life was not meditative and quiet; it involved movement and noise and gesticulation. Ritually, the major holidays are pilgrimage festivals, entailing the entire community traveling to and from Jerusalem. The holidays are called *Regalim* (Exodus 23:14; Numbers 22:28-33), which literally means "feet."

The prevalence of movement in biblical ritual lies against the backdrop of the major theme of travel and movement in the biblical narrative. This theme is clearest in the desert wanderings in the Torah, where four of the five books (Exodus through Deuteronomy) depict the Israelites in constant motion, traveling from Egypt to Israel. This theme, however, is equally important in the Book of Genesis, where journeying plays a major role as well. God's appearance in the Garden of Eden is in walking through the Garden (Genesis 3:8); Adam and Eve are forced to journey out of the Garden (Genesis 3:23-24); Cain is forced to journey (Genesis 4:12ff); Noah journeys during the flood (Genesis 6ff); the people who built the Tower of Babel are punished by being forced to scatter and

---

[9] See, for example, Miriam dancing at the parting of the Sea (Exodus 15:20), Jephthah's daughter's greeting her father with dance (Judges 11:34), Benjaminite women dancing (Judges 21:21, 23), honoring David with song and dance (1 Samuel 18:6; 21:12; 29:5), Jeremiah describing joy and dancing in anticipation of the future return from exile (Jeremiah 31:3.12), the Psalmist describing joy and celebration of God through dance (Psalms 30:12; 149:3; 150:4), and the lack of dance as sign of sadness (Lamentations 5:16).

[10] Moses died at the age of 120, and the Israelites wandered for 40 years, making Moses 80 at the beginning of the Exodus. We also know that Miriam was Moses' older sister.

[11] Many have written about the feminine or queer imagery used to describe David. The fact that there is such emphasis on his dancing (which seems to be women's imagery), and that he is mocked by his wife, Michal, afterwards, adds depth to that reading, as do several other textual supports. See, e.g., James E. Harding, *The Love of David and Jonathan: Ideology, Text, Reception*, New York: Routledge Press, 2014; Dirk von der Horst, *Jonathan's Loves, David's Laments: Gay Theology, Musical Desires, and Historical Difference*, Wipf and Stock Publishers, 2017. A further approach can be seen in Ken Stone, "1 and 2 Samuel" in *The Queer Bible Commentary*, edited by Deryn Guest, et al. London: SCM Press, 2006.

[12] See, e.g., *Mishnah Tamid* 3:8.

separate throughout the world (Genesis 11:8); Abram begins his connection with God by being commanded to travel to Canaan (Genesis 12:1); Abram's father is identified as having begun the journey that Abram then completed (Genesis 11:29ff); Abraham continues to travel throughout his life, even in most important moments such as the wife-sister stories and the Akedah (Genesis 12-22); Isaac travels to Gerar (Genesis 26); Jacob and his sons travel to Egypt, with the sons making the trip back and forth several times (Genesis 37ff).

Each of these journeys plays a major literary role. They lead to growth and development in the patriarchal narratives. Even when the need to journey is a punishment, such as in the Garden of Eden and with the builders of the Tower of Babel, the journeying leads to new life and the further development of humankind. It leads to survival rather than death; it can lead to a more hopeful future. Thus, even in negative situations, journeying is a source of life and a necessary way to move into the future.

Rabbinic understanding of biblical travel further supports its significance. This comes through in the cantillation used in chanting certain "traveling" verses of the Torah. In the section listing the travels of the Israelites in the desert and where they stopped, verses that speak of the travels are read in a festive trope, also called the "desert traveling melody."[13] It is the same festive trope that is used in the Song of the Sea, specifically in the verses that contain God's name.[14] Perhaps this melody was chosen to draw connection between the role of God in the parting of the sea and the role of God in the Israelites' traveling through the desert. Thus, the significance of travel and the idea that biblical journeying is related to divine will is reflected in the traditional cantillation with which the Torah is chanted.[15]

While each text has individual nuance, the theme of journeying is central to the Torah and significant in the remainder of the Bible as well. The great emphasis on journeying can be understood as pointing to the central roles of the Exodus in biblical thought. The Exodus, and the subsequent revelation at Sinai, is the quintessential covenantal moment between God and the Israelites.

---

[13] Miles B. Cohen and Leslie Rubin. *Luah Hashanah*, New York: Miles Cohen, 2020, 186.

[14] Binder, A.W. *Biblical Chant*. New York: Sacred Music Press, 1959, 66-68.

[15] A.W. Binder notes a special chant for the reading of "journeys," which is also known as the "traveling melody." He writes that the special chants add "... majesty to the description of the Journeys of the hosts of Israel as they moved through the desert to the Holy Land..." (Binder, 68). Rabbi Tzvi Hersh Weinreb asks the question: Why would wandering through the desert be considered triumphant or majestic? His answer: Because although aimless wandering can be torture, wandering with a goal (God's promise of a land to settle at the end of the journey— Numbers 33:50-53) elevates the meaning of the wandering. Weinreb adds that the first time we hear the melody is the moment the Israelites leave Egypt. That majestic moment is now echoed in the 40-year march toward the land that will be theirs. See https://outorah.org/p/3013/.

It was during this time of wandering when God fulfilled a patriarchal promise to Israel to save them from their Egyptian servitude and to establish their covenantal relationship for the future.

The Exodus was a long, physical journey, involving a circuitous trek from Egypt to Israel. The Bible goes into detail about the Israelites' travels, emphasizing the physical toll it took on the people. It also makes clear how this movement is part of the self-identification of the Israelites. They suffered hunger and thirst.[16] They felt fear and concern.[17] Their cultic center, the *Mishkan*, was designed to be portable and carried. The Deity moved and traveled with them. God's presence was clear physically in a pillar of smoke during the day and a pillar of smoke at night (Exodus 13:21). Thus, the theme of the Exodus is so significant that it not only plays a central role in an overt way in the Torah, but is also a motif so powerful that it plays a crucial role in Genesis, which precedes the Egyptian experience and Exodus, and then continues throughout the Bible.[18]

This biblical theme of traveling connects with the concomitant theme of longing for Israel. Very little of the Torah actually occurs in the land of Israel; just a small part of the Book of Genesis. However, most of the Torah includes a focus on Israel from afar, and a promise of, and longing for, Israel as a covenantal home. The Torah ends before the Israelites enter the land, thus reinforcing the importance of peoplehood as opposed to arrival in Israel. In addition, it reinforces that this peoplehood is rooted in travel. Significantly, this is not a nomadic ideal; rather, it is a longing for a settled lifestyle, with the understanding of the reality of the need to often be on the move. The biblical eye is always looking toward Israel, although for much of the time the people themselves are living elsewhere.[19]

The Exodus motif and the central role of peoplehood are also directly related to the reality of the Israelite experience of exile much later in its history. It is generally understood that the Torah was canonized during the time of the Babylonian exile (6th century BCE) or very soon thereafter.[20] The Israelite experience of Exile and the impact of that experience on the canonization of

---

[16] For example, an elaborate description of that suffering in Numbers 20.

[17] For example, when they were being chased by the Egyptians (Exodus 14:10), or when they thought that Moses was lost to them (Exodus 32:1).

[18] Although from a "historical" perspective the narratives of Genesis occur before the Exodus, many of the themes of Genesis reflect material that occurs afterward. Among other places, this theme can be seen in narratives such as the wife-sister story in Genesis 12, and the Hagar narrative in Genesis 16. See, e.g., Yair Zakovich, *"And You Shall Tell Your Son...": The Concept of the Exodus in the Bible* (Jerusalem: Magnes Press, 1991), and Phyllis Trible, *Texts of Terror: Literary-Feminist Readings of Biblical Narratives* (Philadelphia: Fortress Press, 1984).

[19] This is discussed further below.

[20] Greenstein, Edward L. *Essays on Biblical Method and Translation*. Rhode Island: Scholars Press, 1989, 29-51.

the Torah logically influenced the central role of the Exodus journeying and wandering, and, we would argue, the centrality of movement and dance.

It is not only the patriarchs, matriarchs, the generation of the Exodus, and the Exiles who move and travel in the Bible. God in the Bible is presented as being very "physically" active and on the move. In God's first real interactions with the humans in the Garden of Eden, God takes a walk in the Garden (Genesis 3:8). At different times in the Bible, we see God riding the clouds (Deuteronomy 33:26) or walking with a walking stick (or perhaps a cane) (Psalm 23:4).[21] God travels through Egypt killing each Egyptian firstborn (Exodus 12:12), and walks ahead of the Israelites showing the Divine self in a pillar of fire during thhe night and a pillar of smoke during the day (Exodus 13:21). God commits to joining the Israelites in Exile (Ezekiel 11:16). In the Bible, our being created in God's image means that we are meant to walk, move, travel, and soar.[22]

Liturgy

This same approach can be applied to Jewish liturgy, where a tremendous amount of movement and choreography is embedded and embodied into the typical prayer life of a Jew. This offers a window into how Judaism has thought of worship, imagined a proper way to show one's devotion, and enjoined spiritual aims to a physical activity.

Traditional Jewish law calls for three daily prayer services: morning (*shaḥarit*), afternoon (*minḥah*), and evening (*ma'ariv*). Although the three services are each different, they all share a few core texts and their accompanying embodied ritual ways of moving. The three common texts are the *Amidah* (standing prayer), *Aleinu* (it is upon us), and *Kaddish Yatom* (mourner's prayer). In addition, the morning and evening prayer services both have a ritualized call to prayer (*barkhu*) which has its own prescriptive movement sequence.[23]

As part of the recitation of these prayers you will typically find the following movements that our ancient choreographers placed within the textual frameworks:

---

[21] See the analysis of Psalm 23:4 understanding the text as God's using a cane in order to walk (Prouser, "Awe-tism and th Biblical God," 1144).

[22] The Bible describes humans as being created *b'tzelem Elohim*, in God's image. See Genesis 1:26-27.

[23] See Michaelson, 21-33. Michaelson discusses how Jewish liturgy offers many prayers accompanied by movement. In one example he discusses the call to prayer, *Barkhu*, and points out that both *barkhu* and *berekh* (the Hebrew word for knee) share a common root: ברך *bet, resh, khaf*. He explains that although the words of this prayer are most commonly translated as "Blessed are You, God, ruler of the universe," a better way of understanding the meaning of these words could be "..YHVH is that-to-which-we-kneel. We are saying, in effect: my ego really wants to throw down a cup of coffee and rush off to work/school/carpool but I'm going to kneel that part of me before the part that acknowledges that I am not the king of the universe—that there's a whole, miraculous world out there."

They are:

> Bending from the knees
> Bowing from the waist
> Bowing left, right, and center—in quick succession
> Taking three steps forward
> Taking three steps backward
> Switching between standing and sitting
> Rising on our toes
> Standing straight up

Movement was considered so important, that in the Talmud, we read that if one does not follow the choreography of the *Amidah*, it would be better that they did not pray at all (Yoma 53B). This is because they understood stepping forward at the beginning of the prayer as stepping into God's presence and stepping backward at the end of the *Amidah* as an action showing respect for God; thus, not doing it properly was seen as a sign of disrespect. It must be noted that this section from the Talmud can feel offensive to those for whom stepping forward and backwards is physically difficult or impossible. Of course, there are also texts that clarify that there are many acceptable methods of praying, including by those who are experiencing sickness or disability.[24]

On another level, there is a movement style called *shuckling* that is not prescribed but has instead become a technology for intense concentration during prayer worship. It is simple, easily performed, and only involves moving the upper body in a repetitive forward-and-back or side-to-side motion. It can be used during silent moments and during those sections where one sings loudly. It is employed during quiet moments of reflection or for times when the prayer is intoned *sotto voce*, in a quiet voice, as if not to be overheard by anyone but God. This rocking motion can appear violent in its energy or soft and undulating. No matter the style, *shuckling* while praying can have the effect of helping the prayer achieve a meditative state or, at least, a state of some greater concentration.

There are many explanations for swaying and moving during prayer. For example, the *Shulchan Arukh*, a 16th-century commentary on Jewish Law, states that it is customary to sway when reading the Torah emulating the trembling that occurred at the revelation at Sinai, where the Bible reads "the people saw and trembled" (Exodus 20:15).

"And those who are exacting have practiced to shake at the time that we read the Torah as an illustration of the Torah that was given with trembling, and so

---

[24] See, for example, *Oraḥ Ḥayyim* 94:6 which makes it clear that someone who is ill can pray lying down in bed. And, if unable to pray due to illness, one can meditate in one's heart.

too at the time that we pray, because of 'all my bones will say to you, Lord who is like You?' (Psalm 35:10)" (Oraḥ Ḥayyim 48). In other words, our swaying during prayer is the embodied recognition of the full-bodied trembling ("all my bones") that took place at Sinai.

Using this same verse, Psalm 35:10, others have stated that we should move our body in prayer to show that we praise God using our whole selves: mind, heart, and body. Another approach is expressed by the Baal Shem Tov[25] who said that just as a person shakes a bit before human intimacy, so too does a person shake before intimacy with the Divine (*Tzava'at Harivash*: 68). Rabbi Akiva[26] was known to move so much during prayer, that he would start in one corner of a room and end up in the other when praying privately due to all of his bowing and movement (*Berakhot* 31a). These representative explanations point to an interesting variety of approaches to embodied prayer.

A further embodied element of prayer that should be mentioned in this context is the importance of praying facing Jerusalem. The direction we face when we stand in prayer, the way we face, adds additional meaning to our prayer. This mirrors the Biblical eye that looks towards Israel, mentioned above.

All this is to say that movement, and even choreography have been part of the Jewish prayer experience for several thousands of years. Embodied learning is a relatively new field of inquiry; embodied praying is not.[27]

Maqom and *Hamaqom*

It's interesting to think about the role of movement in the context of the word *maqom* in Jewish tradition. It literally translates as "place," but is also used in rabbinic contexts as a name for God. The significance of a word like *maqom* in the Bible resides in that, often, "identity formation occurs in relation to movement toward and from particular locations."[28] In other words, biblical texts of national identity naturally bring with them a sense of movement (Jacob, Abraham, Genesis 12, 28). Much of this movement includes an emphasis on *maqom,* place. This can be seen in Genesis 28:11, which involves Jacob's fleeing to Haran and having the famous "Jacob's Ladder" dream. The word *maqom* is used three times in a short verse, emphasizing the centrality of place. "[Yaakov]

---

[25] Rabbi Israel ben Eliezer, a 16th-century mystic who is known as the founder of Hasidic Judaism.
[26] A major rabbinic figure of the first and second centuries CE whose contributions to rabbinic thought and Jewish law are immeasurable.
[27] Similar work can be done in rabbinic literature as well. In addition, looking at mystical texts, significant work has been done on the role of walking in the Zohar. See David Greenstein, *Roads to Utopia: The Walking Stories of the Zohar*. Stanford, California: Stanford University Press, 2014.
[28] Mann, Barbara E. *Space and Place in Jewish Studies*. New Jersey: Rutgers University Press, 2012, 11.

encountered a certain place [*maqom*]. He had to spend the night there, for the sun had come in. Now he took one of the stones of the place [*maqom*] and set it at his head and lay down in that place [*maqom*]."²⁹

In the biblical text, the word has theological and philosophical overtones, but by the rabbinic period the word *Maqom* is used as a divine name. *Bereishit Rabbah* 68:9 contains the traditional explanation for this name of God: that God is seen as the space where the universe exists. God is not a part of nor outside of the space of the world; rather, the world is a part of God.³⁰ Barbara Mann builds on this idea saying that "perhaps the rabbis who produced *Bereishit Rabbah* felt themselves to be in some sort of exile, and therefore invested space with transcendence, and God with the materiality of space."³¹ If we accept that an important part of our national ethos has always been travel, movement, and spatial impermanence, then historically it became all the more important to see that spatial permanence in God.³² If the Jewish community did not feel that where they lived was secure as a permanent home, they could still find that sense of security and reliability of place in the image of God as *maqom*. Perhaps it is no accident that the traditional statement of comfort in times of mourning refers to God as "*Hamaqom*."³³ Given that grief and loss can lead to feeling uprooted metaphorically, again, it was important to express comfort through permanence of space, even in a metaphorical sense.

Movement in Jewish Arts

Jewish Literature³⁴

> ... the Jewish game of hearts between east and west, between self and heart, to and fro, to without fro, fro without to.
> —Yehuda Amichai

The idea of movement continues its impact beyond our sacred literature and into modern Jewish literature with an emphasis on desire for travel, actual

---

²⁹ This is the translation of Everett Fox, The Five Books of Moses. Fox's translation is especially valuable here as his method includes repeating words in English that are repeated in the Hebrew.
³⁰ See a nice explanation of this concept by Rabbi Ismar Schorsch at https://www.jtsa.edu/behind-gods-names.
³¹ Mann, 11.
³² Note Yehudah Amichai's reference to the same idea in his poem, "*Jewish Travel #2.*"
³³ The full statement is "*Hamaqom yinahem etkhem b'tokh she'ar aveilei Tzion v'Yerushalayim.*" "May *Hamaqom* (God, the Omnipresent One) comfort you among the mourners of Zion and Jerusalem."
³⁴ Our gratitude to Professor Anne Lapidus Lerner for her assistance in this section.

travel, and an understanding that they are a part of Jewish consciousness. For example, Israeli poet Yehuda Amichai (1924-2000) has two major poem groups called "Israeli Travel: Otherness is All, Otherness is Love," and "Jewish Travel: Change is God and Death is His Prophet."[35] Amichai brings image after image of transit and travel. He describes sights while traveling and the essential nature of Jewish travel. He relates it to movement in the Bible, and brings it into the idea of the *tiyul* (trip, trek, hike) in modern Israel. He talks about Moses writing the Torah as his personal travel book ("Jewish Travel #3"). He writes about the migration of Jews and what that means for Jewish life, and, perhaps, death ("Jewish travel #2").

Yehuda Halevi wrote, " the East is my heart, and I dwell at the end of the West." That's Jewish travel, that's the Jewish game of hearts between east and west, between self and heart, to and fro, to without fro, fro without to, fugitive and vagabond without sin. Endless journey, like the trip Freud the Jew took, wandering between body and mind, between mind and body, only to die between the two.[36]

He does not conclude that Jewish travel ends with the establishment of the State of Israel, focusing on Israel as the destination. Rather, he emphasizes that Jewish travel is part of Jewish thought and Jewish life, and continues within Israel.[37] According to Amichai, travel is an inescapable part of Jewish life, is part of Jewish heritage, and will be a part of the future of Jwish life.

Amir Gilboa's poem, *Sarai*, describes Sarah's pain as she lived a life without children. We hear of her beauty, of her infertility, of her struggle. But most of all, we hear of her walking. The poem begins: "A long way she went. Over mountains and in valleys, Mountains upon mountains she left behind her and still she walks and walks."[38] There are many ways we could speak of Sarai's life and pain, her beauty and her infertility. The poem, however, gets all this across by talking about her endless walking.

S. Y. Agnon's *Ma'aseh Ha'ez Fable of the Goat* is based around the idea of a goat who regularly travels between Poland and Israel. The owner's son follows it once and rejoices in reaching the land of Israel. The process of the travel is emphasized in the challenges involved. The son writes a note to his father telling him to follow the goat and he too will end up in Israel, tucking the note

---

[35] Both poems are in *Open Closed Open* by Yehuda Amichai. Translated by Chana Bloch and Chana Kronfeld. New York: Harcourt Ind., 2006.
[36] Yehuda Amichai, "Jewish Travel: Change is God and Death is His Prophet, #2."
[37] Vered Shemtov, "Between Perspectives of Space: A Reading in Yehuda Amichai's 'Jewish Travel" and 'Israeli Travel." *Jewish Social Studies* 11 no. 3 (2005): 141-161.
[38] Jacobson, David C. *Does David Still Play Before You? Israeli Poetry and the Bible*. Detroit: Wayne State University Press, 1997, 188-190.

in the goat's ear. However, the father does not see the note, and in a fit of grief believing his son is dead, slaughters the goat, only finding the note when its life has left its body. The combination of the value of travel, the beauty of the ability to travel between locations, and the ultimate tragedy of the loss of that ability to travel emphasizes the point that movement is a central, albeit complicated, part of Jewish life.

These are only a small sampling of what we see as typical of Jewish literature. They express the understanding that Jewish life involves the necessity of movement among locations. In some cases, it involves longing to travel to Israel, or that journey. The essential idea, however, is the significance of travel itself in Jewish life.

Israeli Folk Dancing

> Art is the only way to run away without leaving home.
> —Twyla Tharp

No discussion of movement in Jewish life would be complete without including Israeli folk dance.[39] While Israeli folk dance has been an integral part of Jewish life, its origins lay in the decades before the establishment of the State of Israel. In these early years, creating folk dance was an integral part of life in Israel. People created dances tied to both the land and the Jewish calendar, providing a "secular" way to celebrate Jewish holidays. While folk dances tend to grow organically over centuries, the early Israeli pioneers knew they needed to create their cultural dance quickly, just like everything else in Israel needed to develop quickly.[40] Dance has been studied as not only reflecting a national ethos, but also as helping to create that national ethos. Thus, Israeli folk dance was meant to exhibit the characteristics that were prized in these early time periods in Israel, including athleticism and vibrancy. Israeli dance was meant to transmit pride, confidence, and self-worth. "All the feelings of dedication to our new nation and pride and joy were imbedded in the syncopated, bouncy, fleet-spirited dancing we did."[41] There was also great emphasis on togetherness. They emphasized "the aesthetic of togetherness" which helped to build community.[42] Similarly, it was intended to refute the antisemitic trope of the

---

[39] The role of dance in Israel is examined in great depth in Naomi M. Jackson, et al. *Oxford Handbook of Jewishness and Dance.* Oxford: Oxford University Press, 2022.
[40] Ingber, Judith Brin. "*Shorashim*: The Roots of Israeli Folk Dance." In *Seeing Israeli and Jewish Dance,* edited by Judith Brin Ingber. Detroit: Wayne State University Press, 2011, 102, 109.
[41] Ingber, 127.
[42] Neuman, Gdalit. "From Victimized to Victorious: Re-Forming Post-Holocaust Jewish Em-

weak, powerless Jew, and to reflect the New Muscular Jew as presented by Max Nordau.[43] The physicality was important as the early settlers needed to be muscular and able-bodied farmers and workers of the land. This has also been called "the aesthetic of toughness."[44] This part of folk dance was considered an extension of gymnastics. During the 19th and first half of the 20th centuries, throughout the world, gymnastics was, seen as a form of fostering deep nationalism, by attempting to build the ideal, strong, bodies, in Germany,[45] America,[46] and other countries.[47]

While much of Israeli folk dance consisted of steps developed from many different cultures, there were several movements that were particular to Israeli folk dance. This is clearly seen in the upright posture of Israeli folk dance, meant to negate the antisemitic image of the stooped diaspora Jew.[48] It is no accident that it was important to the Jewish Agency to send an Israeli folk dance company to perform throughout Europe in 1947. The statement they made through their dance was the one that the Jewish Agency wanted Europe, and European Jews in particular, to understand about the New Muscular Jew.[49] It is said that the view of the weak Jewish body was so embedded in the thought process of many European Jews that it was only through the arts, including music, dance, and physical exercise, that some, especially young survivors, were helped to "carefully reclaim Jewish life."[50]

In Conclusion: The Wandering Jew[51]
Our study of text through movement reclaims this complicated identity and transforms it to an enlightening and exciting form of study of Jewish sacred text.

---

bodied Identity Through Dance." In *The Oxford Handbook of Jewishness and Dance*, edited by Naomi Jackson et al. Oxford: Oxford University Press, 2022, 128.

[43] Ibid., 110-112.

[44] Ibid., 129.

[45] See Reicher, D. "Nationalistic German Gymnastic Movements and Modern Sports: Culture Between Identity and Habitus. *Historical Social Research* 45, no. 1 (2020)

[46] Hofmann, A. R. "The American Turners: their past and present." *Revista Brasileira De Ciências Do Esporte* 37, no. 2 (2015): 122. As with many nationalistic ploys, especially those rooted in the body, this was driven by and fostered certain racist, antisemitic, and authoritarian ideologies.

[47] Ingber. "*Shorashim*: The Roots of Israeli Folk Dance." In *Seeing Israeli and Jewish Dance*, 114.

[48] Neuman, 115.

[49] See Neuman, 115, and Ingber, Judith Brin. "Vilified or Glorified? Nazi Versus Zionist Views of the Jewish Body." In *Seeing Israeli and Jewish Dance*, 251-280.

[50] The role of dance in building up post-Holocaust community in Israel is explored further in Ingber's "Vilified or Glorified?", 266

[51] The term "wandering Jew" oftentimes refers to the plant (tradescantia zebrina) whose leaves are a deep purple and sport brilliant stripes of silver. While this name seems to call to mind Moses and the Israelites wandering in the desert, this familiar narrative does not reveal the

It reframes a form of struggle and fear into a joyous act of learning and growth. Studying Bible through circus and movement, in addition to being a powerful form of study, almost becomes a statement of power itself.

---

antisemitic intention of the plant's name. This plant, and others in its genus, are described as invasive plants and tend to spread out. The appellation Wandering Jew derives from a 13th-century Christian legend about a Jewish man who taunted Jesus while on his way to the crucifixion. As punishment for his verbal abuse the man was destined to wander the earth until the second coming. Though there are several versions of this story, all are based on this structure rooted in an antisemitic base. Antisemitism is important to the explication of our work because of its relevance to the vision of the Jew who wanders. Since wandering is such an important aspect of the Jewish identity, and because antisemitism is close to the root of that historic trope, its inclusion cannot be minimized.

References

Agnon, S.Y. "Three Stories: Fable of the Goat." Translated by Barney Rubin. *Commentary*, December 1966. https://www.commentarymagazine.com/articles/s-agnon/three-stories-fable-of-the-goat/.

Amichai, Yehuda. *Open, Closed, Open*. Translated by Chana Bloch and Chana Kronfeld. New York: Harcourt Ind., 2006.

Binder, A.W. *Biblical Chant*. New York: Sacred Music Press, 1959.

Bouissac, Paul. *Semiotics at the Circus*. Berlin: De Gruyter, 2010.

Cohen, Miles and Leslie Rubin, *Luaḥ Hashanah*, New York: Miles Cohen, 2020.

Fox, Everett. *The Five Books of Moses*. New York: Schocken Books, 1983.

Greenstein, David. *Roads to Utopia: The Walking Stories of the Zohar*. Stanford, California: Stanford University Press, 2014.

Greenstein, Edward L. *Essays on Biblical Method and Translation*. Rhode Island: Scholars Press, 1989.

Gruber, Mayer I. "Ten Dance-derived Expressions in the Hebrew Bible." In *Dance as Religious Studies*, edited by Doug Adams and Diane Apostolos-Cappadona. Oregon: Wipf and Stock Publishers, 2001, 48-66.

Harding, James E. *The Love of David and Jonathan: Ideology, Text, Reception*. New York: Routledge Press, 2014.

Hasan-Rokem, Galit. "The Wandering Jew – A Jewish Perspective." *Proceedings of the World Congress of Jewish Studies* Division D, no. 2 (1985): 189-196.

Hofmann, A. R. "The American Turners: their past and present." *Revista Brasileira De Ciências Do Esporte* 37, no. 2 (2015): 119-127.

Ingber, Judith Brin. "*Shorashim*: The Roots of Israeli Folk Dance." In *Seeing Israeli and Jewish Dance*, edited by Judith Brin Ingber. Detroit: Wayne State University Press, 2011, 99-170.

Ingber, Judith Brin. "Vilified or Glorified? Nazi Versus Zionist Views of the Jewish Body." In *Seeing Israeli and Jewish Dance*, edited by Judith Brin Ingber. Detroit: Wayne State University Press, 2011, 251-280.

Jacobson, David C. *Does David Still Play Before You? Israeli Poetry and the Bible*. Detroit: Wayne State University Press, 1997.

Lehrner, Amy and Rachel Yehuda. "Cultural Trauma and Epigenetic Inheritance." *Development and Psychopathology* 30, no. 5 (2018): 1763-1777.

Mann, Barbara E. *Space and Place in Jewish Studies*. New Jersey: Rutgers University Press, 2012.

Michaelson, Jay. *God in Your Body: Kabbalah, Mindfulness and Embodied Spiritual Practice*. Vermont: Jewish Lights Publishing, 2007.

Neuman, Gdalit. "Dancing Between Old Worlds and New: Max Nordau's New Jew Idea and it's Manifestation in Pre-State Israeli Folk Dance." *Performance Matters* 2, no. 2 (2016): 11-24.

Neuman, Gdalit. "From Victimized to Victorious: Re-Forming Post-Holocaust Jewish Embodied Identity Through Dance." In *The Oxford Handbook of Jewishness and Dance*, edited by Naomi Jackson et al. Oxford: Oxford University Press, 2022.

Pritchard, James B. *Ancient Near Eastern Texts Related to the Old Testament*. Princeton: Princeton University Press, 1969.

Prouser, Ora Horn. "Awe-tism and the Biblical God." in *Ve'Ed Ya'aleh (Gen. 2:6) Essays in Biblical and Ancient Near Eastern Studies Presented to Edward L. Greenstein* Vol II., edited by Peter Machinist et al. Atlanta: SBL Press, 2021.

Prouser, Ora Horn. *Esau's Blessing: How the Bible Embraces Those with Special Needs*. New Jersey: Ben Yehuda Press, 2012.

Reicher, D. "Nationalistic German Gymnastic Movements and Modern Sports: Culture Between Identity and Habitus. *Historical Social Research* 45, no. 1 (2020): 207-225.

Samuels, David. "Do Jews Carry Trauma in Our Genes? A Conversation with Rachel Yehuda." *Tablet*, December 11, 2014.

Shemtov, Vered. "Between Perspectives of Space: A Reading in Yehuda Amichai's 'Jewish Travel" and 'Israeli Travel.'" *Jewish Social Studies* 11 no. 3 (2005): 141-161.

Stone, Ken. "1 and 2 Samuel." In *The Queer Bible Commentary*, edited by Deryn Guest et al. London: SCM Press, 2006.

Trible, Phyllis. *Texts of Terror: Literary-Feminist Readings of Biblical Narratives*. Philadelphia: Fortress Press, 1984.

Von der Horst, Dirk. "Jonathan's Loves, David's Laments: Gay Theology, Musical Desires, and Historical Difference." Wipf and Stock Publishers, 2017.

Zakovich, Yair. *"And You Shall Tell Your Son...": The Concept of the Exodus in the Bible*. Jerusalem: Magnes Press, 1991.

Outsider Circus Trapeze Horse Acrobats, Malcah Zeldis, 1982.
© 2022 Malcah Zeldis / Artists Rights Society (ARS), New York

Hafokh Bah, For Everything is In It: The Method of Sacred Arts

AYAL PROUSER, MICHAEL KASPER, ORA HORN PROUSER

In a full length Sacred Arts class that we taught, we set up a tightwire and students practiced walking on it. We studied the *Akedah*, the Binding of Isaac (Genesis 22), and then returned to the wire. We encouraged the students to think about the *Akedah* while walking on the tightwire. We asked them to think about Abraham and his choices during the *Akedah* while feeling the imbalance of wire walking. One student traversed the tightwire while holding the Bible, and reading the text. (Yes, he was holding one of our hands!) In this process he was brought to tears. He told us he had studied the *Akedah* so often that he felt jaded about it. And then, while walking on the tightwire, feeling the imbalance in his being, he thought about Abraham in a whole new light and was deeply touched by Abraham's struggle, his impossible choice, the utter lack of control of his situation. Thinking with his body and mind, instead of his mind exclusively, led him to feel the struggle of a biblical character in a way that he never had: a sense of bodily empathy.

Throughout this chapter we will bring you through the processes of a Sacred Arts workshop or class. This will be a combination of step-by-step moments combined with personal anecdotes. What can we say? We are a chatty trio. Hopefully we don't bring you to tears like that student on the tightwire, though. We will not be giving you instructions that will catalyze a Sacred Arts experience, but by the end of the chapter we hope you will have a fuller grasp of just what Sacred Arts is, and how it works. With any Sacred Arts workshop we always start by asking, *What is it?*

Studying the Binding of Isaac with Academy for Jewish Religion students, 2018.
(Photo: Ora Horn Prouser)

Step 1: What do we mean by Sacred Arts?
Sacred Arts is more than an interesting name; it joins and elevates the two foci of our work, sacred text and artistic exploration, so that together they add new sensory experience to the already vast corpus of interpretation Jewish tradition

embodies.[1] Our understanding of Sacred Arts is a method in which art forms are used as vehicles to process text. It treats both the text and the art as serious academic disciplines. To be clear, this is not art as arts-and-crafts or playtime, (although employing art methodologies can be quite fun). And it is not using the text as a jumping-off point to produce art. Rather, it uses the artistic process as a way to understand the text, as a way to study the text. It entails the use of art methodologies as a rigorous discipline in which we both present and solve problems about sacred literature. Jewish text communicates on a variety of levels to a variety of students possessing a variety of intelligences. Our method affirms to artists that their ways of understanding are essential, valued, intrinsic, and not tangential to their experience of Jewish texts and Jewish life. Examples that have made their way into AJR's curriculum include: using circus pyramid-building to understand the structure of a Talmudic argument; composing poems and songs to understand the perspective of specific characters in biblical texts; engaging in movement activities in order to imagine biblical characters' interactive lives. These examples can each be amplified, showing that the arts can serve as a means of processing—as important as any other approach to study.

We spent so long developing this method not only because we believe in it, its efficacy, and its potential for influence in the Jewish world. It also helps that we are a: 1. Biblicist/circus mom and circus enthusiast (harsh critic, honestly); 2. Dancer turned cantor and Jewish Educator; 3. USCJ poster child turned circus artist and circademic.

Why Sacred Arts?
We are often met with some sort of combination of excitement and cynicism. "Circus… like clowns and acrobats?" Can we really think with our body? Is this a legitimate form of academic study? We say, absolutely, and are happy to explain why.

There is significant literature to support the importance of studying through the arts. Howard Gardner's theory of Multiple Intelligences has been a staple of educational thought for many years.[2] It emphasizes that individuals do not all learn the same way, and that in order to reach the greatest variety of learners,

---

[1] The majority of this chapter focuses on circus rather than dance. We did that as circus is less known, and we feel that if we can get the idea across through circus, most people will know how to apply it to dance as well.
[2] Howard Gardner, *Frames of Mind: The Theory of Multiple Intelligences*. Philadelphia: Basic Books, 2011. There has been significant discussion and disagreement as to the value and success of the theory of multiple intelligences, with some dismissing it as simplistic, unrealistic, too complex, or not valuable for a curriculum (see Shearer, p. 3). Others have found great value in the theory, noting that those who have "debunked" the theory are not sufficiently well versed in what it really means, and how it is meant to be used.

Studying a biblical text with Academy for Jewish Religion students, 2018.
(Photo: Ora Horn Prouser)

it is important to teach to these multiple intelligences. These intelligences have been thought to include linguistic, logical-mathematical, visual-spatial, kinesthetic, musical, naturalist, interpersonal, and intrapersonal.[3]

It is important to note that the theory of multiple intelligences is not synonymous with learning styles. Learning styles refers to ways that people prefer to learn, while multiple intelligences refers to the skill of creating a product, or problem solving. For our purposes, both of these are important. In our work, one of the most relevant intelligences is kinesthetic education. That includes the ability to use the body for both expressive and goal-directed activities: using the body for artistic purposes and using the body in areas such as sports and activities, which includes working with one's hands. Studying through movement (and by movement we mean dance or circus) is advantageous to those whose learning style is kinesthetic (as opposed to visual or auditory) and is powerful to those whose strongest "intelligence" is kinesthetic.

Significantly, however, we have found that this process is also valuable to those whose learning styles and intelligences are not primarily kinesthetic.

Perhaps we are just a couple of academic nerds here, but as original practitioners of Sacred Arts, we have a bit of a tangent or confession to illustrate the value of the range of learning styles in a community and even within one

---

[3] Branton Shearer, "Multiple Intelligences Theory After Twenty Years." *Teachers College Record*, 106, (1)2004: 2-16. Many have built on Gardner's approach in a variety of ways, and there are many analyses of multiple intelligences that go beyond Gardner's original list; depending on the scholar the number of these multiple intelligences has varied widely.

individual. In a discussion about experiential education in one of our academic courses on studying Bible through circus, a guest lecturer asked everyone to describe a favorite learning moment. He fully expected everyone to describe an experiential moment: singing at camp, working on a Purim spiel, etc. Two of us were co-teachers of the course, who believe deeply in the value of alternative forms of education such as Sacred Arts. In response to this question, both of us referred to moments of conventional classroom study as having been completely central to our educational background, and even *fun*. This in no way discounts the benefits of kinesthetic learning. Rather, it emphasizes the value of this kinesthetic learning to everyone, not only to self-described kinesthetic learners.

There has also been significant research on the impact of arts education on students as a whole. That is, the role of the arts in the educational system and the opportunity for students to be actively involved in the process has led to higher test scores and more integrated and effective learning. The arts have been used in educational curricula to lead students to be more efficient problem solvers, to enjoy more satisfying lives, to become more thoughtful, and to have a better understanding of the larger world.[4]

In combining art with other disciplines, students will develop skills by manipulating and perfecting the materials they work with. They will perceive information in a fresh way. They will heighten their awareness, their ability to associate, and their ability to discern between related and non-related topics. They will learn to actively express themselves by creating or fashioning a product and creating a more in-depth understanding of the process by engaging both with their hands and with their minds in the process. They will learn to evaluate by analyzing, valuing, and showing appreciation for not only their own development but the development of others.[5]

We have seen all of the above with our approach to studying text through circus. Students have approached text in ways they did not expect. Even though they were studying texts they had read many times, they were finding new understandings and making new connections because they were approaching the text through movement.

Why the body?

We do Sacred Arts because of our backgrounds. We do, however, believe in the potential for other forms of study. For instance in one of our courses, we had a student who really got Sacred Arts. He could apply the concept, and follow the

---

[4] Lorraine W. Cowe, "*The Concept of the Theory of Multiple Intelligences and an Interdisciplinary, Arts Inclusive Curriculum: A Model for Teaching Whose Time Has Come.*" MA Thesis, (Western Michigan University, 1993).

[5] Ibid, 83-84.

guidelines set out in the method, as well as a deep appreciation for its benefits. By the end of the course he said, "I know exactly how I'd study Bible through basketball drills now." We are still waiting on him to show us Sacred Sports, and cannot wait to see it in practice.

One may ask, why introduce new learning models of sacred text? Biblicists, lay people, believers and non-believers alike have successfully engaged in the study of religious sacred texts for some two thousand years by reading, thinking, and discussing deeply. So why suddenly add to the process? Why upend the natural order of things? Why replace the well-worn study tables of the *beit midrash* (house of study/study hall) for the open space and smoothed wooden planks of a dance studio or the mats of a circus gym? Indeed, what makes the case for dance or circus as legitimate tools that can help unlock the ancient mysteries of some of the world's most foundational texts? In other words, what does this have to do with using dance or circus as vehicles for learning? More to the point, what does this have to do with the study of sacred texts?

Movement of the body is inextricably linked with feelings in the mind. Those feelings may originate as brain activities but they are felt throughout: in the stomach, the heart, the rush of blood and the contractions of muscle and tendon, even a breath. Movement is first: it is primary, primal, and essential. It comes before control of body function, before speech, before artistic ability, before everything! Movement is life itself. It is how we know we are alive. We watch the uncontrolled full-bodied throes of the newest born. We watch the undulating respirations of a sleeping neonate. We watch, and delight in the watching, as the crawler becomes a toddler, a walker, a runner, and then maybe a bodily artist, perhaps dancing on the ground or in the air. So, how is it possible that in the evolution of our thinking about the pedagogy of learning we have forgotten to remember our collective history, that very essence that helps define us as human beings?

If we are made holy because we are made in the image of God, *B'tzelem Elohim*, then we must recognize that this pertains to the body as well, and all the information it holds. We need to pay it the respect we offer our mind and our intellect. And not because there is a Divine physical body that we are patterned after but, rather, because our essence, our intellectual perception, our humanity is fashioned in God's image.[6] To forget the majesty of this image is to discount the history of our personal experience—which is always a mistake.

---

[6] There is wonderful work on the image of God's body in the Bible, as there are many biblical images of God's hand, face, back, nose, etc. Yochanan Muffs has made the point that since in ancient Israel they were prohibited from creating visual images of God, the biblical authors created literary images of God. (Muffs, 97-98.) See also, e.g. Benjamin D. Sommer, *The Bodies of God and the World of Ancient Israel*. Cambridge: Cambridge University Press, 2009.

Maimonides, in his *Guide for the Perplexed*, gives voice to the understanding that being made in God's image, in God's *tzelem*, refers to the elevation of spirit and of soul and not to the idea that God is made of a face and limbs, as humankind is.[7] S.Y. Agnon, in his 1945 novel *T'mol Shilshom* (*Only Yesterday*) picks up the image of an elevation of the soul. As Agnon imagines it, the act of dancing, the raising of limbs[8] signaling the dance about to emerge, sets in motion the elevation of the human to the place of a soul. Agnon's vision imagines our ability to move as the medium that catapults humanity toward God's *tzelem*.

Studying the Book of Ruth with Academy for Jewish Religion students, 2018.
(Photo: Ora Horn Prouser)

If to move is to be human, then movement, in any of its capacities, (dance, circus or others) is at the heart of human activity, even when it is movement for studying. This is more potent in studying Sacred Literature when the ethos of one being made in God's image is fundamental to Jewish study. We are using our bodies, our physical representation of God's image, to study the Bible, the text we use as our source of understanding God's image. The "what" we are studying and the "how" we are studying are inherently connected.[9] The concept of unifying the vehicle for study and the subject of the study is further discussed below. That said, the Jewish connection to movement is further legitimized and practiced through study.

Step 2: Underlying principles of Bible study

One of the most famous adages about studying Torah is *Hafokh bah, v'hafokh bah d'kulah bah*—"Turn it over and over for everything is in it" (Pirkei Avot 5:24).[10] We agree; if you do enough flips, you start to see things differently.

The idea of *hafokh bah, hafokh bah d'kulah bah*, that there is so much in the Torah that we can come back to it over and over and continue to find new

---

[7] *Guide for the Perplexed*, Part 1, 1:2
[8] See his connection to Psalm 35:10 "All my bones/limbs will say to you..."
[9] This can be connected to the methodological concept in Biblical Studies of "form and content." That is, the form of the text often parallels the content of the text. (Rendsburg, 559-578 and Trible, 91ff).
[10] Interestingly, different versions of Pirkei Avot cite this verse as anywhere between 5:22-5:26.

things, is inspirational. It pushes us to continue to return to the Torah in new ways and with new directions.

In order to understand the process of studying Bible through circus, we first need to lay out the assumptions and methodology of Bible study that we employ. The first methodological assumption is that we aim to study the *peshat* of the text. Two broad approaches to biblical study include *peshat* and *derash*. *Derash* is an interpretive method, reading text through broad interpretation and homiletic approaches. *Peshat* is a contextual approach. That is, when we read the *peshat* of the text we look to see our readings as supported clearly by the language and context of the text.[11] Reading the *peshat* of the text is beneficial for a number of reasons. It forces us to read carefully and to really pay attention to the language of the text. It also enables us to focus on the biblical text itself as opposed to the rabbinic understanding of the Bible. By focusing on the biblical text, we often find that the Bible is more open to modern sensibilities, such as approaches to feminist views,[12] than millennia of patriarchal biblical interpretation left room for.

This study is often done in heterogeneous groups. That means that we need to leave real room for many different approaches to biblical study in any given group. A group studying together through circus may include students who understand the Torah as being of divine authorship, and others believing that it is totally a product of human creation. It can include those who find the text historically accurate and those that read the Bible mythologically. Focusing deeply on the text itself is something that diverse groups can do together, while avoiding conversations on these topics of great controversy. This is not to say that those conversations are unimportant, but rather that this method enables us to place our focus elsewhere and thus is very beneficial to diverse groups.

The biblical methodology we use is literary in focus. We do a close reading of the text, with special attention paid to word choice, themes, structure, and character development within the narrative. We ask questions such as who speaks and when, and what are the relationships among the characters. Given that we are working on a *peshat* reading of the text we require participants to support their views within the text itself. We make it clear that we are not looking for

---

[11] A good classic formulation of these terms is in Greenstein, 215-227.
[12] This may sound counterintuitive to those who have been led to read about women in the Bible as unimportant and as subjugated, deep analysis of women characters shows them to be characters who think, who use their power in creative and valuable ways, and who are instrumental in moving the sacred history forward. Similar statements can be made, for example, about Disability Studies, where many have only focused on the negative statement about those with disabilities in Leviticus 21:16-24; 22:20-25, while ignoring the fact that major biblical characters were those with disabilities. See, for example, Prouser, *Esau's Blessing*, and Prouser, "Awe-tism," pp. 1149ff.

one reading of the text. Rather, we believe in many different *peshat* readings of the text, even mutually exclusive readings.[13] That is, as long as participants can support their reading, the reading is a possible *peshat* reading. In fact, we actively promote alternative readings, emphasizing the richness of the Bible, and the fact that no matter how well we think we know a narrative, there are ways of approaching it that we have not yet considered.[14] We carefully make the point that none of us needs to fight for our reading over all other views. Rather, there is tremendous space for diversity of opinion.

The richest/most accessible texts to use for this method are narratives with multiple characters that speak and act. For example, the stealing of the birthright (Genesis 27-28), the story of Hagar (Genesis 16, 21), The Binding of Isaac (Genesis 22), The Garden of Eden (Genesis 3), The Book of Ruth, the Joseph story (Genesis 37ff), and the like are all rich texts with multiple active characters which enable us to delve into those relationships, and tease out a variety of defensible readings.

At Limmud NY, a non-denominational communal learning event, we led a workshop with others who study through the arts. All of our methods were very different, and there was beauty in the range of approaches. We led both a dance and circus Sacred Arts crash workshop. All the artists were tasked with teaching the same text. Genesis 24, the beginning of the narrative of Rebekkah and Isaac. One line in that text describes how Isaac takes Rebecca into his mother's tent. Most of us in the room found this text to be awkwardly Freudian and hard to contextualize beyond that point.[15] During the circus Sacred Arts section, three women created a pyramid in which they all balanced each other, and if any one did not commit to doing their part the whole pyramid would fall. It was in this pyramid that they found a new reading. One of the women stated that she felt the support of the other women. She then understood this sentence as referencing intergenerational maternal and female support—everyone doing

---

[13] See, for example, multiple conflicting readings of the Binding of Isaac in Genesis 22. The classical traditional reading is that Abraham passed the test. Other *peshat* readings, however, have been offered, such as that Abraham failed the test (Fewell and Gunn, 90-100), and that Abraham was testing God as much as God was testing Abraham (Gros-Louis, 71-84).

[14] Even Rashi, the great medieval biblical commentator of the eleventh century, according to his grandson, Rashbam, "admitted to me that, if he had had the time, he would have found it necessary to write new commentaries, based on the insights into the *peshat* that are newly created each day." See Rashbam's commentary on Genesis 37:2 (note that in some versions this is listed as Genesis 37:1).

[15] Freudian developmental theory would suggest that sons want to replace their fathers and become the love object of their mother: the Oedipal Complex. The text points to this archaic love and seems to say that Isaac took Rebecca to Sarah's tent with the idea of turning Rebecca into his mother. For more on this see Rashi, the French medieval biblical commentator from the eleventh century on Genesis 24:67)

their part. This was a new reading of an old text, one devised by bodily/circus thinking. Just as we learn how to study Bible, so too we can learn how to study in circus or dance.

Step 3: Let's get moving!
In the workshop we typically start learning circus or movement-based prompts at this point. In lieu of recklessly trying to use the written word here to teach circus arts or to convey choreography, we will instead contextualize those artforms a bit more deeply for you here. In our full length courses we spend serious time studying specific nuances of each art.

As we establish the importance of using circus and dance to study text, it is important to have real clarity as to how we are defining these two art forms. Most any source one looks at describes dance as a way of moving one's body rhythmically…to music. Although this definition is clear and accurate it must be said that music (at least music that can be heard) is not necessary. Dance happens when a body moves. The rhythm of that movement, the identifiable steps, the coherence of the patterns, they may not be easily apparent but they are there for the discovery.

We would add a few more things to a description of what dance is. In the broadest sense. any movement, all movement, is dance whether it is intended or not. But what makes it dance and not, simply, life? The answer to this question relies on context and nimble thinking. Any movement is dance but just because it is dance doesn't mean we have to pay it any attention. In other words, movement is dance because we say it is, because we choose to see it that way, because we choose to be interested in it, because it can have meaning, because we experience it as meaningful. And, because looking already changes it - from just life to something special, to dance.

Circus, on the other hand, is much less familiar and is going through rapid changes. There has been the rise of Cirque du Soleil, an elevation of contemporary circus, the beginnings of post modern circus, a decline in the prominence of traditional circus shows, shifting politics around animal rights in performance, the grounding of Circus Studies in academic settings, and an enormous expansion of recreational as well as pre-professional and professional level circus training[16]. While it is true of any art form in general, any attempt to define circus is complicated by the continuous shift of circus. All that said, it is important to understand what we mean when we say circus. Reductively, we are referring to a range of skills that traditionally make up the form of circus.

---

[16] For further reading on these meteoric shifts in circus see Leroux, Batson (2016), and Lavers, Leroux, Burtt (2020).

Studying a biblical text with Academy for Jewish Religion students, 2022.
(Photo: Ora Horn Prouser)

This may include, though is not limited to, tumbling, partner acrobatics, pyramid, aerials, juggling, clowning and equilibristics such as tightwire walking and rolla bolla. Beyond the form however, we do recognize the heritage, codes, and history of circus, beyond just the technique. We believe that the more you understand an art form the more you are able to think in that form.

To this end, in order to support our physical approach to circus, we also study circus through a traditional academic approach. This varies based on whether we are working in one-time workshops, or, in full semester courses. Using the example of circus, in quick sessions this may only include discussions of trust, communication, and a foray into basic circus language such as the use of "hup" as an action word instead of "go!," or alternatively calling the bottom of the pyramid "a base" and the top "a flyer" etc. During the semester course in circus Sacred Arts, we were able to do a deeper dive into the academic field of Circus Studies, from theoretical, historical and cultural perspectives.[17] With a

---

[17] We studied the evolution and histories of juggling and acrobatics. We looked at flying trapeze through a gender studies lens (Tait, 2005), (Stoddart 2000). We looked at contemporary and traditional circus through a dramaturgical lens (Maleval 2016). We researched what Walter Benjamin may have to say about circus from a critical theory and labor theory perspective (Benjamin, 1999, 541-542; 171-121).

deeper understanding of the circus arts themselves the ability for one to study Bible through circus is expanded.

Now that you have been introduced to Sacred Arts, our approach to biblical study, and are virtuosic acrobats/dancers, you have now reached the fun stage of the Sacred Arts.

Step 4: Putting the method to use

A number of years ago the Academy for Jewish Religion began to develop an initiative called Sacred Arts. The idea was to allow students to approach their study of sacred texts in a new way, in which a study session included both a close reading of a particular passage and an artistic exploration of that same text. What was innovative was the idea that the end result was not meant to be a new work of art. A student did not need any particular artistic ability in order to fully participate and flourish. The outcome would be a new experience, and was fully process based.

It will help to give a picture of the process we use. We will begin with an example using circus as the art form. We begin by reading the text together and asking open-ended questions. The amount of time we have determines the depth we can go to in studying together. When time is short we may just raise the questions. If we have enough time then fuller analyses are possible. Once participants have a good sense of the text, we move on to learning circus moves. If the work is based in partner acrobatics, the next step is for students to learn a variety of partner acrobatic moves. These moves are designed to enable participants to engage with concepts such as support, tension, and structure. They need to start thinking about questions like who is supporting whom? Who is in tension with whom? Who knows that they are being supported by others?

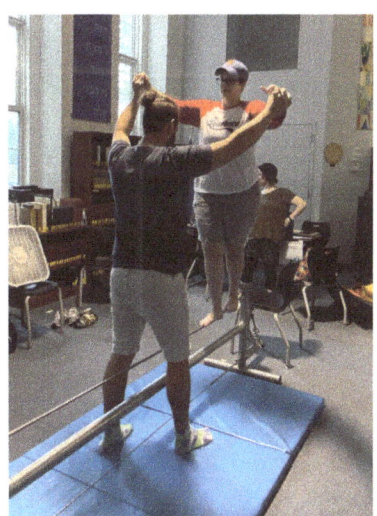

Students are asked to embody characters in the text through these partner acrobatic structures. They actually experience the moves through their understanding of the text. The steps are as follows. They choose what partner acrobatic move to do, how many others to involve in that move (can range from two to many), and how they imagine this experience internally

Studying a biblical text with Academy for Jewish Religion students, 2022.
(Photo: Ora Horn Prouser)

physicalizing the characters. In other words, they may choose to engage in a partner acrobatic move in which one student (the flyer) is standing upon the legs of a second student (the base), with the two of them facing each other. They then think through what it meant to be supported by another while looking at them face to face, if that support was strong and helpful, or felt weak and fragile. They may try the same move again with the flyer facing away from the base thus relying on someone else while seemingly not engaging with them. They then think, for example, whether they felt independent or dependent, if they felt gratitude to their base or if they did not focus on their base and simply felt free. Once they are done, participants then reflect on the experience. How did the embodiment impact on their understanding of the text and the characters? What did they feel as they were embodying the text? That discussion then generally leads to a deeper engagement with the text and the characters. It should be noted that often participants anticipate one reading, but once they embody the text, they experience something totally unexpected. For example, a sense of security while "flying" will lead to a different reading than a sense of fragility and insecurity. This may lead to an alternative reading of the text, at which they perhaps would not have arrived otherwise. Those moments bring out the richness of the method, and the text.

Another model of this process involves a more leader-centered approach. This example uses dance as the art form. Following discussion of the text, looking at it to understand as much as possible in a traditional way, the instructor asks the class to solve a problem using movement (dance) as the language of exploration. The movement puzzle requires of the students that they enter the exercise not knowing how it might relate to the text; it involves trust. The movement problem asks students to move in ways that might push their physical ability but is never designed so that one need be a proficient dancer in any way. Actually, the opposite is true. Every student is able to solve the problem because the level of ability does not factor in. Rather, the only thing we look for is the experience a student has during the exercise. It is that experience that offers a new perspective on the text to be studied.

The experience of moving produces a set of feelings—what does it feel like to concentrate on walking a straight line? What does it feel like to move across a room, facing another person, but never touching? Or, the opposite: what does it feel like to move across a room holding the shoulder of your partner. In other words, what emotions are activated by simply following the instructions? Then, a level of complexity is added. What emotions are felt when you are instructed to do something uncomfortable? How does it feel to solve a movement problem that calls for you to dance in close proximity to a stranger? You get the idea—every movement instruction, every bit of improvisation, each moment, is laden with emotional content... just like life... just like the text. The instructor, by keeping the text in mind while devising the movement problem, is making a parallel process between reader and biblical character. Once the dance work is done we have the possibility of viewing the two processes together, to see how they resonate, to see where they influence the way each is experienced.

This model works well for us at the Academy. While this approach is possible with a variety of texts, we find it to be especially beneficial in Bible study.[18] In addition, we find these art forms very democratic ways to read the Bible. While people have varying experience with the biblical text, generally, reading the text through circus is new to all participants. In addition, this method of studying through dance does not assume nor does it privilege previous dance experience. Therefore, even a group of very diverse participants are generally on a relatively even playing field.

At a Jewish education conference we studied the text of Sarah and Hagar's relationship. In trying to understand what it might have been like for each character, (two women of different social statuses living as co-wives) we devised a series of improvised movements for each participant to work with, within the group context. Each participant-dancer had their own movement vocabulary to be performed within prescribed lanes, pathways. As imagined the initial improvisations were relatively conflict free; the dancers had enough space to fulfill the required instructions. However, with each new round, the instructions became slightly more complex and personal space became more precarious. We felt increasingly more crowded as we went on. By the end, frustration showed on each face as participants struggled to find a way of accomplishing their task while finding and preserving their physical place. There was general agreement that studying the dilemma posed by this family living in conflict and complicated social status, and yet, sharing the intimacy of person and space was made painfully explicit by the danced physical experience. Reading, imagining, and thinking produce one sort of understanding. Making and doing produce another.

Sacred arts and experiential education

This method holds a unique space in experiential education. Experiential Learning Theory (ELT), the result of David A. Kolb's research, published in 1984, and based on the earlier work of psychologists Kurt Lewin, Jean Piaget, and John Dewey is a theory of learning based on the idea that it is through having a concrete personal experience, experimenting within and about the experience, reflecting on it, and finally, abstracting and conceptualizing the experience so

---

[18] The first Circus Sacred Arts workshop, however, was in studying Talmudic structure.

that it can be successfully absorbed into the brain of the subject, that learning happens. The theory is compelling because it feels complete and full circled. Students study by engaging and doing. They learn by processing and reflecting which results in an expanded map of brain experience and neuronal pathways. Students learn content, but they also learn about how they individually learn.[19]

This second point, learning about your own learning process, can go unnoticed but it is ultimately a very important part of one's learning. We find that students come away, after the final stage of abstraction and integration, with a clearer sense of their own learning needs and natural ways of obtaining information. Studying and learning in the body is new for many and brings with it a sense of excitement and possibility. The knowledge that can be gained when a student receives information from a singular source (a teacher) is markedly different from the knowledge gained when the group engages in a knowledge seeking shared activity to be experienced and directed communally.

Students wanted to experiment with non-narrative texts and they chose the building of the *Mishkan,* the Tabernacle (Exodus 25). The *Mishkan* contains a combination of holiness and risk, a dangerous sacred space if boundaries are not observed and protected. As an individual with orthopedic limitations, I, Ora, am very conscious of maintaining careful balance. I was very careful during our circus work not to be put in a position where my balance would potentially be compromised. The class decided to use my hesitancy for the purposes of our reading. They built a two level human pyramid in a circle around me; I was standing on the ground. The students knew I was worried about my balance and they felt cautious and concerned about the potential of falling on me, or even simply impinging on my space. I was worried that I would be pushed or knocked to the point of losing my balance and falling. Ultimately, the embodied pyramid enabled everyone involved to feel and process the presence of clear boundaries and impending danger, viscerally, all while couched in a framework of care and concern for others. This was also, however, a great example of students taking a text they did not find naturally and easily fruitful, and figuring out how to study and research it using our approach.

Now that we have won you over with our enthralling approach, charming anecdotes, and you have danced the moves of Genesis or built the pyramids of Exodus (human pyramids, that is) we are almost done.

---

[19] For an in-depth analysis and explanation of Experiential Learning, see David Kolb, *Experiential Learning: Experience as the Source of Learning and Development*. New Jersey: Pearson, 2014.

STEP 5: Para-practice-led research
Educationally there is a lot that makes Sacred Arts interesting. Among other forms of practice-led research (PLR), there is a defining factor that makes Sacred Arts unique. It is practiced by complete amateurs. For many it is the first choreographed dance steps they take, or the first time they build a pyramid or walk on the wire. Other forms of PLR require experience in the art or the practice.[20] We are not even quite at the form of practice, just a tasting; there is no show at the end, novel techniques for artistic practice, or even glamor to the level of skills practiced. For this reason participants are exercising what we have named para-practice-led research. We continue to unpack the theoretical nuances of Sacred Arts in this section.

Sacred Arts finds its methodological grounding in the concept of practice-related research, practice-led research and creation as research, all terms explicated in this section. Professor R. Lyle Skains states: "Practice-related researchers push [artists'/academics'] examination into a more direct and intimate sphere, observing and analyzing themselves as they engage in the act of creation, rather than relying solely on dissection of the art after the fact."[21] Understanding the nuances of practice-based and practice-related research offers a background in which to contextualize Sacred Arts.

Montreal-based academics Owen Chapman and Kim Sawchuck neatly organized such research categories in relation to performance. While their work is specifically about performance, it relates well to our work since, for our purposes, the difference between performance-based research and non-performance-based research is minimal; they both call on active forms of doing art.[22] Therefore we will be discussing approaches that call on performance, such as creation as research, as well as theories that call on practice alone, such as practice-led research, without much distinction.

The categories Chapman and Sawchuck define are as follows:

---

[20] Professor R. Lyle Skains, relates practice-led research to auto-ethnomethodology. She refers to the father of ethnomethodology, sociologist Harold Garfinkel, who "favors observing activities carried out by individuals whose competence is high enough that the activities are taken for granted—essentially, activities that are familiar and practiced, even those with significant cognitive loads—then making the activities visible by applying a "special motive" to make them of "theoretic interest" (Skaines, 2018, 87-88).
[21] Skaines discusses that artists intellectualizing their practice is nothing new. Similarly she states that academics practicing the form that they critique is not a novel idea. However, the idea of in-the-moment, intellectualizing one's practice as a form of academia is new (Skaines, 2018, 83-84).
[22] The idea of what constitutes part of one's practice is somewhat debated. Some say it is just in the moments of actively practicing. We, however, believe in a much more expansive definition. If reading a book informs one's artistic practice, then that moment of reading is part of one's artistic practice. Here it refers to the more active acts of art practice.

- "Research-for-creation," the gathering of materials, practices, technologies, collaborators, narratives, and theoretical frames that characterizes initial stages of creative work and occurs iteratively throughout a project;

- "Research-from-creation," the extrapolation of theoretical, methodological, ethnographic, or other insights from creative processes, which are then looped back into the project that generated them;

- "Creative presentations of research," a reference to alternative forms of research dissemination and knowledge mobilization linked to such projects;

- "Creation-as-research," which draws from all the aforementioned categories, an engagement with the ontological question of what constitutes research in order to make space for creative material and process-focused research-outcomes.

Research for creation may consist of something similar to what contributors to this collection, Stav Meishar and Roxana Küwen, have accomplished. They interviewed relevant individuals and conducted extensive historical research to guide their creation. For us it also includes the study of biblical text and Circus Studies to best inform our practice.

Research from creation can be understood through the work of the Montreal-based circus company, Lion Lion. Their immersive circus show entitled *Se Prende* takes place entirely in an apartment, in close proximity to a very small audience. About this show they state:

> This project is an essay on our intimate relationships, on the complexity of our attachments and distances, on the understanding of our bodies and our minds. We are inspired by this negotiation between ourselves and the Other in the storm of our identity crises. Driven by the challenge of meeting, we enter the precarious cathedral of simultaneous existences, that complement, support, and confront each other.... Intimacy being a key factor of our research, we stage our piece in ex-

treme proximity, inviting the viewer to join us in an atypical space of performance: an apartment.[23]

Claudel Doucet, the director and co-star of *Se Prendre* spoke to the students of the 2019 summer circus seminar, *Writing (about/on/with/at/the) Contemporary Circus* at Concordia University, led by circademics Professors Louis Patrick Leroux and Alisan Funk. Doucet explained that their performances act as research about conveying intimacy. They use the information sourced from performing as continued dramaturgical guidance to further their performance.[24] That is, there is a continuous loop in which performance yields research which then is used to shape the performance.

For Sacred Arts this includes simply engaging in deeper and wider ranging circus practice. Though it may appear that the continued circus practice is just for fun, it actually is a process of learning more circus in order to increase the frame of reference to use in further study. Trying anything further in circus simply expands one's viewpoint. Perhaps Sacred Arts participants may be able to compare the ease of stability in partner acrobatics in juxtaposition to the effort of walking a tightwire. Or perhaps the need to depend on someone else for balance in partner acrobatics may be juxtaposed with the autonomy of balancing in tightwire. Alternatively, this type of research also includes asking more research questions through circus in order to have other contexts/circus-related inquiries to reference. To process this through more traditional forms of literary analysis, research across circus disciplines can be compared to finding source texts, or even intertextual readings.

Creative presentations of research was elegantly articulated and executed by Professor Camilla Damkjær, another contributor to this collection, who presented her research on Western philosophy while performing a *corde lisse*, aerial rope act.[25] Her work on the rope was just as integrated as a point of presentation and a source of information, as was the paper she delivered.

> "Roperesentation" is simply a conference paper. In rope. It follows a classical structure for a conference paper. But in

---

[23] Lion Lion. "Se Prendre" (performance). https://web.archive.org/web/20220816200706/https://www.lionlion.ca/se-prendre
[24] Personal notes.
[25] Rope in this context refers to aerial rope: a circus act in which an aerialist climbs, wraps, drops, and performs other maneuvers from a hanging rope.

rope. It examines a particular question, quite typical of an academic conference paper. But in the material of rope. It has the matter-of-fact character of a serious paper at a philosophical conference. Yet in rope.

"Roperesentation" was first conceived as a paper for a philosophical conference on the work of Gilles Deleuze... the theme of the conference was trans-disciplinary perspectives, and my idea was to connect Deleuze not simply to another academic discipline other than philosophy... but to a physical discipline and practice: circus performance and more specifically vertical rope.[26]

In her proposal for this performance-lecture she writes, "How can we use rope to reflect on Deleuze without making the choreography mimetic, and yet construct tangible analytic connections between the two?" Damkjær used the circus demonstration to articulate her interpretations of philosophy. For Sacred Arts, this includes students showing their partner acrobatic work to the group and walking colleagues through their thought processes, explaining how the acrobatics phenomenologically influenced, and were fully integrated into, their study. They are once again receiving the acrobatic information as they share the experience with their colleagues, who, in turn, are having their own informative circus moment.

Creation as research builds on all three prior categories and is a more loosely defined term than the other three. It pushes the definitions of what is considered research and explicitly makes space for creative contributions. There is no question that Sacred Arts calls on this legacy of creative, art-based, academic exploration. Sacred Arts deals with what constitutes research and whether it can be done with physical skill. This looser definition brings us back to Skains, specifically reflecting on creative research and the use of practice to inform research and vice versa:

> When we as practitioners pursue our art as research, we not only offer insights into art and the practice of art as it occurs, but can throw new and unexpected light onto a range of topics including cognition, discourse, psychology, history, culture, and sociology... The outcomes of such research are intended to develop the individual practice and the practice of the field,

---

[26] C. Damkjær, *Homemade Academic Circus: Idiosyncratically Embodied Explorations into Artistic Research And Circus Performance*. Iff Books, 2016.

to build theory related to the practice in order to gain new knowledge or insight.[27]

The research influences the art as much as the art influences the research.

Sacred Arts pulls from different aspects of these categories but does not fully fit into any one. It is in the intersection with practice-led research (PLR) that Sacred Arts can more fully be articulated, and through which Sacred Arts' methodological solidity can be demonstrated. Brisbane-based researcher Andrew McNamara further dissects the academic politics of PLR and sets out specific rules for maintaining its academic integrity:

Rules 1 and 2: "Eliminate—or at the very least, limit—the use of the first person pronoun, 'I', as a centerpiece of a research formulation…Avoid recourse to one's own experience as the basis or justification of the research ambition." This forces an artist/researcher to work to seek academic objectivity and to contribute to the field, rather than only emphasizing their own artistic perceptions and agendas. In addition, McNamara argues that all research should be to explain something beyond oneself, either to the world at large or to a specific field.

Rules 3 and 4: "Avoid PLR instrumental relations between theory and practice; and avoid conflating practice with research.… Always write an abstract that equally encompasses one's creative practice and the exegesis and/or thesis component." That is, recognize the difference between research and practice and do not replace one with the other. While they feed one another and may fall under the category of "art" or "research" they will always have conceptual differences. They will inform you as an artist differently, and inform your art differently, to provide you with unique information.[28]

---

[27] Lyle R. Skains, "Creative Practice as Research: Discourse on Methodology" *Media Practice and Education* 19 (2018): 82-97. Though she is specifically discussing practice-led research (PLR), it should apply to creation as research as well, because, as previously stated, there should be minimal theoretical difference between the two.

[28] For example, creating a circus act alone in the studio will not teach you about the complications of defining "when did circus start." Western European circus is said to have "started" less than 300 years ago with Phillip Astley. In Asian countries, however, there has been a continued presence of acrobatic, theatrical performances for millennia, although it is now only called circus. In European countries, Romani and other nomadic people were performing shows that would now be perceived as circus. In certain African countries there are old acrobatic and stilt dancing rituals, but these were not considered circus. In South America there were aerial feats, and acrobatic tricks performed as part of cultural and religious rituals. Defining when circus started and what it is can be tricky and, at times problematically, full of erasure. Inversely, retroactively ascribing a Western concept of circus to these other rituals and practices can have its own conceptually quasi-imperialist problems. One may process some of this through art, and through one's own practice, but it still requires traditional research in order to gather this information. For information on this subject see Duncan Wall's book *The Ordinary Acrobat*,

Rules 5 and 6: "Good PLR can acknowledge other research paradigms…. Avoid defining PLR as more self-reflexive than other research methods." PLR is overly lauded as an enlightened interdisciplinary technique over all others; it is important to respect the other techniques and disciplines of one's research approaches as equals.[29]

These rules provide strong underpinning to our approach to Sacred Arts. For clarity specific to Sacred Arts, we are presenting them in a different order.

Rules 5 and 6: Acknowledge other research paradigms, and do so as equals. Sacred Arts, although dependent upon artistic methods of study, is based in a deep respect for biblical study and its strong methodological basis. This can be seen in our attention to the rigorous literary methodology used in biblical study and starting our sessions with such an approach. We recognize that this literary approach enables students to gain significant textual insights within the biblical text.

Rules 1 and 2: The removal of "I" and personal experience is complicated in a method so rooted in individualized experience. As Skaine states, "Practice-related researchers push this examination into a more direct and intimate sphere, observing and analyzing themselves as they engage in the act of creation, rather than relying solely on dissection of the art after the fact." This is why research parameters must be placed on this creative practice, primarily in the form of focusing on the *Peshat,* or contextual interpretation of the biblical narrative, as defined above in the "Underlying principles of studying Bible" section. McNamara writes in regard to rule 1: "The challenge for the creative field is, however, this shift from quasi-confessional mode of the artist statement to a research model that requires a critical reflection involving the communication of the contribution of knowledge and its finding." By being able to ground and identify the source of one's reading in the text, there is an element of rigorous textual method included in the process. While all reading is subjective, and influenced by the reader, grounding the reading in the language of the text keeps the work from becoming purely agenda-driven. The vehicle of arriving at one's reading is generally different than is typical of academic study, and that contrast is fundamental to understanding Sacred Arts, and the final two rules.

Rules 3 and 4: Avoid the conflation between research and practice. In Sacred Arts we believe in a deep respect for both Biblical Studies and Circus Studies. We hope it has been present in this chapter, and, in practice, we

---

specifically pp. 43-47, 108-122.
[29] Andrew McNamara, "Six Rules for Practice-led Research." *TEXT: Journal of Writing and Writing Programs,* (S14) 2012: 1-15.

dedicate significant time to the study of each field in Sacred Arts courses and workshops as discussed above. We recognize that not every artist will have the critical approach to their art that an academic may exercise, and we also recognize that an academic may miss the very important information that actually doing the art may inform. This is why we dedicate time to both, to create something altogether unique from each discipline.

There have also been times that the use of Circus Studies was corroborated by bodily research to yield new analyses. During a full-length course on studying biblical texts through Circus Studies we looked at Genesis 22, the Binding of Isaac, through the lens of tightwire. We based our Circus Studies reading on *Thus Spake Zarathustra* by Nietzsche, a reflective piece by Philippe Petit on his walk between the Twin Towers, and an article by Giulia Schiavone about the Zen of wire walking. Each of these readings discusses the need for intense focus in wire walking. While we were analyzing Abraham's actions in the biblical text, we all were fixed on how time seemed to slow down. In one single verse Abraham accomplishes a three-day-long journey while in another it takes the full verse to describe Abraham reaching out his hand to pick up a knife. Many of us we thought Abraham was either afraid, or hesitant, or hoping that God would tell him to stop. One circus reader, however, reflecting on this text while walking on a wire, realized that it was intense focus and dedication that Abraham was experiencing, not any sort of hesitation. This was a new reading of an old text, discovered through walking on a wire and understanding the nature of wire walking.

By obeying similar rules, Sacred Arts maintains a level of academic integrity, similar to the project-led research approach laid out by Andrew McNamara.

What is it?
With all these rules and categories, what is Sacred Arts? Damkjær's work is of particular importance in terms of understanding Sacred Arts as she uses circus arts to study a distant field, such as philosophy, just as we use circus to study Bible. In addition, she is not a professional circus artist, and we have made it very clear that proficiency in circus arts is in no way a prerequisite to achieving depth and creative conclusions through Sacred Arts. She writes:

> This is the story of a "professional amateur in circus performance" (an alter ego of mine), or even an "academic freak" (yet another one). Or of a theoretical researcher who increasingly started engaging in practice-based and artistic research

in circus disciplines—a process in which these alter egos became necessary.[30]

Unlike Damkjær, who is a "professional amateur," training regularly, performing on the semi-professional level, and dedicating real time and effort to her practice, Sacred Arts has been practiced by complete amateurs facilitated by professionals. Similar to Damkjær, Sacred Arts uses circus, dance, writing, and other art forms to study a subject distant from practice, Jewish Sacred Literature. As with every discrete method, Sacred Arts has its own peculiarities, but it is deeply connected to both creation as research techniques and project-led research. It is from these roots that Sacred Arts can be described as para-practice-led creative research. To put it simply, Sacred Arts allows all individuals, regardless of technical proficiency, to use the praxis of movement, circus, dance, or other art forms in pursuit of the academic study of sacred literature.

In a continued deeper study of the method, specifically via Circus Studies, we see its strong connections to Jewish pedagogy as well.

How circus analysis is Jewish analysis: *havruta*

I, Ayal, was once teaching at a flying trapeze school and there was a birthday for a child. Her grandfather, who was wearing a kippah and had a Hebrew name, wanted to try. He began climbing up the ladder and looked down at me and said, "Ayal, I am winded, can you help me?" My boss suggested that I put my shoulder under him and push him up the ladder one step at a time. This is not typical practice. He finally got up to the board from which he would be jumping (it hangs at about 23 feet). I attached him to the safety lines and was holding his harness. That same boss suggested I hold him in a way that's more comforting for the student but *much* less safe for the instructor. Unfortunately, I am here to say the trainwreck continued. I almost fell off the board, and seconds after the flier began to swing he flew off the bar. Luckily the safety lines were there, and he was over the net. I rushed down the ladder to check on the man in the net, and as a joke said to him, "So, are you going to *bench gomel*?"—asking him if he would recite the Jewish prayer one says after a dangerous experience. He asked how I knew about the prayer. I explained my Jewish lineage: a rabbinical school dean mother, a rabbi father, and an extensive Jewish education. He responded, after this long process I took with him, "Your father is a rabbi, and you teach trapeze?" Little did he realize, they are very connected.

Circus studies scholar Peta Tait discusses that within acrobatic circus arts

---

[30] Damkjær, p. 5.

there is what she describes as a "body to body form of communication."[31] Acrobatic feats catalyze audiences to have physical reactions such as gasps and applause, as well as visceral anxiety. For example, when a flying trapeze artist performs multiple flips and twists in the air, an audience member may hold their breath, drop their jaw, or experience visceral anxiety until the trick is finally accomplished successfully, prompting them to applaud. A gifted circus artist can curate these bodily affective moments in a specific order to create an act, or even a narrative.

There is a further bodily communication among circus artists in the form of another type of communication called "touch language."[32] This is the ability for acrobatic partners to perceive micro physical expressions of another's physical and emotional state through touch. One can tactually intuit whether someone feels physically balanced, nervous, or anxious, for example, or alternatively one can feel the presence of physical pain, or the absence of strength. Good partners call on this information in training to best support each other physically and emotionally.

At the heart of circus communication is a bodily dialectic, involving the bodies of the artists and the audience. These perceptions are exactly where the art of circus lives. Whether it be between audience and artist in performance or among acrobats in their art, circus (hopefully) reveals a union of mind(s) and body(ies). A third dialectic is between artist and apparatus.[33] A fourth is between one's self and one's mind. Whether it's mitigating fear, taking care of one's own body, or anything else that may come up in such a bodily art form, the connection to one's self is a fundamental point to recognize. This circus-specific characteristic, paying attention to both the internal mind-body reactions and the interpersonal union of minds and bodies, drives circus Sacred Arts.

It is here that the unlikely pairing of Jewish text study with traditional circus reveals itself to be quite historically grounded—it is, after all, a form of the ancient craft of *havruta* study, or religious study in pairs.

---

[31] Peta Tait, *Circus bodies: Cultural Identity in Aerial Performance*. London: Routledge, 2005.
[32] This term is taken from a show by the duo Henrik & Louise titled "Extreme Symbiosis" which was performed at the Berlin Circus Festival in 2018. The show was about their process as partners, and how they discussed the concept of touch language in that capacity.
[33] Apparatus is a complicated term to define, while some define it as anything outside of the person themselves including art codes, and politics (Foucault), it also refers to any circus apparatus from a juggling ball to a trapeze. In our approach to circus theory, there is little separation between perception of apparatus and acrobat. Within circus theory there has been a deep deconstruction of the concept of apparatus, wherein sometimes a body acts more as an apparatus, e.g. someone doing a handstand on a contortionist's hips. Alternatively what may be conceived as more of an apparatus acts more like a fellow artist, e.g. certain aerial work. The ability to fully articulate this concept is beyond the scope of this book.

In *The Philosophy of Havruta*, education scholars Orit Kent and Elie Holzer discuss *havruta* study as a triangle of study consisting of:

- *Textual* practices, which focus on the interaction between the learner and the text;

- *Interpersonal* practices, which concentrate on the interaction between the student and the *havruta* partner;

- *Intrapersonal practices,* which concern the student's active engagement with their own preconceptions, values, and beliefs as they are activated during *havruta* text study.[34]

Circus is thus a form of *havruta* study, as these categories can be paraphrased as interaction between one and their partner, one and their apparatus, and one and themselves. As stated, circus consisting of both touch language and body-to-body communication involves the same interactions. They include the interaction between the artist and the apparatus, the interaction between the artist and their partner(s), and the interaction between the artist and their own internal ideas, approaches, moods, and the like. This approach fosters circus Sacred Arts.

Through the vignettes, we hope you have seen how our method of studying with circus requires:

- relating to circus partners, such as in the story of building the *mishkan* at the end of Step 4;

- relating to apparatuses, such as the tightwire story at the beginning of this chapter;

- building upon one's own approach, understanding, and all that one brings to study, in all the stories.

It is thus clear how circus Sacred Arts is truly the joining of the codes of traditional circus and ancient approaches to Jewish study.

---

[34] E. Holzer & O. Kent, *Philosophy of Havruta: Understanding and Teaching the Art of Text Study in Pairs.* Boston: Academic Studies Press, 2014.

References

Benjamin, Walter. "The Destructive Character." In *Walter Benjamin: Selected Writings Volume 2 1927-1934*. Edited by Michael W. Jennings, Howard Eiland, and Gary Smith, 541-2. Cambridge: The Belknap Press, 1999.

— "Toys and Play." In *Walter Benjamin: Selected Writings Volume 2 1927-1934*. Edited by Michael W. Jennings, Howard Eiland, and Gary Smith, 117-21. Cambridge: The Belknap Press, 1999.

Chapman, O. & Sawchuk, K. "Creation-as-Research: Critical Making in Complex Environments." *RACAR : Revue d'art canadienne/Canadian Art Review*, 40(1) (2015): 49–52. https://doi.org/10.7202/1032753ar.

Cowe, Lorraine W. "The Concept of the Theory of Multiple Intelligences and an Interdisciplinary, Arts Inclusive Curriculum: A Model for Teaching Whose Time Has Come." MA Thesis, (Western Michigan University, 1993).

Damkjær, C. *Homemade Academic Circus: Idiosyncratically Embodied Explorations into Artistic Research And Circus Performance*. Iff Books, 2016.

Fewell, Dana Nolan and David Gunn. *Narrative in the Hebrew Bible*. Oxford: Oxford University Press, 1992.

Foucalt, Michele, "The Confession of the Flesh" interview. In *Power/Knowledge Selected Interviews and Other Writings*. Edited by Colin Gordon, 194-228. California: Vintage, 1980.

Gardner, Howard. *Frames of Mind: The Theory of Multiple Intelligences*. Philadelphia: Basic Books, 2011.

Greenstein, Edward L. "Medieval Bible Commentaries," In *Back to the Sources*. Edited by Barry W. Holtz, 213-59. New York: Summit Books, 1984.

Gros-Louis, Kenneth R. R. "Abraham II." In *Literary Interpretations of Biblical Narratives, Vol. II*. Edited by Kenneth R. R. Gros-Louis and James S. Ackerman, 71-84. Nashville: Abingdon, 1982.

Holzer, E., & O. Kent, *Philosophy of Havruta: Understanding and Teaching the Art of Text Study in Pairs*. Boston: Academic Studies Press, 2014.

Kolb, David A. *Experiential Learning: Experience as the Source of Learning and Development*. New Jersey: Prentice Hall, 1984.

Lavers, Katie, Louis Patrick Leroux, & John Burtt. *Contemporary Circus*. Oxfordshire: Taylor and Francis Group. 2020.

Leroux, L. P., & C.R. Batson *Cirque global: Quebec's expanding circus boundaries*. Montreal: McGill-Queen's University Press, 2016.

LION LION. "Se Prendre" (performance). https://web.archive.org/web/20220816200706/https://www.lionlion.ca/se-prendre

Maleval, Martine, and Jane Mullet. "An Epic New Circus." In *The Routledge Circus Studies Reader*, Edited by Peta Tait and Katie Lavers, 50-64. New York: Routledge, 2016.

McNamara, Andrew. "Six Rules for Practice-led Research." *TEXT: Journal of Writing and Writing Programs*, (S14) 2012: 1-15.

Muffs, Yochanan. *The Personhood of God: Biblical Theology, Human Faith, and the Divine Image*. Vermont: Jewish Lights, 2005.

Prouser, Ora Horn. *Esau's Blessing: How the Bible Embraces Those with Special Needs*. New Jersey: Ben Yehuda Press, 2012.

— "Awe-tism and the Biblical God" in *Ve'Ed Ya'aleh: Essays in Biblical and Ancient Near Eastern Studies Presented to Edward L. Greenstein*, Volume 1. Edited by Peter Machinist, et al, 1143-50. Atlanta: SBL Press, 2021.

Rendsburg, Gary. "Form Follows Content in Biblical Literature," *Ve'Ed Ya'aleh: Essays in Biblical and Ancient Near Eastern Studies Presented to Edward L. Greenstein*, Volume 1. Edited by Peter Machinist, et al, 559-78. Atlanta: SBL Press, 2021,

Shearer, Branton. "Multiple Intelligences Theory After Twenty Years." *Teachers College Record*, 106, (1)2004: 2-16.

Skains, R. Lyle. (2018) "Creative Practice as Research: Discourse on Methodology" *Media Practice and Education* 19 (2018): 82-97.

Sommer, Benjamin D. *The Bodies of God and the World of Ancient Israel*. Cambridge: Cambridge University Press, 2009.

Stoddart, Helen. *Rings of Desire: Circus History and Representation*. Manchester: Manchester University Press, 2000.

Tait, Peta. *Circus bodies: Cultural Identity in Aerial Performance*. London: Routledge, 2005.

Trible, Phyllis. *Rhetorical Criticism: Context, Method, and the Book of Jonah*. Minneapolis: Philadelphia, Fortress Press, 1994.

Wall, D. *The Ordinary Acrobat: A Journey into the Wondrous World of the Circus, Past and Present*. New York; Alfred A. Knopf, 2013.

One Plate from Le Cirque, Marc Chagall, 1967.
Lithograph in colours on wove paper.
© 2023 Artists Rights Society (ARS), New York / ADAGP, Paris

Conclusion

Ora Horn Prouser, Michael Kasper, Ayal Prouser

Throughout this volume we have presented our understanding of what we call Sacred Arts. In chapters 15 and 16 we laid out its origins, its purpose, and the theory that went into developing this model of learning. The many contributors to this book widen and enrich the discussion by expanding on a number of areas surrounding the art forms and their use in educational and religious contexts.

We believe as a basic tenet of our work that the more one knows about an art form, the more one can think in that art: in the traditions, affects, and modes of thinking typical among its creators and informed spectators. This allows educators and students to use the art more effectively as a learning tool. For this reason we included work on circus and religious thought and history. Learning about the connections between acrobatics and Eastern or Middle Eastern religions provides a grounding on which to build; learning about ancient Babylonian jugglers, the history of Jews in circus during the Holocaust, and current work being done with circus in St. Louis serves to broaden one's understanding of circus, and adds to one's ability to think more critically about their own work.

The theory and practice sections of this volume provide educational theory as grounding to the work. We included a range of models and theories which employ circus and dance to study science, language, culture, and sacred text for a full range of ages, from preschool through adult. This exposure to a variety of approaches to using the body in learning provides a larger framework within which to understand Sacred Arts.

Throughout these different chapters the goal was to give the reader a fuller image of how to think about Sacred Arts, as well as critical perspectives on bodily thinking. That said, our analysis is based on our experience, as well as with students who are complete circus and dance amateurs. We believe there is still much work and exploration to do with Sacred Arts.

One area we are looking to explore is Sacred Arts research with professional artists. As we have operated thus far, the academic investigation has been guided heavily by both the academic and artistic styles of the facilitator. In circus workshops, for example, certain acrobatic moves and structures are taught as our main points of research. There is, of course, always the opportunity for participants to request alternatives to the acrobatics that were taught as they engage in the research, and those are often the most interesting moments. Given that the students are circus amateurs, however, they still rely on the instructor to help them actualize their new ideas. There is a similar limitation with dance-based Sacred Arts where movement challenges are presented and facilitated by the teacher, who has spent considerable time thinking about the shape and the language of movement. Sacred Arts work has yet to be brought to students fluent in the language of that art. What would it mean to complete Sacred Arts research with a group of professional artists? What would it mean to attempt a Sacred Arts approach with individuals whose first language is circus or dance? What would it mean to dissect a text with someone who says, I don't think I want to research this by executing a handstand but by being flipped by two other people? On a flying trapeze? On a highwire? In tap shoes instead of ballet slippers, or maybe in sneakers or barefoot? This raises some interesting questions.

- Is this method contingent upon working with amateurs?

- How would the Sacred Arts interpretations of text change with students who are fluent in the artforms we use for research?

- Would aptitude in circus or movement be a distraction or yield new unprecedented readings of text?

Another area we have yet to explore with Sacred Arts is longer-form research and exegesis. As it stands, we have never spent more than a few hours on one text. In the full-length courses we may revisit a text, but each session of the course is typically allocated to different texts or skills. What would it mean for an academic, such as a biblicist, to study a text in-depth using Sacred Arts as the main method of research? Some research questions we have considered but have yet to explore for this type of work include:

- How does Sacred Arts inform intertextual readings?[1] Does having similar bodily experiences while reading two different texts provide enough of a basis to declare an intertextual reading, regardless of language, narrative or form? How could that be developed?

---

[1] This entails reading two seemingly unrelated biblical texts in conjunction with each other based on similarities in theme, language, etc.

- What would it mean to focus on the race, gender, or ability of multiple researchers in embodied readings of the same text?

Similarly we are looking forward to exploring alternative forms of Sacred Arts research. Sacred Arts has primarily been explored in a workshop setting where experiences are verbally discussed immediately, without the opportunity to distance oneself from the experience. We have yet to explore the most effective way to deliver the outcome of Sacred Arts research that combines a literary focus with a bodily methodology. This would be especially interesting with longer, more in-depth investigations. Is writing the best mode? Or would it be possible to present the results of Sacred Arts research in some other artistic form? Perhaps we are looking for a verbal/nonverbal combination? We have reiterated that Sacred Arts is a process-based research approach. It is *not* about performance. Of course, there could be the potential for the inclusion of performance while maintaining the *peshat* specificity of Sacred Arts. This will require much experimentation.

We are also interested in seeing alternative applications of Sacred Arts. First of all, we believe it could be applied in many literary settings. While the Bible is a fruitful literary text, the Sacred Arts method is not contingent on being applied only in conjunction with sacred texts. We would also be interested in replacing the word *Arts*. One student who took a Sacred Arts full-length course told us he could imagine how to run similar workshops with basketball drills. Maybe Sacred Sports is next. Sacred Games? Sacred *fill-in-the-blank*. A major pillar of the method is alternative forms of learning for different forms of thinking. It is not dependent on being rooted in art.

These are all areas that require significant time and research via Sacred Arts, and we believe they have much to offer to the field of biblical studies. However this work proceeds, what is most evident is that it is an essential contribution to Jewish life and Jewish learning. In many circles, artistic passions and pursuits are not sufficiently valued. Jewish educational institutions often do not give the arts their due focus. When art is involved in Jewish education, it is typically not approached in a sophisticated, nuanced manner. Of course there are gifted artists who have brought significant contributions to Jewish study, but they have often needed to go against the grain in order to be appreciated. Sacred Arts work puts great emphasis on the idea that the art form needs to be approached with the same level of seriousness and respect as the biblical text. This is significant not only in that it elevates the use of the art; it also makes the point to all participating that our appreciation for the art form is deep and meaningful. This leads to more powerful readings of text and also emphasizes that art is an integral part of Jewish study and Jewish life.

The emphasis on *peshat* readings of text also makes room for Sacred Arts as another voice in modern biblical studies. Early in feminist biblical studies, Judith Kates and Gail Twersky Reimer made the point that their dream was for feminist criticism to have a voice in conversation with our traditional commentators. "We envision a new *Mikraot Gedolot*, in which the voices surrounding the text would include those of women and the conversation would include women's perspectives and interactions with the traditions of commentary."[2] Their point was that bringing feminist criticism into the conversation could be a corrective and significant contribution to millennia of patriarchal commentary. So, too, we believe that Sacred Arts, or other forms of bodily research, can be a corrective and significant contribution to millennia of studying in *yeshiva,* which can be translated both as a place of Jewish study, or literally, as a seated position. We offer this collection as our contribution to this correction because it expresses our belief in Sacred Arts, integrating creative thought, intellectual rigor, fun, seriousness of purpose, devotion to our textual tradition, and innovation, with the body's potential for thought and research. We hope to see that integration expand further in the future.

---

[2] Judith A. Kates, Gail Twersky Reimer, eds. *Reading Ruth: Contemporary Women Reclaim a Sacred Story*. New York: Random House, 1996, xix.

Glossary of Circus Terms

Aerial Rope: Sometimes called *corde lisse*, aerial rope is a smooth rope that an aerialist climbs, wraps themselves in, and on which they perform a variety of aerial tricks.

Base: The position in partner or group acrobatics/aerials that refers to the acrobat who supports/lifts/throws/balances other acrobats.

Flyer: The position in partner or group acrobatics/aerials that refers to the acrobat who is supported/lifted/thrown/balanced by other acrobat(s). Also refers to the performer in a flying trapeze act who performs a trick and is caught by the catcher.

Flying trapeze: The iconic circus spectacle that involves an aerial acrobat jumping off of a suspended platform and swinging on a horizontal bar suspended by two cables, performing a trick, and then either being caught by another acrobat, grabbing on to another trapeze bar, returning to the platform, or dropping into the safety net.

Human Pyramids: In circus, human pyramids are not just kids on their hands and knees stacking up 3, then 2, then 1 at field day. It consists of three or more acrobats stacking and hanging from each other in a wide variety of configurations. In a pyramid, acrobats typically stand on each other's thighs, shoulders, feet, backs, heads, or hands.

Partner Acrobatics: A catchall term for a movement language in which acrobats balance upon and climb on each other. It is adjacent to acroyoga and human pyramids.

Rolla Bolla: A balance-based apparatus and circus act. It is a fairly simple apparatus consisting of a plank of wood placed on top of a tube. Performers sway back and forth to maintain their balance, resembling a combination of a seesaw and a person miming surfing.

Tightwire: A rope or wire pulled tight between two points so that an acrobat can walk and perform tricks while balancing on it. In modern times, tightwires are almost exclusively metal wires with platforms at each end. A tightwire can be rigged at a range of heights; highwire indicates that the tightwire is rigged up high.

About the Authors

Dor Abrahamson, PhD, Professor at University of California Berkeley, is a design-based researcher who develops and evaluates theoretical models of mathematics learning and teaching by analyzing empirical data collected during implementations of his pedagogical design. Drawing on embodiment and sociocultural perspectives, Abrahamson focuses on students' reconciliation of perceptually immediate and culturally mediated constructions of dynamically situated phenomena.

Ofra Arieli Backenroth, EdD is the Associate Dean at the William Davidson School of Jewish Education of The Jewish Theological Seminary. She has taught Hebrew literature and modern dance in numerous schools in New York City and Israel. Her interests reflect an integration of the arts in Jewish education, Hebrew language, Hebrew and Israeli literature, and teaching Israel. She earned an MFA in dance education from Teachers College, Columbia University, and an EdD in Jewish education in 2004 from The Davidson School.

Esther Bagno, PhD is a Senior Staff Scientist in the Science Teaching Department at Weizmann Institute of Science, and has a major role in the research and development activities of the Physics Group. She has been the director of the National Center for Physics Teachers since its establishment in 1995.

Yuval Ben Abu, PhD teaches advanced courses in physics and mathematics at Ben Gurion University, Tel Aviv University, and Sapir Academic College. His research deals with biological physics, solid and soft state physics, and physics education. In recent years he has been engaged in joint and advanced research with the physics department of the University of Oxford on the issues of a non-Markovian approach.

Camilla Damkjaer, PhD is Assistant Professor in Performing Arts in the Department of Performing Arts at Stockholm University of the Arts. Her research concerns the performing arts, movement practices, philosophies of the body and first-person methodologies of research. Her research focuses on the analysis of the phenomenal and socially constructed experiences of circus, dance, and yoga. She is the author of *Homemade Academic Circus: Idiosyncratically Embodied Explorations into Artistic Research and Circus Performance* (2016).

Bat-Sheva Eylon, PhD is a Professor Emerita at the Weizmann Institute of Science. She studies the learning and teaching of high school physics, and the long-term professional development of teachers and teacher educators. Eylon received the 2015 Israel EMET prize for social sciences and education. She is a Fellow of the American Association for the Advancement of Science and the International Society of the Learning Sciences.

Jessica Hentoff has been teaching and performing circus arts for over 47 years. Jessica is Artistic/Executive Director of Circus Harmony where she uses circus arts and her remarkable vision to build character, expand community, and help children defy gravity, soar with confidence and leap over social barriers.

Michael Kasper (co-editor) is Dean of Student Life and Cantorial Studies at the Academy for Jewish Religion. He holds an MSW, an MA in Jewish Studies, and cantorial ordination. His career path includes being a touring dancer/choreographer, a private practice and teaching psychoanalyst, pulpit cantor and seminary teacher/administrator. He is a past winner of a National Society of Arts and Letters choreographers competition and has published papers in both psychoanalysis and liturgy.

Roxana Küwen graduated in 2013 from Fontys Academy for Circus and Performance Art in Tilburg, Netherlands. In her second study year she specialized in static trapeze and foot juggling. Roxana likes to take her audience into her world and astonish, confuse, or amaze them by playing with categories and presence. The diversity of her audiences is a decisive factor for her artistic vision.

Stav Meishar is an award-winning performance maker, stage artist, researcher, and educator. Her stage work explores the amalgamation of history and current affairs using theater, circus, and contemporary performance. Stav holds an MA in Contemporary Circus Practices from the Stockholm University of the Arts, and a BFA in Musical Theatre with a double minor in Jewish Culture and Gender Studies from The New School.

Daniella Pressner is the Head of School at Akiva in Nashville, Tennessee. She received her BA in Religion and Dance from Barnard College, her MA from Vanderbilt University, and completed the *semicha* program at Yeshivat Maharat. Daniella was awarded a fellowship by the Day School Leadership Training Institute of the Jewish Theological Seminary and has taught nationally on curricular design and children and spirituality.

Ayal Prouser (co-editor) is a circus artist, choreographer, coach, academic, and co-founder of Time Flies Circus. Ayal has performed and taught circus professionally across North America, as well as in Asia, Africa, and Europe. He received his MA from Columbia University. He has secured funding for circus research and creation from the Jerome Foundation, Clark University, Columbia University, and the Streb Lab for Action Mechanics. His research can be found in academic journals and textbooks on circus theory.

Ora Horn Prouser, PhD (co-editor) is the CEO and Academic Dean at the Academy for Jewish Religion. She holds a PhD in Bible from the Jewish Theological Seminary. She has worked with educational institutions to develop Bible curricula and pedagogical materials for all levels and learning styles. Her book, *Esau's Blessing: How the Bible Embraces Those with Special Needs* was a National Jewish Book Council finalist and a Gold winner in the 2016 Special Needs Books Awards.

Shirah Rubin is an artist and educator. She has an MA in Jewish Education from the Jewish Theological Seminary. She co-founded Hebrew Play which teaches young children Hebrew in playful, immersive classes. In 2015 Rubin received an award from Hebrew College for her leadership and commitment to Hebrew education.

Alexander Volfson, PhD is a physics lecturer, science education researcher, and circus artist. Alexander earned his PhD in Science & Technology Education at Ben-Gurion University and did postdoctoral research at the Weizmann Institute of Science. His research concerns physics education, dialogic teaching, misconceptions, and conceptual change. These come together in developing methods for physics teaching via circus arts.

Thom Wall is an American juggler who specializes in juggling disciplines of the past. He holds an MS in Nonprofit Arts Administration. He was honored by the Mesoamerican University in Mexico for revitalizing forgotten juggling disciplines, and by the International Juggler's Association for Excellence in Education. He toured for five years with Cirque du Soleil's *Totem*. Wall lives in Philadelphia, teaching, coaching, and consulting, and performs a solo show on cruise ships and stages around the world. He is the founder of Modern Vaudeville Press.

Lori Ayela Wynters, EdM, MFA, PhD is a faculty member and Jewish College Chaplain at SUNY New Paltz and Goddard College. She values the complexity of our multiple identities, epistemologies, and theologies located in intersectional feminism, queer, and critical race theories, interdisciplinary art practices at the intersection of the sacred and healing/social justice, ancestral knowledges, and our bodies' wisdom for constructing knowledge, meaning making, collective healing and liberation.

Roni Zohar, PhD is a researcher, educator, and improvisation and dance instructor. Roni is a postdoctoral fellow in the Department of Neurobiology at the Weizmann Institute in Israel. Her doctorate is in science teaching, in which she developed and researched an approach to combining physics studies and movement. Her current research connects embodiment, eye movement, learning sciences, and art.

Artwork Credits

Cover: Guillaume Azoulay, *Le Grand Cirque*, 1988,
Serigraph on paper
Courtesy of Guillaume Azoulay.

Marc Chagall, *Le Cheval de Cirque, 1964*.   Page ix
Gouache and brush and India ink on paper.
© 2023 Artists Rights Society (ARS), New York / ADAGP, Paris

Man Ray, *Barbette, 1926*.   Page xxi
Photograph
© Man Ray 2015 Trust / Artists Rights Society (ARS), NY / ADAGP, Paris 2023

Zamy Steynovitz, *Circus A*.   Page 17
All rights are reserved to the Steynovitz Estate, www.steynovitz.info.

Irene Aronson, *Seated Clown*.   Page 31
Photo
© The Israel Museum, Jerusalem by Zohar Shemesh.

Ringling Brothers: The Lorch Family, 1909.   Page 59
Ink on paper.

The Lorch Family.   Page 79
Ink on Paper. Date unknown.

Purim Box.   Page 85
Photo
  © Collection of the Mishkan Museum of Art, Ein Harod, Israel by Ran Arda.

Irene Aronson, *The Circus Performance*.   Page 101
Lithograph, 1958.
Image: Art Resource, NY © The Metropolitan Museum of Art.

K'tonton in the Circus book cover   Page 117
Reproduced by permission of the University of Nebraska Press.
Published by The Jewish Publication Society

Wimpel (Torah Binder)   Page 135
Photo
© The Center for Jewish Art, Gross Family Collection, Jerusalem,
by Zev Radovan

Guillaume Azoulay, *Le Grand Cirque,* 1988,   Page 159
Serigraph on paper.
Courtesy of Guillaume Azoulay.

Nahum Gutman, *Circus,*   Page 181
Ceramic Plate;
with special permission by the Nachum Gutman Art museum

Pann (Pfeffermann), *Circus Parade,* 1930-1940,   Page 203
Ink on Paper,
Photo from The Bezalel Narkiss Index of Jewish Art,
Center for Jewish Art, The Hebrew University of Jerusalem

Irene Aronson, *Clown.*   Page 217
Photo
© The Israel Museum, Jerusalem by Zohar Shemesh

Marc Chagall, *Circus Horse and Rider*, 1964,   Page 241
Lithograph,
© 2023 Artists Rights Society (ARS), New York / ADAGP, Paris

Malcah Zeldis, *Outsider Circus Trapeze Horse Acrobats,* 1982   Page 259
© 2022 Malcah Zeldis / Artists Rights Society (ARS), New York

Marc Chagall, One Plate from *Le Cirque*, 1967   Page 287
Lithograph in colours on wove paper.
© 2023 Artists Rights Society (ARS), New York / ADAGP, Paris

Anthologies from *Ben Yehuda Press*

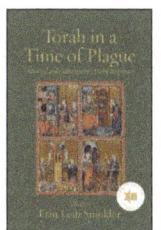

Torah in a Time of Plague: Historical and Contemporary Jewish Responses. Edited by Erin Leib Smokler. **Winner of the 2021 National Jewish Book Award for Modern Jewish Thought and Experience.** A collection of essays using Torah – broadly understood to include any canonical Jewish text or tradition – to illuminate, explore, bemoan, or grapple with our current moment of plague.

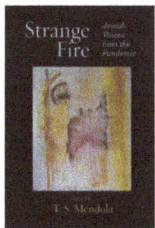

Strange Fire: Jewish Voices from the Pandemic. Edited by T S Mendola. In this anthology, award-winning essayist and cultural critic T.S. Mendola presents a collection of previously unpublished art, poetry, essays, and short stories that explore our more-or-less heretical relationship to Judaism in times of crisis.

Liberating Your Passover Seder: An Anthology Beyond The Freedom Seder. Edited by Rabbi Arthur O. Waskow and Rabbi Phyllis O. Berman. This volume tells the history of the Freedom Seder and retells the origin of subsequent new haggadahs, including those focusing on Jewish-Palestinian reconciliation, environmental concerns, feminist and LGBT struggles, and the Covid-19 pandemic of 2020.

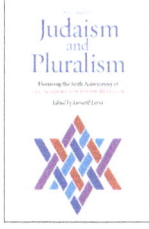

Studies in Judaism and Pluralism Honoring the 60th Anniversary of the Academy for Jewish Religion. Edited by Leonard Levin. From questions of philosophy and law to matters of liturgy and practice, this volume explores how Jewish communities can live with co-existing commitments to non-negotiable, contradicting beliefs.

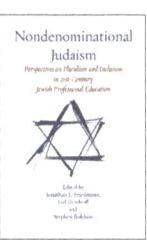

Nondenominational Judaism: Perspectives on Pluralism and Inclusion in 21st-Century Jewish Professional Education. Edited by Jonathan L. Friedmann, Joel Gereboff, and Stephen Robbins. This volume collects personal, academic, and philosophical reflections on learning, teaching, administrating, and leading in pluralistic Jewish settings; the unique roles of pluralism vis-à-vis denominational models; and the benefits and challenges of nondenominational Jewish education.

Ra'u Or: Essays in Honor of Dr. Ora Horn Prouser. Edited by Joseph Prouser. A collection of scholarly essays in celebration of Dr. Ora Horn Prouser on her 60th birthday. Dr. Prouser is CEO and Academic Dean at The Academy for Jewish Religion, a pluralistic rabbinical, cantorial and graduate school.

www.ingramcontent.com/pod-product-compliance
Lightning Source LLC
Chambersburg PA
CBHW061249230426
43663CB00022B/2954